citadel

eviscerated P.83

archaic.

Relic

jurisprudence

irrelevance.

CRUEL JUSTICE

CRUEL JUSTICE

THREE STRIKES AND THE POLITICS OF
CRIME IN AMERICA'S GOLDEN STATE

JOE DOMANICK

UNIVERSITY OF CALIFORNIA PRESS
BERKELEY · LOS ANGELES · LONDON

University of California Press

Berkeley and Los Angeles, California

University of California Press, Ltd.

London, England

© 2004 by the Regents of the University of California

Library of Congress Cataloging-in-Publication Data
Domanick, Joe.
   Cruel justice : three strikes and the politics of crime in
America's golden state / Joe Domanick.
      p.   cm.
   Includes bibliographical references and index.
   ISBN 0-520-20594-4 (cloth : alk. paper)
   1. Prison sentences—California.   2. Mandatory sen-
tences—California.   3. Imprisonment—Government
policy—California.   4. Punishment in crime deter-
rence—California.   5. Murder—California—Case stud-
ies.   6. Reynolds, Kimber, 1973–1992.   7. Klaas, Polly
Hannah, 1981–1993.   I. Title.
HV9305.C2D66 2004
364.6'5—dc22

                                          2003022764

Manufactured in the United States of America

13   12   11   10   09   08   07   06   05   04

10   9   8   7   6   5   4   3   2   1

For David Deitch, a great man, and a Greek dancer;
and Carol Domanick, who's been there for me
from the beginning

CONTENTS

Photographs follow p. 90
Acknowledgments / xi
Prologue / 1

PART ONE. SENSELESS ACTS

1. Kimber Reynolds: Outside the Daily Planet / 13
2. The Natural / 18
3. Justice Seldom Seen in America / 22
4. Mike Reynolds's World / 26

PART TWO. THE STEAMROLLER

5. Mike Reynolds's Law / 37
6. A Menace to Society / 44
7. A Child of the '50s / 48

8. Roots of the Backlash / 58

9. The New Yellow Press / 67

10. Tough Love: Sue Reams and Her Boy / 69

11. "Weird Ducks and Blind Fools" / 76

PART THREE. THE POSTER CHILD AND WILLIE HORTON

12. Right Out of Her Own Bedroom / 93

13. Another Piercing Scream / 100

14. "Guns Don't Kill People" / 106

15. The Prince of "J" Street:
Don Novey Comes On Board / 111

16. Polly Klaas: America's Child / 116

17. Happily Shaking Fate's Sorry Hand / 123

18. Checking the Weather Vane / 142

PART FOUR. ROCKS THE SIZE OF PEAS

19. Looking East, Looking West / 149

20. Say Hello to Hitler, Dahmer, and Bundy / 153

21. Pizza Face / 156

22. Another Reynolds Bill: "Ten, Twenty, Life" / 167

23. Jean Valjean Redux / 174

PART FIVE. THE COUNTERREVOLUTION (SORT OF)

24. The More Committed Executioner / 195

25. Lenny, Drug Court, and Three Strikes / 200

26. The Modification / 223

27. Shane and A. J. / 231
28. A "Taliban-Type" Law / 240

Epilogue / 257
Notes / 267
Selected Sources / 301
Index / 307

ACKNOWLEDGMENTS

My first reaction to California's 1994 three strikes law was astonishment. Then I realized that I was witnessing one of the strangest, yet most emblematic, stories of America in the 1990s, and knew I had to write about it. It was not, however, an easy tale to understand and I received an enormous amount of help.

Among the scores of people with whom I spoke, the following were particularly generous in sharing their expertise and insights and deserve special thanks: Michael Butler, Catherine Campbell, Erwin Chemerinsky, Steve Cooley, David Deitch, Jackie Goldberg, Tom Hayden, Joe Klaas, Marc Klaas, Stephen Manley, Aubrey Nelson, Gary Nichols, Shane Reams, Sue Reams, Mike Reynolds, Alex Ricciardulli, Bernardo Saucedo, Geri Silva, and Bill Zimmerman.

Others whose insights and expertise proved useful were Ray Appleton, Howard Berman, Ed Bervena, Nancy Chand, Dale Cutler, Richard Allen Davis, Gil Garcetti, Gary Giarretto, Charles Greenberg, Peter Greenwood, Ernest Gualderon, Jan

Hall, Marcelita Haynes, Marylou Hillberg, Ricardo Hinojosa, Kathryn Jett, Bill Jones, Michael Judge, Doug Keiso, Mark Lessem, Dan Lungren, Don Novey, Lael Rubin, Vincent Schiraldi, Jim Serles, Khaled Taqui-Eddin, and John Vasconcellos.

The reporting of Jeffrey Toobin in the *New Yorker* about Richard Allen Davis was as critical to me as it was invaluable. The same was true of Associated Press reporter Martha Bellisle's profile of Gregory Taylor; the work of the filmmakers who made the superb documentary "The Legacy: Murder, Media, Politics, and Prisons"; and of University of Southern California Law School and graduate journalism student Shannon Seibert, who served as my eyes and ears and did the hard work of reporting from Washington, D.C.

Additionally, I'd like to express my thanks to Dan Abatelli, professor of style; Luci Abatelli; Frances Ring, charter member TMG®; Donald Freed; Clancy Sigal; Jeff Berg; Limar Bar-Cohen; David Dotson, great cop and teacher; Shannon Seibert, graduate assistant extraordinaire, who will one day walk with Brennan, Warren, and Marshall; my friends at the Institute for Justice and Journalism, Marc Cooper, Dr. Julie Silvers, Bobby Kirkwood, Bob Berger, Victor Merina, and Elyse Glassberg Montiel; my editor, Naomi Schneider, she of infinite patience and faith; my copyeditor, Nancy B. Ranney, for her superb work; and Dan Noyes and Burt Glass of the Center for Investigative Reporting, for their generous and crucial last-minute project underwriting.

To my family: Andrea, Mom, Teresa Tanka, Carol, David, Uncle Tony, Teresa Domanick, Jason, Alex, Phillip, and Ovram.

To Judy Tanka, without whose encouragement, support, and love, this book would not exist.

To Steve Montiel, the Director of the University of Southern California Annenberg Institute for Justice and Journalism, for his quiet, steadfast support and commitment to this book's completion.

And most especially to A. J. Langguth, irreplaceable friend, indispensable mentor, and inspiration to two generations of students, who took with him the soul of the School of Journalism at the University of Southern California when he retired.

PROLOGUE

"GET BACK IN LINE," BELLOWS THE CAPITOL COP. "Anyone cutting in line, or anyone *allowing* anyone to cut in line, will be barred from entering the courthouse." He sounds serious, but by now it doesn't matter. By now, it's 7:30 in the morning and all those must-have, sky-blue admittance cards have already been passed out to the first fifty people in a queue long enough to snake across the platform in front of the Court's main entrance, down the steps, and around to the side of the building.

The first fourteen had arrived by 3:00 A.M., curling up like embryos in thick sleeping bags, trying hard to keep the bitter D.C. cold from biting deeper into flesh more accustomed to warm southern breezes or the endless summers of sunny California.

They were cocky, mostly white law students, equally divided between men and women and still energetic after traveling up from Duke University in Chapel Hill, North Carolina, or flying in on the LA red-eye from the University of Southern California. They'd all come for exactly the same reason: to hear the historic oral arguments that would unfold later that morning within the imposing, neoclassical grandeur of the United States Supreme Court.

Earlier, a woman in the Court's Public Information Office had warned them that interest in the arguments was *huge*. "Get in line early," she'd advised. "No time is too early to claim your place in line" and to be among the first fifty—the lucky fifty—who would make the cut.

At 9:00 A.M., they'd be permitted to pass through the thirteen-ton bronze doors guarding the Court's front entrance and into the Great Hall. There, among the marble busts of the Court's former chief justices, they'd await their moment to be ushered into the visitors' section of the red and gold Court Chamber to watch the morning's events.

They all understand the stakes involved. For anyone interested in law and order and crime and punishment in America at the dawn of the twenty-first century, the constitutionality of the law to be argued is among the most important, emblematic, and controversial questions to come before the Court in decades.

But it isn't just the case that's brought them to D.C. They're bound together by Erwin Chemerinsky, a thin, meek-looking man with thick glasses, a soft voice, and a hesitant manner who teaches at both universities and will be arguing against the law and its constitutionality on this November 5 morning in 2002.

Chemerinsky, the holder of the distinguished title of Sydney M. Irmas Professor of Public Interest Law, Legal Ethics, and Political Science at USC, had grown up in Chicago in a traditional Jewish family. His father had worked in a home-improvement store; his mother was a homemaker. Both had stressed a central tenet of Judaism called "Tikkun Olam," which obligates each individual, as Chemerinsky understood it, "to heal the broken world." It was an obligation he took very seriously.

His heroes while he was at Northwestern University and then Harvard Law School during the '70s were giants—the U.S. Supreme Court's first African American justice, Thurgood Marshall, and the pioneering NAACP litigator Jack Greenberg—attorneys who'd dedicated their lives to winning the landmark civil rights cases of the '50s and '60s that transformed racial justice in America. Now, this very morning at 10:00 A.M., it would be Erwin Chemerinsky's chance to move the nation.

- - - -

The day breaks with billowing gray clouds giving way to a spectacular sunrise. At about 6:30, a new group joins the students in line. Many are wearing black T-shirts emblazoned with a picture of a man clutching prison bars. Like the students, these members of FACTS, Families Against California's Three Strikes Law, have a special reason for being there. But theirs is far from academic. All of them are desperate to have the law in question—a law that has put their loved ones in prison for twenty-five years to life—overturned or at least modified. All have flown in from California to watch Chemerinsky argue their collective case, and to pray for the best.

Newsweek magazine had gotten it right when it called California's three strikes law "the toughest in the nation"—an assertion that was irrefutable. After a man received twenty-five-to-life for attempting to steal a bottle of vitamins from a drugstore, U.S. Supreme Court Justice John Paul Stevens declared California "the only state in [the Union] in which a misdemeanor could receive such a severe sentence."

The vitamin case was no aberration, no misapplication of a statute by a mad-dog judge. It was, in fact, a quite ordinary example of three-strikes justice, California style.

There was, for instance, the case of Willie Turner, who received a twenty-five-to-life third-strike sentence for attempting to buy a $5.00 rock of cocaine (actually a disguised macadamia nut) from an undercover cop. And the cases of many others who'd received the same sentence: Rene Landa for stealing a spare tire; Johnny Quirino for shoplifting some razor blades; Michael James for forging a check for $94.94 at an Alpha Beta supermarket; Scott Benscotter for stealing a pair of sneakers; Robert di Blasi for shoplifting $2.69 worth of AA batteries; Eric Simmons for being in possession of three stolen ceiling fans; Joey Arthur Fernandez for aiding and abetting the theft of some baby formula and Tylenol; Bernice Cubie for possessing forty-six *milligrams* of cocaine; and Richard Banales for possessing $3.00 worth of a controlled substance while in jail.

One of the FACTS members is Sue Reams, a tall, determined, fifty-two-year-old white woman from suburban San Diego who'd been working for the past thirty years as an account manager in the insurance industry. She'd been one of the 72 percent of voters who'd approved California's three strikes proposition when it was placed on a statewide ballot in 1994. Many people thought it had sounded right on the money—a simple law that would keep all those rapists, kidnappers, armed robbers, cold-blooded gang-banging murderers, and irredeemable psychopaths off the streets.

It was about time *something* was done. People were fed up with all those liberal mantras about the links between crime, social and economic deprivation, and pathologically self-destructive intergenerational behavior, fed up with blaming crime on the pull of the streets and on schools no better than jail holding tanks, fed up with that genetics nonsense about inherited predispositions to drug and alcohol addiction and with psychobabble about kids being scarred by growing up with crackhead mothers and convict fathers.

Crime, they knew, was *not* some complex social problem. It was a simple matter of right and wrong and its solution was simple: stop revolving-door justice and start locking up—for a very long time—every baggy-panted, hair-net-wearing cholo, gray-bearded Hell's Angels muscle-head, sign-flashing, in-your-face boyz-in-the-hood gangbanger, and white, suburban, teenage serial killer.

Sue Reams, however, had found out that it wasn't all that simple when her son, Shane, who was certainly no violent predator, had gotten caught in the three strikes law's iron fist. Now she was working day and night to change both the three strikes law and a "political climate of fear where we promote public safety at the expense of a guy who stole $150 worth of videos."

- - - -

In November of 2000, the United States Court of Appeals for the Ninth Circuit had asked Erwin Chemerinsky to serve as defense counsel in an appeal of California's three strikes law called *Andrade v. the Attorney General of California*. Bill Lockyer was California's attorney general at the time, Leandro Andrade the defendant. It was a "great set of facts," Chemerinsky had quickly realized, with which to mount a challenge to the law.

Here was Leandro Andrade, a thirty-seven-year-old army veteran from East LA without a single violent crime on his record, who had been sentenced to fifty years to life for stuffing $153.54 worth of videocassettes into his pants and trying to walk out the door without paying.

The cassettes were not exactly instructional videos from Osama Bin Laden. On November 4, 1995, for example, Andrade had stolen five videos from a Kmart in Ontario, California. Among the titles were *Snow White*, *Casper*, and *The Fox and The Hound*. Two weeks later, at the Kmart in Montclair, he shoplifted some others, including *Free Willy 2*, *Cinderella*, *The Santa Clause*, and *Little Women*. Andrade's initial trial attorney, public defender C. Christian Cruz, later told the *Los Angeles Times*, "You know who the videos are for? Family. I believe his sister had some kids."

That, of course, was Cruz's *position*. In fact, Andrade, who'd been a junkie for more than twenty years, had stolen the videos to get cash to buy a fix and get *right*.

That, in fact, was the story of Leandro Andrade's life. Every time he got out of prison or jail, Andrade told his probation officer, he'd do something stupid to get high. He'd been stupid when he'd done those three residential burglaries in '82, stupid for selling that marijuana in 1988, and stupid again for selling more marijuana in 1990. No doubt about it. Andrade had a long criminal record. But he was a junkie, not a violent thug; he had *no* record of violent crime.

His prior "strikes" had been committed twelve years earlier; his most recent crimes had been petty thefts that otherwise would have resulted in a maximum of six months in county jail. But under the three strikes law, Andrade's projected release date from his cell in Tehachapi state prison was far different. His best-case scenario was now the year 2046. If lucky, he could then celebrate his eighty-seventh birthday as a free man.

In the appeal to the Ninth Circuit, Chemerinsky argued that a defendant's repeated commission of crimes should, of course, impact his sentence, but within the realm of rational proportionality. In effect, Chemerinsky asked the court the following question: If fifty years to life for two petty thefts wasn't a violation of the United States Constitution's Eighth Amendment prohibition against cruel and unusual punishment, what was?

In November of 2001, with post-9/11 vengeance in the air and the Patriot Act mocking the very notion of civil liberties, the Ninth Circuit answered Chemerinsky's question. Such a sentence, ruled the court, was indeed "cruel and unusual punishment" and thus violated the Constitution.

Not long after his victory, Chemerinsky received word that California's Democratic attorney general, Bill Lockyer, intended to appeal the decision to the United States Supreme Court.

- - - -

Andrade's would not be the only three strikes case to be argued before the United States Supreme Court that morning. There was another that would be separately argued, this one flowing out of the California courts rather than the federal courts. A defendant named Gary Ewing was appealing *his* third strike conviction as well.

If Leandro Andrade's kiddie-video case was a scene straight out of "The Simpsons," Gary Ewing's was classic comedy of the absurd. One day in March 2000, the forty-year-old Ewing had dressed himself in a dark trench coat, entered a suburban LA pro golf shop, and shoved three Callaway golf clubs worth a total of $1,197 down his pants leg. After purchasing a small bucket of golf balls, he then limped, stiff-legged, out the door. This understandably aroused the store clerk's suspicions, given that when Ewing had entered the shop, he'd been walking normally.

Ewing, too, was a hapless junkie, with eight previous convictions. At the time of his trial, he was already blind in one eye and was going blind in the other as a result of complications from AIDS. Before sentencing, he pleaded with the judge for a little compassion. "I don't have much time left," he said, "and in the little time I do have left, I want to do something; make myself better." In March of 2000, Superior Court Judge Deanne Myers responded by sentencing Gary Ewing to twenty-five years to life in prison.

- - - -

At 8:30, Erwin Chemerinsky walks up the courthouse steps dressed in a dark suit and a shirt and tie, holding a soft brown briefcase. Striding into the courtroom, he promises himself that he will not play the optimistic fool, that whatever decision the justices hand down, he'll be *prepared*, come what may. For the preceding eight years, California's three strikes law had been a political third-rail issue. No one dared touch it. Then the Ninth Circuit Court of Appeals, one of the most liberal federal courts in the country, had decided to launch a frontal attack on what Chemerinsky considered a Kafkaesque throwback to another time and place. The three strikes law was a child of the politics of fear in a media-saturated culture—a perfect metaphor for America's war on crime and drugs and its obsession with the quick fix. A new philosophy of punishment with heavy racial and class overtones had arisen—a radical notion of preventive detention.

Its underlying rationale was that a petty criminal *might* commit a more serious crime in the future and therefore should be taken off the streets for decades, or for the rest of his life. It was an astounding concept—a throwback to another time—and he was now standing smack in the middle of the controversy swirling around it.

Shoving open the courtroom doors, Erwin Chemerinsky has a feeling deep in his gut—a feeling he will win. Sentences as grossly disproportionate as these, and the fact that human beings are being put in prison for life for shoplifting, would have to provoke a sense of outrage in a majority of the justices. The most elemental humanity and decency would require that, wouldn't they?

PART ONE

SENSELESS ACTS

1

KIMBER REYNOLDS

OUTSIDE THE DAILY PLANET

AS SHE LOCKED THE DOOR of her champagne-colored '85 Isuzu, Kimber Reynolds turned, and with her childhood friend, Greg Calderon, strolled into a popular late-night restaurant known as the Daily Planet.

At just eighteen, Reynolds was a slim, self-possessed young woman with thick, honey-blond hair that cascaded down her shoulders, a smooth, oval face set off by languorous brown eyes and a wide smile that complemented an infectious, ready laugh.

Kimber had always liked the Daily Planet. The place was art deco, yuppie heaven—an oasis of relative sophistication in the gritty, sun-baked city of Fresno and in the endless produce fields and citrus orchards that stretch over the desolate flatlands of California's San Joaquin Valley.

It was a slow, quiet Monday night in June of 1992, and the background buzz of people absorbed in drinks, dinner, and conversation was muted as Reynolds and Calderon, who was home on leave from the Marine Corps, moved past a huge palm and a polished piano and into the dining room, where they seated themselves and ordered dessert.

Despite her young age, Reynolds felt right at home. After all, she'd been brought up in a big, rambling house not far away. And until just recently, she'd lived there with her wedding photographer father, Mike, her mother, Sharon—who was a registered nurse—and her two older brothers, who were in college.

She was, in fact, just wrapping up a long weekend visit home from the Fashion Institute of Design and Merchandising in Los Angeles where, several months earlier, she'd begun attending school. A longtime friend whom she'd known since grade school had just gotten married, and Kimber had been one of her bridesmaids.

That Saturday night at the wedding had been one her father would always remember: Kimber, eyes flashing with all the excitement of an eighteen-year-old asserting her independence and coming-of-age at a friend's wedding, dancing and laughing, and he, as the wedding's official photographer, snapping away, picture after picture.

At the age of forty-three, Mike Reynolds was a short, balding, big-bellied man, one of those people so unremarkable in appearance that he seemed part of the furniture.

He'd spent most of his adult life working as a freelance wedding photographer out of the basement of his cluttered home, an arrangement that had allowed him to spend many of his business hours around the house taking care of Kimber while his wife was off working at the VA hospital.

Back then, Kimber had loved designing clothes for her dolls. Scraps of cloth would become dresses, and old stockings, stretch outfits. She'd then pose and photograph the dolls in the miniature studio her father had built and lit for her. Mike Reynolds took great pleasure in doing that, or anything else he could for her. When she'd fall asleep on the living room floor, Reynolds would carry her up the stairs to her room. He did that until she was ten, despite the fact that he was developing a hernia and the lugging sent shooting pains through his back. Ever since she'd been a little girl, Kimber had evoked in him that tender yet fiercely protective emotion fathers can have for their daughters—an emotion he wore like a badge of honor.

- - - -

Mike Reynolds had always liked the way his daughter looked in his red-and-black-checkered sports coat, the one she was wearing on this night with Greg Calderon at the Daily Planet. It was a classic—Abercrombie & Fitch, beautifully cut, a gift from the widow of a family friend— that no longer fit him. When Kimber wore it, men's heads turned.

After coffee and dessert, she and Greg headed over to a nearby café to see what was happening. The answer was nothing. The café was dead, the evening over. So they wandered back to Kimber's car.

There, keys in hand, she opened the passenger door for Calderon and walked around to the driver's side, facing the street. At that instant, two strangers sitting astride a stolen gray Kawasaki motorcycle, their faces concealed by shaded visors attached to helmets, rolled out of the parking lot near the restaurant. In full view of the Daily Planet's customers through the restaurant's plate glass windows, they rode up next to Kimber Reynolds and pinned her against the car door. The rider jumped off the motorcycle, blocking Calderon. The driver then pulled on

Kimber's purse. When Kimber pulled back, he whipped out a .357 Magnum and placed it near her right ear. Then, with twenty-four people looking on, he pulled the trigger. Leaving Kimber's purse behind, he gunned the bike and the two men roared off into the night.

Blood was gushing out of the hole in Kimber's head as a customer ran out of the Daily Planet and tried to stem the bleeding. By the time an ambulance arrived to speed her to the hospital, Kimber was already in a deep coma.

Meanwhile, the muggers blew past a red light as they zoomed away, heading to Fresno's west side. There, they abandoned the motorcycle in a deserted alley near a Kentucky Fried Chicken outlet and tried to grab a woman's car as she sat in the drive-through line. But she gunned the car and managed to speed away. Finally they stole a pickup truck and disappeared.

That night Mike Reynolds, who normally watched the eleven o'clock news, was so tired he decided to skip it, going to bed and missing the first reports of a young woman being shot. At about 2:30 in the morning the phone rang and his wife answered. Greg Calderon was on the line. Mike Reynolds then heard his wife Sharon screaming, "In the head! She's been shot in the head!" as his life changed forever.

- - - -

Kimber Reynolds was already stabilized and on life support when the Reynoldses arrived at the hospital. She had a fifty-fifty chance of surviving, they were told. But that was simply a kind, transitional assessment designed to temporarily minimize the ghastly truth: a .357 Magnum had been placed near Kimber Reynolds's ear, and an exploding bullet had severed part of that ear before lodging in her brain.

About twenty hours later, that brain began to swell. Sometime after midnight, the transplant team asked the Reynoldses if they'd consider donating Kimber's heart, kidneys, and liver if the worst happened. They said they would. Twenty-six hours after being shot, the worst did happen, and Kimber Reynolds died.

2

THE NATURAL

THE NEXT MORNING, A STILL STUNNED Mike Reynolds received a call from the producer of Fresno's answer to Rush Limbaugh: Ray Appleton. Appleton hosted his own highly rated talk show on Fresno's KMJ 580 AM, and he was pissed, "really pissed" about Kimber's murder. So pissed that, years later, he still could reel off the reasons: (1) it had happened in front of a restaurant where he ate all the time because of its close proximity to KMJ; (2) it had taken place in a district of Fresno "that was once on the downside, but was going through a great renaissance and rejuvenation—just the last place you'd think this type of crime would occur;" (3) crime in Fresno "seemed to be at a pinnacle, and his hometown felt like the murder capital of the world and the car-jacking capital of the world;" and (4) he wasn't the only one that felt that way, "the whole damned town" felt that way. And that was why he'd asked Mike Reynolds to appear on his show just twelve hours after Kimber's death.

A former '60s hippie and radio DJ—"the only guy," he'd later say, "to leave Fresno to spin records in London and then *come back*"—Appleton had been a radio man since 1968, evolving, like Don Imus and so many other AM talk show hosts, from rock-jock to outrage-of-the-moment, right-wing screamer.

He was, as local civil rights attorney Catherine Campbell would later describe him, "a big, greasy man with dyed hair and a gold chain, who was featured in ads for a cure for snoring . . . as well as being the spokesperson for every man's basest impulses in the San Joaquin Valley on [his] daily talk show."

Ray Appleton, on the other hand, had a far more benign view of Ray Appleton. He regarded himself as "a conservative, a life-long Democrat who'd become a 'middle-aged Ronald Reagan.' " He saw himself not as some kind of political sage, à la Rush Limbaugh or Fox's Bill O'Reilly, but as an entertainer, a guy who felt that scorching Bill Clinton's ass was no different from talking about J Lo and Ben or the Material Girl. It was just a different cast of characters, gossip of a different kind, another way to help listeners pass the time. "There were way too many people in talk radio," he'd say, "puffing themselves up, playing the role, legislating from the microphone, thinking they were important—both in front [of] and behind the mike."

Whether Ray Appleton actually thought of himself that way, or was just responding to the angry politics lying deep in the belly of the white man, his radio talk show would be the first in a long list of others on the AM dial that would prove pivotal to Mike Reynolds in the astounding battle that lay ahead.

Mike Reynolds agreed to appear on Appleton's show, and twelve hours after Kimber's death they engaged in the theater of talk radio at its rawest and most compelling. "There isn't a damn thing that's easy," Appleton began. "Mike Reynolds and I spoke earlier and he agreed that this [killing] needs to be addressed while emotion is high. It was just a couple of days ago that eighteen-year-old Reynolds was shot . . . while resisting an assailant who wanted her purse. She died early this morning."

Appleton then set both the tone and the theme for all that was about to follow in Mike Reynolds's life. "But though one tragic death occurred, there is another message here, [that] this can happen anywhere. This is about people and neighborhoods . . . we can no longer have our neighborhoods traumatized."

Then Reynolds spoke, and in terms of pure dramatic pathos made Appleton appear like some broadband, two-watt amateur. Kimber, he said, was "like a flower that was really starting to bloom. She loved her art and she loved dress design. She even designed her own dress to wear to the Christmas formal. This morning her mother and I went up to her room and chose that particular dress for her final interment."

It was a remarkably powerful moment, made even more so by the fact that it came from a man who'd never been on radio before. What he did, thought Ray Appleton, was amazing to behold. Here was a guy, just hours into the grieving process, playing the role of clear-eyed political activist, thinking aloud, asking questions on air, taking the first steps in formulating a plan—a plan of prevention, a plan of revenge. "He just basically announced to the world," recalls Appleton, "that he was going to continue to grieve and then he was going to kick some ass."

But Mike Reynolds had always had a flair for the moment, a natural brashness and a hail-fellow-well-met salesman's persona perfectly suited for talk radio. "I've always been an extrovert—always," Reynolds would later point out. "I'm the first to open up a conversation—to walk up to a stranger, say, 'hey, how the hell are you,' reach out, shake his hand, and tell'm who I am. I've never had a problem with that."

As Appleton and Reynolds continued talking, calls were invited. They trickled in, calls of sympathy, of outrage, and even of remembrance. But the call that mattered most came not into KMJ, but to the Fresno police. It was a local snitch phoning his detective-handler. He said he'd been listening to Appleton's show and knew who had shot Kimber. After some initial hesitation, he met with the detective and fingered her killer: Joseph Michael Davis.

3

JUSTICE SELDOM SEEN
IN AMERICA

JOE DAVIS TOO WAS A NATIVE of the San Joaquin Valley. At twenty-five, he was a short, slight, square-jawed, pale-skinned man with vacant-looking eyes and razor-cut black hair sprouting above a bull neck, who, thought Mike Reynolds, "looked as if he might have been a ladies' man under better circumstances." He was one of seven children, and at fourteen he had lost his father to kidney disease. Joe Davis then began running wild, ending up with an assortment of convictions for drug and gun crimes. He never married, but had fathered two children. Just two months before he murdered Kimber Reynolds, Joe Davis had been paroled from Wasco State Prison, where he'd been doing time for auto theft.

His accomplice in the killing, twenty-seven-year-old Douglas Walker, was a wild-haired, dissipated man whose life had also been framed by his drug addiction. His parents had divorced when he was twelve and his earliest arrests had been for glue sniffing and heroin dealing. Walker was addicted not only to heroin, but to cocaine and methamphetamine ("speed") as well. As a hard-core addict in a parole system that required perpetual drug testing and offered little in the way of treatment, he would inevitably test dirty, be rearrested, test dirty again, and be rearrested a pattern he repeated at least seven times. Just three months prior to Kimber's killing, Walker had been granted a temporary release from county jail to be home with his pregnant wife. The stipulation of release was that he later return to serve the rest of his term. He never did.

When Davis murdered Kimber, he and Walker and the informant who fingered Davis were part of a band of crystal-meth-speed freaks loosely held together by their common urge to get high and feel good in a San Joaquin Valley that was then the methamphetamine-manufacturing capital of the west. Meth is a vicious drug. The coming down inevitably turns sweet bliss into a fierce agitation that can be calmed only with a new fix. Nevertheless, it was the drug of choice for many marginalized people throughout impoverished rural America.

The good, established people of the valley had a derisive term for these people dating back to the days of the Dust Bowl. "DBOs," they called them. Ditch Bank Okies—poor white trash so down, so out, and so dirt poor that they'd live anywhere, including the ditch bank of an irrigation field on the side of a road.

It was meth that had set Joe Davis's nerves on edge the night he killed Kimber Reynolds. But it wasn't the precipitating factor. At least, not according to Mike Reynolds. "I've talked to family friends who knew Joe and his brother, and they asked him why he shot Kimber," says Reynolds. "And he said that he already had the purse, so that wasn't an issue. But that he'd shot her, instead, because of the way she was looking at him. He shot her because he didn't think she was 'taking him seriously and wasn't giving him any respect.' "

Twenty-four hours after Joe Davis had been fingered, a Fresno police SWAT team and four plainclothes officers surrounded his girlfriend's apartment. There, according to the police, Davis spotted the cops from her living room window and jumped from a second-floor staircase, firing one shot and hitting an officer (spared injury by a bulletproof vest) before his Saturday night special jammed. The officers' return fire from pistols and shotguns smashed into Joe Davis fifty-two times.

Four days later, with a bandanna wrapped around his head and his wounds undisguised by mortuary makeup, Joe Davis lay in an open casket, just as his mother had requested. She told the *Fresno Bee* she wanted everyone to see what had happened to her son, "what happens when you abuse drugs, when you get involved in drugs."

Soon afterward, Douglas Walker was captured without a struggle by a Fresno motorcycle cop. There was talk at first of charging him with murder. But it was Davis, not Walker—who had been in a deep, drug-induced haze during the killing—who'd driven the motorcycle and pulled the trigger. And with Davis dead, Walker could plausibly claim that he was just along for the ride and had no idea what Davis was about to do. (The night the murder occurred, he told the television news magazine show "20/20," "I wasn't in no state of mind to even think about it.")

So Douglas Walker took a nine-year plea bargain for robbery and being an accessory to murder. In a presentencing letter to the judge, Walker wrote: "The loss, the sorrow and the pain is a heavy weight on me. . . . That pretty girl most definitely deserved more for her courage [when she] defended herself."

Within a week, the police had exterminated Kimber Reynolds's murderer and locked up his accomplice. Her death was an inconsolable loss, but justice, insofar as it could ever be, had been swift and proportionate and thus should have insured that the story of Kimber's star-crossed life ended there. But, of course, it had only begun.

Mike and Sharon Reynolds were overjoyed when they heard Joe Davis had died in a hail of police bullets. For Mike Reynolds, Davis's bloody execution represented a kind of "justice seldom seen in America." "Think about it," he'd later say. "Somebody kills your daughter, and forty-eight hours later, the cops shoot *him*. Usually there's a trial three years later, and if you're lucky, the killer gets a death sentence that's never carried out. Then, the dirtbag starts coming up for parole and you have to go to endless parole hearings to keep him in prison." But with all that swiftly out of the way, Reynolds's energy could be directed elsewhere.

4

MIKE REYNOLDS'S WORLD

SITTING MIDWAY BETWEEN THE PALMS of LA and the fog of San Francisco, the San Joaquin Valley rarely makes the news in either city. And when it does, it's usually portrayed as an inland backwater filled with "gimme" caps and cowboy boots, Okie bikers, politicians dressed in Kmart suits, agribusinessmen with Trent Lott hair, fire and brimstone Pentecostal preachers, and Mexican migrants doing stoop labor for peon wages under a sweltering sun. They are all clichés, of course, but like many clichés they're grounded in some reality.

There is, of course, another Fresno and another San Joaquin Valley—the one that succored William Saroyan and Pulitzer Prize–winning poet Philip Levine. "Levine used to say it was a town for losers," says Catherine Campbell, who grew up and lives in Fresno. "He hated teaching at Princeton and Yale because those kids had never lost a thing. So how could they write poetry? His students at CSUF [California State University, Fresno] were losers already. After all, they were living in Fresno and going to

CSUF—a good start for poets." So the images of the valley as blighted, smoggy, and owned by corporations "are true, but hackneyed for me. The valley is a robust, gritty, authentic place—lots of action, political and otherwise, and it has its own sad, neglected beauty."

William Saroyan once wrote lyrically of the natural beauty of the valley; Woody Guthrie sang of its fields of plenty. But that was before the Army Corps of Engineers began damming the mighty Sierra rivers lying to its southeast and north and draining the mammoth Tulare Lake basin, leaving bone-dry what had once been the largest body of fresh water west of the Mississippi. They had irrigated the valley and transformed it into some of the richest farmland in the world. But in the process, as Marc Reisner points out in his epic work on western water, *Cadillac Desert*, they'd destroyed all that had been beautiful and eternal. The beneficiaries, it would turn out, were not small family farms, as originally envisioned by a special act of Congress, but gigantic, government-subsidized, multinational corporate farm money machines, owned by insurance, energy, and chemical conglomerates such as Prudential, Tenneco, Chevron USA, Getty, and Exxon.

During the 1920s, the mayor and a quarter of the police department of Fresno were members of a powerful local liquor syndicate that made a joke of Prohibition in the region. In the 1930s, John Steinbeck's Dust Bowl Okies, their drought-stricken lands in Oklahoma, Arkansas, and Texas turned to windblown sand, desperately pushed into the valley, where the Ku Klux Klan and massive corruption were the order of the day.

Political graft, gambling, and prostitution all flourished in Fresno well into the '50s. In the '70s, just as President Nixon fired the opening salvos of the war on drugs, prominent Fresno businessmen and farmers were caught financing the importation of huge loads of Mexican cocaine and marijuana into the United States.

It was the most supreme of ironies that out of such a place would arise a law that symbolized all that was wrong with California's and the nation's carpet-bombing approach to drugs and crime in the waning years of the twentieth century.

- - - -

Mike Reynolds was a sort of Fresno version of Woody Allen: a hometown boy whose horizons, values, and worldview were limited to the place that had suckled him. If Allen's brain ceased to function beyond the western banks of the Hudson River, Mike Reynolds's horizons ended at the outermost edge of the last San Joaquin Valley broccoli field.

He'd grown up to be a tenacious man, a trait that would prove extraordinarily important in the journey on which he was about to embark. Once he took an interest in a subject—whatever it might be—he'd find out everything he could. And then, in sharp, utterly self-assured sentences, he would regurgitate the information at will—the words tumbling out as if he were a Dennis Miller on crank racing through a stand-up routine on HBO.

And, in fact, Reynolds might well have been juiced. But not on speed. His drug of choice was caffeine-rich Diet Coke. He would run through one or two six-packs a day, opening one to take a slug, setting it down or forgetting it somewhere and then cracking open another. He always kept that six-pack close by, either stored in his home or on ice in the back of his battered white van.

The caffeine, combined with his sharp recall and lust for gossip, would sometimes produce extraordinary recitations.

Once, six years after Kimber's murder, he stood in front of his home on a residential block in Fresno with a reporter and, unsolicited, broke into his rapid-fire cadence and began describing his neighbors: "A Hispanic couple lives there, they're getting their doctorates out of UC Berkeley. Over there is a young man, he bought that house—he's got two roommates, one male and one female—they're all straight, and they're kind of splitting up the rent. The gentleman in that house is six-foot-seven—and his wife has got to be six-foot-two, and they have a baby, the biggest baby I've ever seen . . . , but you know what, they're getting a divorce; and this couple here, the husband, he's bald like me. . . ."

His parents had migrated to Fresno from Dayton, Ohio, in 1939. His father was a cash register repairman, his mother, a registered nurse. Traumatized by the Depression, the Reynolds wanted nothing more than a steady, secure job. A bird in the hand, as tens of millions of Americans had learned in the '30s, was always preferable to risky aspirations and thinking big. The only luxury Mike Reynolds remembers his parents allowing themselves was a new '57 Pontiac and one family trip outside Fresno to visit their midwestern roots.

By the early 1990s, however, the California and the Fresno they'd known had been radically transformed into one of the most racially and ethnically diverse places on Earth—a liberal state both culturally and on the national political stage. Nevertheless, it would elect two conservative, law-and-order Republican governors who served a total of sixteen years during the '80s and '90s and were followed by a Democrat equally conservative on the issue of crime and punishment.

Their criminal justice policies reflected the wishes of the majority of the California electorate (despite its growing diversity and liberal nature), and were in line with the state's tough law-and-order tradition, which had its roots deep in the anarchy of the Gold Rush.

As David J. Garrow pointed out in a review of Christopher Waldrep's book *The Many Faces of Judge Lynch:* "The state where lynching was most popular in pre-Civil War America was not Mississippi, but California, where the word took on the meaning of 'an act of violence sanctioned, endorsed or carried out by the neighborhood or community outside the law.' San Francisco was [then] the lynching capital of America . . . as vigilante action against suspect[ed] criminals created a 'pervasive and long-lasting' public acceptance." The logical alternative to vigilantism was to have tight, big-muscle law enforcement.

Beneath the rosy patina of the Golden State, in short, always lurked California's darker hues. What, after all, had "liberal" Hollywood's cop-show worship been reflecting for decades, if not that strong law enforcement mind-set? Where had the more than twenty-five LAPD series that had appeared on network TV as of the mid-1990s originated, if not from the heart of Southern California and the world capital of entertainment?

The Bay Area and other, smaller, enclaves of progressive thought would become enlightened exceptions to the rest of California, of course. But for the most part, from the old-growth forests of Eureka through the cabbage fields of the Central Valley down to LA and San Diego, California was a heavily policed state with an astoundingly powerful, punitive, and well-financed criminal justice industry, a huge number of laws, cops that rarely gave anyone a break, and governors who throughout the 1990s were the creatures—the tools—of law enforcement unions and associations.

The reality of California has been quick-drawing, head-thumping police departments as exemplified by the LAPD, nightmare prisons where guards literally sit in towers and shoot prisoners for sport, and O. J. juries that naturally assume that cop frame-ups are as Southern Californian as a double-cheeseburger.

But all those journalists back east, all those West Side New York intellectuals, all those German and English television film crews rolling tape and tooling down Sunset Boulevard, continued to get California wrong. They saw what they wished to see and confirmed their lazy clichés of a state dominated by Hollywood glitz, San Francisco drag queens, and rioting Bloods and Crips bustin' up the 'hood. When it came to crime and punishment, they understood nothing.

Their images were of Patti Hearst, Sin Que and the SLA, Charlie Manson, George Jackson, Angela Davis, Governor Moonbeam, Watts, Baghdad by the Bay, Berkeley radicals, boyz in the 'hood, the Menendez brothers, the Rodney King beating, the '92 riot, O. J.'s acquittal, and Mr. Johnnie's jive. Those images were real, of course, but they were only part of the story.

- - - -

Throughout his high school years, Mike Reynolds wasn't, as he later put it, "the most likely to succeed, straight-A student." He "got through high school, didn't flunk out." But he remained firmly lodged in the bottom half of his high school class. An asthma condition had precluded him from participating in high school PE classes, so he became designated towel boy. Other than his burgeoning skills with a camera, there was nothing to make Mike Reynolds stand out.

He moved on to Fresno Community College, left before earning a degree, and began working as a salesclerk in the Fresno Camera Exchange. In 1968, at the age of twenty-five, he met Sharon Fandel, a quiet, introverted registered nurse at the VA hospital. She was immediately drawn to Reynolds and his outgoing personality. She thought he was smart, far smarter than he seemed to realize. Several months after their first date, they married.

Decades later, Reynolds would take great delight in leading strangers on unsolicited tours of the home the couple later bought and that he had slowly refurbished, proudly pointing out redeemed acquisitions: "This is an old piano," he'd say, "the guts are gone, ruined in a flood, but there's like three inches of thick rosewood here, it weighs about four hundred pounds. . . . Here's our breakfast room, these chairs all have their own stories—that was Dad's chair over there . . . , this is an old-time kitchen with an old-time stove . . . , here in the living room are the antique barber chairs I managed to save" (and which, scattered around the room, were used for furniture). Moving to the backyard, he'd show off the salvaged motel ice machine, the cast iron bathtub he'd converted into a barbecue pit, and a beat-up old stove that he'd bought for fifty bucks from a restaurant just down the street from the Daily Planet. To an outsider, much of it looked like the junk it had been. But for Mike Reynolds, it was part of who he was.

For twenty years he'd carved out a quiet, deeply rooted, remarkably provincial existence in his boyhood neighborhood with Sharon and his three children. They lived moderately. During his life he had bought only one new car, mostly making do with his used 1965 Chevy van. It was a modest life filled with small, familiar routines and memories. Rarely had he ever left the San Joaquin Valley. He'd never been away to college or felt a desire to see the world. His life, his work, his entire past—everything that Mike Reynolds knew and cared about—centered around his small, tranquil, tree-lined Fresno community. By the summer of '92, his life seemed particularly sweet. His children were grown. Kimber was in school in Los Angeles, his twenty-four-year-old son Christopher was enrolled in Fresno Community College, and twenty-two-year-old Michael was in law school at UCLA.

Then one evening his daughter was suddenly murdered—not in foreign, big-city LA, but in front of a favorite restaurant, within eyeshot of a place that had once housed his mother's antique shop, and in the heart of a beloved neighborhood. For Mike Reynolds, the violent death of his daughter was thus not only an unspeakable loss but a profound violation of his very existence.

PART TWO

THE STEAMROLLER

5

MIKE REYNOLDS'S LAW

SO IT WAS THAT ONE HOT INLAND summer night, a little more than a month after Kimber's death, Reynolds invited about ten people to meet in his tree-filled backyard. They were all white men—people with whom Reynolds had come into contact over his long years in Fresno or had been able to contact through friends and associates, people who had political clout and special expertise. They all shared Mike Reynolds's crime-and-hard-time conservative politics, and for the most part worked in California's law enforcement industry. Among them were a couple of local judges, a Fresno police lieutenant, a prosecutor, a defense attorney, a high school administrator specializing in juvenile justice, and several local businessmen.

One of those present was Richard Machado, a glad-handing Republican power broker. In Fresno, he represented the Portuguese agribusiness community, which was a *big* community and major constituency for any politician seeking money and votes in the San Joaquin Valley. Any time a major Republican politician came to Fresno, be it a president or a governor, as Ray Appleton later told it, Machado was the guy who would introduce the visiting dignitary to the Valley dignitaries. He was the guy who rode shotgun; a man who could smooth a trail and get you an appointment with the attorney general or governor to pitch a scheme or a dream. He had that walk-in ability. When the time came, he would put that to work for Mike Reynolds.

Also sitting at the table was Buck Levis, a local municipal court judge, and James Ardaiz, then an associate justice of California's Fifth District Court of Appeal. A former Fresno County chief deputy district attorney in charge of homicide prosecutions, Ardaiz, at forty-four, was known within state judicial circles for his long-winded legal opinions (once writing an eighty-paragraph introduction to a single opinion) and for being among the most conservative and outspoken judges in the state on criminal justice matters. That Levis and Ardaiz were participating in the drafting of criminal justice legislation at the same time that they were sitting judges seemed not to have disturbed their personal or professional ethics.

Everyone meeting with Reynolds felt he had good reason to be there. From 1982 to 1992, the largest increase in crime in California's fifteen largest counties had come not in huge urban metropolises like Los Angeles or San Francisco but in Fresno County.

By the early '90s, large swaths of Fresno's farmland had been rezoned, replaced by mini-malls and cookie-cutter housing developments, as Fresno's population doubled to over four hundred thousand in the preceding fifteen years. Fresno's ethnic population of immigrants was rapidly growing as diverse as LA's, and its concentration of impoverished Mexicans and blacks and poor semirural whites and Southeast Asians had grown along with the rest of the city. And with their growth had come gangs, crack wars, and a steep rise in crime. In 1990, homicides in Fresno reached a record high of sixty-nine. Two years later, Kimber Reynolds's murder helped boost the annual total to eighty-eight. In 1993, the total would rise again, to ninety-eight. That same year, as crime rates in California and the nation began their historic decline, Fresno's would buck that trend and continue upward.

But numbers are abstract. What stoked the emotions of the people of Fresno were all the newspaper headlines, radio talk shows, and local television newscasts making the vaguely abstract concrete. A series of drive-by shootings that occurred in 1994 would crystallize the fear that had been mounting in the city and county since the late '80s: an eleven-year-old girl shot five times at close range in her front yard, a six-year-old girl grazed by a bullet in the back, a man killed in a hail of fifty bullets, an eight-year-old boy shot in the head as he stood in the kitchen of his home, and an ice cream man murdered for $8 as little kids stood by with their ice cream money clutched in their fists.

Crime blossoms in the decay and rot of poverty, and in the San Joaquin Valley the fertilizer was rich. Mark Arax, in a stunning series of stories in the *Los Angeles Times*, focused on just one of its impoverished groups. "More than seven out of ten black children in the San Joaquin Valley are born out of wedlock," wrote Arax. "Of the 6,000 blacks in Tulare County [southeast of Fresno], 45 percent receive welfare or food stamps. Tulare may rank as the Number 1 milk producer in the world, but it stands as the poorest county in California, with nearly one-third of its residents living below the poverty line." The crack and crank trade and the gangbanging lifestyle had done the rest.

Sitting together at his picnic table, Mike Reynolds and his guests feasted on various "theme night" offerings Reynolds whipped up on the Victorian bathtub he'd converted into a grill—fried chicken, watermelon, and barbequed ribs on American Theme Night; Chinese, Italian, and Mexican food on other nights. And then they began discussing simple, direct ways to reduce crime. They "talked about the gambit," recalls Mike Reynolds. "Everything was on the table. And we got down to what would work. Not what feels good. Not what makes me warm and fuzzy. Because, obviously, when that doesn't work—when an offender isn't reformed, then part of his therapy becomes his next victim. And what we were really unwilling to do was to commit more victims as part of some guy's crime therapy."

In short, what was not on the agenda was crime *prevention* through drug treatment, therapeutic communities, and other forms of rehabilitation; serious commitment to early intervention and job training; higher wages and better working conditions for the subsistence-level workers whose kids were involved in much of the crime; community-based policing; gang truces; and other multipronged approaches to crime reduction.

What *was* on the agenda, it turned out, was finding the best way to lock up as many people as possible, for as long as possible. Period.

"Right away," as Reynolds later wrote, they "began to zero in on repeat offenders. . . . All of us would throw out ideas. . . . We wound up having a couple of these meetings where the whole group would get together and work, and we had minigroups working on researching and drafting as we went along."

"I was at the meetings because of my mouth," recalls Ray Appleton. "I was the messenger. I sure as hell wouldn't pretend to know anything about law. But they would look to me like, 'OK, can we sell this to the public?' And I would say yes or no. [During] one conversation, we discussed making [the proposed] law automatically kick down to sixteen-year-olds. There was big concern from the more public figures involved: 'Can this be sold to the public without us looking like a bunch of whip-cracking bastards?' That was a *heavy* conversation, I remember."

"So, I was the barometer of what could be sold to the public and what couldn't . . . and I told them that kicking the age down to sixteen was a very easy sell because of gang violence in California—especially in this area. The idea floated around the table that night and [was incorporated into the proposed bill]. I remember I really tried to drive that point home."

Once the group had written their proposal, they considered calling it "The Street Sweeper" because, as Reynolds later pointed out, "[our] law was designed to get all the criminal garbage off the streets—we thought long and hard about that one."

Instead, they settled on a term that had just been used in some legislation passed in Washington state: "Three Strikes and You're Out!" What Reynolds's group had produced, however, was not just a codification of some old repeat offender laws to put repeatedly violent criminals behind bars, as was essentially the case in Washington. What they were proposing instead was a new criminal statute that was as astounding in its scope and radical in its ambition as it was audacious in its intent—a sweeping repeat offender law like no other in the country—one of an entirely different magnitude.

Shortly after a completed draft had been cobbled together, Reynolds, along with Judge Ardaiz and Richard Machado, brought it to the attention of Reynolds's state assemblyman, the influential veteran legislator Bill Jones.

Jones, who'd just stepped down as assembly minority leader,

was a valley Republican whose twin political passions were fighting crime of the kind committed by poor people—as opposed to the white-collar, corporate type historically endemic to Fresno—and fighting for the rights of corporate farmers against the heirs of that Chicano shining star Cesar Chavez and his United Farm Workers.

A tall, broad man then in his early forties, Jones looked like a dude ranch version of Hoss, just stepped out of a Channel 9 rerun of "Bonanza" for a chat. He'd grown up on his family farm outside of Fresno, and along with his duties in the assembly, he continued to row-crop about a thousand acres of tomatoes on his family spread, along with raising some cattle and running a feed lot.

A staunchly conservative assembly member for more than a decade, Jones had always believed, as he'd later say, "in certain fundamental rights." One of those rights, to which he gave top priority, was "protecting people from fear itself."

His political campaign contributors, both in the assembly and when he later ran for statewide office, would reflect his priorities. Among Jones's most imposing supporters were some of the most powerful big-money law enforcement lobbying organizations in the state: the California Correctional Peace Officers Association, the California Sheriffs' Association, the state's Police Chiefs Association, the State Police Association, and the Coalition of Law Enforcement Agencies.

Jones's other passion was protecting valley agribusiness from anyone who dared question the mammoth government subsidies and water rights given to his paramount constituents: the California Grocers Association, the Food Processors Association, the Cattlemen's Association, the Grape and Tree Fruit League, the

Farm Bureau Federation, the Fertilizer Association, the Grain and Feed Association, and the Poultry Industry Federation.

In any case, Jones liked the proposal, and although he thought its chances of passage were slim to none, he agreed to be the principal sponsor of an assembly bill based on "Three Strikes and You're Out!" and to carry the legislation in the assembly. (Wanting the bill to appear bipartisan, Reynolds then convinced another Fresno assemblyman, a Democrat named Jim Costa, to cosponsor the bill.)

Before actually introducing the bill, however, Jones decided to do Mike Reynolds another favor by placing a phone call to Sacramento.

6

A MENACE TO SOCIETY

IT WAS ONE OF THOSE NIGHTS when Sue Reams couldn't sleep. One of those nights when there was only one thing on her mind. So she arose in the dark, taking care not to wake her husband, Wayne, quickly dressed, and drove to an area near the Orange County jail in Santa Ana, California. There, in a homeless hovel reminiscent of one of Dante's lesser circles of hell, the tall, solidly built, forty-eight-year-old woman wandered from one cardboard-box bedroom to another looking for her twenty-four-year-old son, Shane, hoping he'd agree to go home with her, take a shower, put on some fresh clothes and get something to eat, all the time silently praying that he wasn't dead.

Nineteen ninety-two had been a bad, but typical, year for Shane Reams. In May he'd been stopped while driving and arrested for possession of a crack pipe. Later in the year he tested dirty for coke four times in violation of his parole, and wound up doing half of a sixty-day sentence.

The following year had started out no better. In early January, he'd been busted for running off with seventeen garments that had been hanging on a sales rack outside of a store called The Clothesline. When the Anaheim police found him, they also found a bunch of the sweaters he'd swiped, still on their hangers, price tags and antitheft devices still attached. For that, he went back to state prison.

But that's the way life had gone for Shane Reams; junkie crimes were the subtext of his life, getting high the main story line. He'd burglarized his mother's house and that of some neighbors when he was sixteen. He'd been caught stealing a pair of jeans from a local Mervyn's department store, intending to return them in exchange for cash. In fact, almost every time he got out of prison, he'd been caught stealing: stereos, VCRs, and jewelry from the homes of his girlfriend and neighbors, or from Orange County discount stores. But then, what else could he do?

At six-foot-one and one hundred eighty pounds, Shane Reams was a compelling-looking young man with "Hawaiian complexion, base-tan skin," as one girlfriend described him, and a thin, "very muscular" body. But he already had more than twenty cheap-looking prison tattoos inked all over that base-tan bod, and his green eyes had grown preternaturally hard from living behind bars or on the street since he was sixteen. Fortune 500 companies were consequently not exactly in a bidding war for his services. Instead, he was earning barely ten bucks an hour at the Remedy Temp Agency, hiring out as a warehouseman. His income would have made it difficult to get by had he been living straight. But having also to juggle a crack habit that cost far more than he was earning simply made the entire notion a joke.

In reality, Shane Reams could think of nothing but sucking on his crack pipe and pulling in that smoke, tasting it, and then feeling the exquisite, intense euphoria—that sweet escape—surging through his body. That elusive bliss, the search for that moment, was Shane Reams's life. He had no hobbies, no interests, no job skills, no religion, no military record, no car, no apartment, and no prospects. All he had was his habit, a record of petty thefts and burglaries, a five-year-old son born out of wedlock, an ex-girlfriend who wanted absolutely nothing to do with him, and a desperate mother racked with worry and guilt.

To Americans like Mike Reynolds, he deserved no pity. Shane Reams was a weak-willed, pathetic piece of garbage, who, having made his own bed, deserved to lie in it. For those familiar with the latest in biochemical research and the causal links between heredity and addiction, and for those with a more nuanced understanding of human complexity, he was Robert Downey Jr. without the money or talent, tormented by the gods, a pitiful annoyance as opposed to a menace to society.

As the early '90s progressed, Shane Reams seemed to be realizing that his life had to change. During one of his last trips to prison he'd been sent to a firefighting camp in northern California. And he had loved it there. He was drug-free, he was outdoors, he'd learned to operate big power saws, and he was working with people he respected in the Department of Forestry and Fire Protection who seemed to respect *him* as well. He'd found his calling, he told his mother: fighting forest fires. "He really did seem to start realizing," remembers Sue Reams, "that his life was floundering."

But it didn't matter. He still could never manage to stay clean for more than a couple of weeks. Gradually, an awareness began to grow in him that had been obvious to everyone around him for half a decade: that he *needed* treatment and couldn't stop using by himself. As he himself would later put it: "Drug addiction can be quite dangerous to those who have no boundaries. I myself never knew any when drugs were involved. Sink or swim was never an option for me; for some strange reason I was always on the sink side. My addictive behavior began way back before my days of substance abuse. I could have become addicted to gambling, drinking, et cetera, just as easily as I became addicted to cocaine." An addiction to addiction, Shane Reams was coming to realize, was a part of who he was, something that simply existed "in [his] character." Once that awareness grew into a desperate certainty, Sue Reams would watch Shane call some cops he knew, cops who'd busted him and put him in jail, begging them to use their influence to get him into a residential drug treatment program *immediately*. All they could, or would, do was to tell him to put his name on a list of applicants who, like him, couldn't afford to pay for their treatment themselves. "I can't wait," he kept telling them, "I can't wait."

7

A CHILD OF THE '50S

ONCE BILL JONES REACHED CALIFORNIA'S Republican attorney general, Dan Lungren, he came straight to the point. "There's been this terrible crime committed in my district," he said, going on to fill in the details of Kimber Reynolds's murder, Mike Reynolds's reaction to her killing, and the bill that he, Jones, was intending to introduce in the assembly.

Jones's call to Lungren was no quick, look-good gesture to show a media-savvy, increasingly high-profile constituent that he was on a case that Reynolds was already turning into a local cause célèbre; no fishing expedition in search of support for his bill.

In approaching Dan Lungren, Jones knew, he was not only approaching an attorney general who headed a law enforcement colossus with an annual budget of $462 million, nine hundred twenty-seven support employees, a thousand lawyers, and six hundred sworn peace officers; he was also contacting a kindred spirit—a highly ambitious, crime-fighting true believer, a successful former congressman now bent on squeezing every possible vote out of the ever-accelerating wars on crime and drugs on his way to the governorship of California.

As attorney general, Dan Lungren never tired of saying, his mission was to reduce California's crime rate to the level it had been at in the 1950s, during the glory days of Vince Lombardi—the tough, iconic Green Bay Packer football coach for whom winning wasn't just everything; it was the *only* thing. Lombardi had been God for tens of millions of men like Lungren who'd come of age in a Cold War America where men were men, women were girls, and banging your opponent into submission was how to make things work.

The reference to Lombardi, as obscure as it must have been to many younger Californians, was also Lungren's shorthand statement of longing for an idyllic time and place—for the white Republican world of his youth, where one could meet Ronald Reagan at fund-raisers at the Lakewood Country Club in Long Beach and go to parties with the Nixon girls.

Lungren had grown up in an affluent, middle-class enclave of Long Beach called Bixby Knolls, on a quiet, beautifully landscaped, winding street of old English Tudor, Spanish colonial, and colonnaded southern plantation–style homes interspersed with modest cottages.

During the 1950s, Long Beach appeared—as it does now—to be just another suburban coastal backwater rolling south from LA. But as Dan Lungren grew up, so did Long Beach, becoming a vibrant port city of over four hundred thousand people and a crucial nexus for the prodigiously profitable Alameda industrial corridor—a wellspring of Los Angeles's stunning economic success following World War II.

The city was a provincial place in the 1950s, a Southern California citadel dominated by the descendants of the conservative, small-town midwestern transplants who had stamped their mark on Southern California, and by the big-money corporations owned and run by them.

Jan Hall, a Republican consultant who grew up there with Lungren, recalls their world as small-town America, Peoria with palms, a place of "Iowa picnics, the flag, and fireworks being fired over the Pacific Ocean on the Fourth of July; of beach parties, barn fires, Senior Day rides on the Great White Steamer to Catalina, church youth groups, [and] school dances and proms at high school gyms. . . ."

"When I went to [college at] Berkeley, it was a vastly different world," remembers Hall, "and the mind-set of the students very different than anything I'd ever encountered. Our world—*Dan's* world—was one of rules, consequences, and personal responsibility. Drugs were terrible. There were no degrees of usage. They produced a devastation to society that *demanded* retribution."

Lungren's father, Dr. John Lungren, was a local cardiologist. In 1952, his impressionable six-year-old son saw him named campaign-trail personal physician to Southern California native son and Republican vice presidential nominee Richard M. Nixon. Over the next eight years, John Lungren would serve Nixon during five of his campaigns.

John Lungren was a quiet man, recalls Jim Serles, a former Republican candidate for the Long Beach City Council, "who became prominent in Long Beach's Republican Party due to his relationship with Nixon—which everyone knew about." And, according to a longtime Lungren family friend, Catholic Msgr. Ernest Gualderon, "Nixon loved John Lungren. When Nixon had that leg problem—phlebitis," says Gualderon, "he came here to Long Beach Memorial because John Lungren was there. That's de facto. I *know* that."

Long Beach then had one of the few full-time Republican headquarters in LA County, and John Lungren's wife, Lorraine, was perhaps even more visible than was her husband in party circles and organizations.

Lorraine Lungren was also a "very big force in the Lungren family," as Msgr. Gualderon tells it, "an ardent Catholic whose husband converted to the Church when he married her; a mother who bore seven children, and, with her husband, oversaw a close-knit family and insured that every one of her children got a terrific religious, Christian education."

But the biggest force in Dan Lungren's life, "his strongest feelings," as Jim Serles puts it, "related to his father, and seeing political life through his father's eyes." Leaving his practice for as long as six weeks to travel with Nixon, John Lungren would call home nightly to his wife and his three boys and four girls. As the legend now goes, it was during his father's first campaign trip, in '52, that Dan Lungren first displayed his predilection for politics, passing out leaflets for the Eisenhower-Nixon ticket and for a family friend running for Congress from Long Beach.

Dan Lungren learned the old-time religion of rigid adherence to the rules, not only from his mother and father, but "from the Holy Cross brothers from South Bend," who used to teach at Lungren's Long Beach high school, St. Anthony's, says Gualderon, who looks not unlike the aged, twinkle-eyed priest portrayed by Barry Fitzgerald in *The Bells of St. Mary's*. "That's why graduation after graduation, students from St. Anthony's went to Notre Dame University. It was a sad blow when we lost the brothers, they were a strict order, you know. For the brothers, like the Jesuits, there were just two things you must have in any successful school: discipline and character development. They stressed that here. If you did something wrong you were in trouble." In fact, Notre Dame University was Lungren's next stop, followed by law school at another Catholic institution, Georgetown University.

After being elected to Congress in 1978, Lungren banded together with Newt Gingrich and other House Republican newcomers who were far more conservative, and unabashedly partisan, than their more established Republican colleagues. During decades of being in the minority, the House Republican leadership had been getting along by going along. That kind of thinking, as Lungren and Gingrich saw it, was for losers. So they and some like-minded colleagues formed the Conservative Opportunity Society, out of which flowed that public relations masterpiece known as the Contract with America—a document so slickly drawn that it would help Republicans gain control of the House in 1994 for the first time in forty years.

As one of the key players on the House Judiciary Committee, Lungren was a driving force behind the radical nature of the 1984 Comprehensive Crime Control Act—a "reform" of the nation's criminal justice system that institutionalized the mandatory federal sentencing guidelines that have filled the nation's federal prisons with low-level drug offenders.

It also created RICO (Racketeer Influenced and Corrupt Organization) statutes, and sentences so stiff that they virtually insured that anyone indicted for a federal crime would plea-bargain with the government rather than gamble on going to trial and being sentenced to twenty, thirty, or forty years in prison for what used to be considered relatively minor felonies.

"Lungren," recalls Howard Berman, the veteran liberal Democratic congressman from Los Angeles, "was the chief implementer of the Republican strategy that ran over the Democratic leadership in the House, and got a [punitive] bill far more to the Republicans' liking." "He was," adds Berman, who served with Lungren for a decade in Congress, "an effective, articulate, prepared, and stubbornly hard-nosed conservative."

- - - -

As Dan Lungren listened to Bill Jones explaining the proposed bill, he found his interest rising. Number one, as a relentless advocate of tougher sentencing when he'd been on the Judiciary Committee, he was now searching as attorney general for ways to "firm up" California's criminal justice system— ways that included drastically reducing, if not entirely eliminating, a convicted defendant's rights of appeal and passing "tougher laws for repeat offenders."

He also liked the name of the bill: "Three Strikes and You're Out!" Some supporters would regard it as a glib title that cheapened the seriousness of the legislation. Not Lungren. He found it "catchy," a "simple mantra" that people could easily understand, relate to, remember, and repeat.

It reminded him of his days working on the federal Crime Control Act and of *his* catchy phrase: "Truth in Sentencing." Before the passage of the act, a federal prisoner could reduce his sentence by fifty percent for good behavior. It was time, Lungren argued to his House colleagues, for a little Truth in Sentencing. Twenty percent time off, *that* was closer to the truth, and today that is all federal prisoners can get off their sentences. The phrase, as Lungren later told it, "had gone to the essence of what [he and his Republican colleagues] had been trying to do, and 'three strikes and you're out,' " felt Lungren, "did that as well."

Eavesdropping on Lungren's conversation with Jones, or reading his quotes in the *Los Angeles Times*, made it easy to picture him looking like some grim, purse-lipped, prune-faced, wrath-of-god crusader. Seeing him in person, however, was another matter. Lungren was a tall man, handsome in a wavy-haired, twinkle-eyed sort of way, who kept in shape by playing racquetball and training in the strenuous martial art of tae kwon do, maintaining his six-foot-two-inch frame well enough for the bow tie–wearing, anemic-looking, East Coast conservative pundit George Will to gush over Lungren's "almost alarming robustness."

Lungren's looks were complemented by an unpretentious demeanor that political friends and foes alike described as "amiable." And he was, in fact, the kind of guy you'd be comfortable standing with at the back of a bar during an early Sunday afternoon playoff game, engaging in an animated, nuanced conversation about the relative merits of the Sacramento Kings versus the Los Angeles Lakers.

Lungren liked what he was hearing from Jones over the phone. A law like three strikes fit in perfectly with his long-range plans. Had he quit Congress after serving for ten years for nothing? Of course not. He craved the big prize: the governorship of California.

Becoming governor of that mammoth, trend-setting state with over thirty million inhabitants would enable him to set California's priorities, influence the direction of legislation, appoint the state supreme court justices, who might or might not rein in the cops and the corporations, choose the state commissioners who would direct the state's huge bureaucracies, and have a major impact on the state's legislative and congressional redistricting.

And as California's attorney general, Lungren had a shot—a real shot—at fulfilling his ambition. Had not California attorney generals Earl Warren, Pat Brown, and George Deukmejian all leapt from their seats in the AG's office directly into the governor's mansion?

If Republican governor Pete Wilson was elected to a second term in '94, he would be term-limited out of office in four years, and the governor's seat would be wide open, just waiting for Dan Lungren.

But it would be a mistake to think that personal glory was all it was about for Lungren. It was as much about the fight as the glory. The fight for *his* political beliefs; the fight for *his* values; the battle for *his* America. The expansive humanity and reemphasis on economic and social justice that followed the liberalizing reforms of 1962's Second Vatican Council seemed to have drifted right past Dan Lungren.

While in Congress, he had opposed the South African sanctions that played such a crucial role in toppling a virulently racist ruling regime, voted against virtually all social programs assisting the poor, been militantly antiabortion, and fiercely opposed reparations for Japanese Americans interned during World War II. "His view was internment had been necessary," recalls Howard Berman, "and he just disregarded the injustice visited on the people interned. There's that touch of the true believer about Dan, the absence of doubt that there's merit to other positions."

But if Dan Lungren was to the extreme right of the American

public on many social issues, on crime, he *was* the American public. Or at least much of the middle-class voting public, who—from the mid-1960s to the early 1990s—had watched large swaths of American cities once considered the nation's crown jewels burn down in riots and insurrections or disintegrate into violent, improvised ghettoes.

The black rage that had been building for centuries erupted first in Newark, New Jersey, in 1964, and then again the following year in a section of South Central Los Angeles known as Watts.

LAPD chief William H. Parker—the founding father of the modern-day LAPD—reacted by speaking the white man's fear: "By 1970," Parker proclaimed, "45 percent of the metropolitan area of Los Angeles will be Negro. [If whites want] any protection for [their] homes . . . [they are] going to have to get in and support a strong police department. If you don't," warned Parker, ". . . God help you."

Come 1970, the nation was indeed reeling. In 1968, Bobby Kennedy and Martin Luther King Jr. lay dead at the hands of assassins as more than sixty cities throughout America, including Chicago, Denver, and Baltimore, went up in flames and riots.

Meanwhile, a 1968 Gallup Poll found that, for the first time in the survey's thirty-three-year history, Americans regarded crime as the country's number one domestic problem. That same year, the FBI reported that urban crime had grown by 88 percent since the start of the decade. In response, a ceaseless drumbeat began, demanding more cops, more prisons, and more and everharsher laws.

- - - -

Before hanging up, Bill Jones told Dan Lungren that he was about to have a meeting with Mike Reynolds. Would Lungren be willing to send some of his deputies from the AG's office down to attend? "Well," replied Lungren, "this looks like a proposal that I might be called on to defend as attorney general, so I think we should take a look at it."

Lungren's lawyers then traveled down to Fresno as promised, winding up seated at Mike Reynolds's much-visited backyard picnic table. Together with members of Reynolds's original group, they carefully edited three or four different drafts of Reynolds's proposed three strikes law, pointing out what they thought was unconstitutional, what was practical, what could fly politically, and what could not.

Dan Lungren's blessing was the second major milestone on Mike Reynolds's journey. He now had Bill Jones, a well-established Republican political leader, introducing his bill, and California's attorney general lending his expertise, support, and the official weight of his office to an effort to pass a law that a different attorney general might have looked upon with incredulity.

8

ROOTS OF THE BACKLASH

IF DAN LUNGREN WOULD PROVE immediately useful to Mike Reynolds, it was an earlier attorney general and two-term governor of California named George Deukmejian who had set the long-term political stage upon which Reynolds would act.

Deukmejian was both a mentor and a booster of Lungren. The two had a lot in common. Both had represented the same general area of Long Beach. Both identified with the politics of the more conservative wing of the Southern California country-club set but were not country-club guys themselves—neither particularly enjoying that social milieu of golf, drinking, and bonhomie.

Cool, thin, tan, and handsome, known as "the Duke" by many of the Republican Party faithful, George Deukmejian was always perfectly groomed but otherwise was so understated and lacking in charisma that it was sometimes difficult to know if he was dead or alive.

Yet Lungren was fortunate to have been taken under Deukmejian's wing. Like Nixon and Reagan, Deukmejian was a skilled politician who early on saw that people's rapidly escalating concern about violent street crime, drugs, and what they viewed as revolving-door justice—concern exacerbated by sensationalist media coverage—was making crime and punishment *the* issue in America. Riots, street crime, soft judges, lax laws, and the Supreme Court's brief moratorium on the death penalty would all be holes punched on Deukmejian's ticket to ride into the attorney general's office in the mid-'70s and then into two terms in the governor's mansion.

The son of Armenian immigrants, Deukmejian grew up in upstate New York hearing the vivid horror stories of the 1915 Turkish genocide of 1.5 million of his people and of the centuries of oppression they'd suffered. Out of such a background come many people who instinctively identify with the underdog, and others with the warm security of the ruling class. George Deukmejian was a security man, having found a snug womb in southern and central California, where three hundred thousand of his fellow Armenian Americans had congregated.

In 1963, Deukmejian, who'd been working for a prominent Long Beach law firm, stepped into politics and was elected to the state assembly. In politics, timing is everything, and George Deukmejian's timing could not have been better.

Historians will differ about when America's hostility toward its criminal justice system began. But as good a turning point as any might be 1954, when Earl Warren's and William Brennan's freedom-loving Supreme Court started to flower, first desegregating America and then forcefully expanding the civil liberties and criminal rights of the people traditionally on the margins of the nation's life.

Back in the '50s, blacks, women, gays, Mexicans, Asians, and other minorities had all known their place, and for the most part were forced to stay in it. Communism was the enemy; corporate men in gray flannel suits and skinny ties were the national ideal; political and social conformity was the guiding ethos; living the safe, white, suburban life was the dream. Crime rates were low, prison cells lay unoccupied, and the theory of criminal rehabilitation was at the vanguard of social science.

But a torrent of cataclysmic events would change all that. At the dawn of the '60s, Anglo-Saxon America had almost completed the social and economic integration of the children and grandchildren of the tens of millions of Irish, Jewish, Italian, and Eastern European immigrants who had flooded the nation at the turn of the twentieth century. During and after World War II, an epoch-defining mass migration of impoverished blacks from the South began to replace the older immigrants in America's industrial cities and were soon making their presence felt and their demands known.

During the '50s, '60s, and '70s, they were joined by Puerto Ricans and West Indians in the northeast, and in the '80s, by Mexicans and Central Americans in the southwest—further accelerating white America's post-war retreat to the suburbs.

Meanwhile, by the early '70s, the war in Vietnam, the great civil rights and anti-war movements, and the fires, crime, and anarchy that were wreaking havoc upon urban America had all hacked away at the myth of America as the land of the free and the benevolent upholder of freedom and democracy throughout the world.

The response of white America's voters to the turmoil was to elect Republican Richard Nixon as president in 1968. Nixon defeated the Democratic candidate, Hubert Humphrey, in large measure by exploiting urban white America's fear of crime and the white South's general loathing of uppity Negroes daring to demand—to *demand*, mind you—the full measure of their humanity.

Nixon's George Wallace–inspired southern strategy of exploiting racial divisiveness worked wonders not only in the South, but among urban, working-class white Americans throughout the nation. Many of them simply shared the southern man's racism; others feared black street crime and despised the well-meaning but sometimes wrong-headed demands of those leading the urban civil rights and social justice movements.

Integration through forced busing was throwing previously white schools into ugly racial turmoil, and most white parents with other options quickly pulled their kids out of the public schools or fled to the suburbs.

Building low-income government housing projects was a noble idea to replace the dilapidated housing and alleviate the unspeakable living conditions in America's urban slums. But dropping them in the middle of stable neighborhoods to achieve integration was an utterly misguided scheme that backfired. It vastly increased crime in those previously safe neighborhoods and helped, in the process, to shatter white Americans' faith in the great liberal movements that had forced government to provide social security and Medicare, an eight-hour workday, a forty-hour work week, and social welfare programs for the poor and handicapped. Meanwhile, running for governor of California, Ronald Reagan was successfully harnessing the same backlash—against integration, civil rights, student protests, the counterculture, and rising crime rates—as was Richard Nixon.

Into this turmoil stepped George Deukmejian. After winning

an assembly seat in '63, Deukmejian moved up to the state senate in 1972 and authored a death penalty ballot initiative that passed overwhelmingly—putting himself on the statewide stage. In 1978, he was elected attorney general by successfully advocating a "use-a-gun, go-to-prison" law.

During his tenure as attorney general and later as governor, a succession of grotesque, highly publicized crimes sickened the California public and produced an even greater cry for a tougher criminal justice system.

In 1978, for example, Lawrence Singleton picked up a hitch-hiking fifteen-year-old girl, raped her, chopped off both her fore-arms, dragged her into a ditch, and left her there naked and writhing in pain, presumably to die. (She lived.) Singleton was caught and sentenced to fourteen years in prison, but was paroled after serving just eight years and four months. The public outcry was so intense that the state was forced to stick him in a mobile home on the grounds of San Quentin Prison for an extra year before his release. (In 1997, Singleton went on to stab a thirty-one-year-old Florida woman to death in his Tampa home. He was sentenced to sit in Florida's electric chair and die, but cancer got him first.)

For Deukmejian, such travesties of justice were political gifts from God. They, and the growing disenchantment with American liberalism, set the stage for Deukmejian to run for governor in 1982 against the popular black liberal mayor of Los Angeles, Tom Bradley. Bradley was a man revered in LA by blacks and whites alike, but Deukmejian again used crime as his wedge issue and won the election by less than a single percentage point.

About a year after Deukmejian took office, another abominable outrage occurred—one that provided ghastly new evidence that something was critically wrong with criminal sentencing and the early release of convicts in California. A man named Charles Rothenberg decided to douse his young son with kerosene and set him ablaze. Incredibly, the boy lived, although scarred over ninety percent of his body. For the unspeakable, Rothenberg was sentenced to thirteen years in prison but wound up serving just six and a half before being released. Who could not feel sickened and vengeful? As LA County Deputy Public Defender Alex Ricciardulli later wrote, "The real trouble lay in the generous early-release provisions in the California law . . . defendants . . , routinely spent only fifty percent of their sentence in prison by accruing credits for good behavior and working in prison. The result was that even with sentences as tough-sounding as twelve or fourteen years . . . defendants got out in a mere six or seven."

The public blamed liberals for the system's failures, and in 1986, George Deukmejian beat Tom Bradley again, this time resoundingly.

His '86 campaign was a case study of the politics of race and crime in California, and of why the stars would be so perfectly aligned for Mike Reynolds less than a decade later.

The campaign revolved around the issues of gun control, the reinstatement of the death penalty, and whether or not Bradley supported the reconfirmation of the liberal and controversial California Supreme Court Justice Rose Elizabeth Bird—a champion of civil liberties, abortion rights, and the poor and disenfranchised, and an ardent opponent of the death penalty. These positions resulted in her being savagely attacked by powerful law firms, law-and-order conservatives, the Catholic Church, and the big growers of the San Joaquin Valley, whose huge campaign contributions had been vital to George Deukmejian's election as governor.

Although Bradley tried to ignore Bird and finesse his positions, conservative and swing voters were sure they had him pegged: He was black, he was a Democrat, and he was the mayor of racially tumultuous, crime-scarred Los Angeles. Therefore, he had to be soft on crime. In fact, Bradley, who had served twenty years as an LAPD officer, was relatively conservative on the issue.

Like Bill Clinton a decade later, he recognized that crime was the Democrats' Achilles' heel. So gun-shy on the subject was he, in fact, that he'd permitted the Los Angeles Police Department to run amok in the city's poor black and brown neighborhoods for most of his two-decade-long reign as mayor, creating, in the process, the rage that finally ignited in the violent 1992 riot that followed the acquittal of the four LAPD officers who'd savaged Rodney King.

And so it was George Deukmejian, with his dour view of human nature, and not Tom Bradley, the personification of Dr. King's dream of bringing black and white together, who would leave his mark on California's criminal justice system. In the dozen years he served as attorney general and governor, the California legislature—ever fearful of a public driven mad by a broadcast media feeding off the very real problem of crime—passed more than a thousand bills toughening criminal penalties and lengthening sentences, often by three to four times what they had been. From 1979 through 1994, eleven hundred changes were made to California's penal code, lengthening and toughening prison terms, while the state's prison population exploded from less than thirty thousand to over one hundred twenty-six thousand.

Meanwhile, in the decade between 1984 and 1994, the Department of Corrections budget rose from $728 million to $3.1 *billion.* At the same time, Deukmejian and his successor, Pete Wilson, appointed judges to the bench that passed their litmus test on law and order—judges for whom the words "compassion" and "rehabilitation" were anathema.

- - - -

In 1990, as his tenure as governor was drawing to a close, George Deukmejian dedicated Pelican Bay State Prison, which was soon to become a notorious example of cold-steel, high-tech incarceration and of hideous brutality against inmates.

"While we were trying to 'understand' these criminals, California's crime rates soared," said Deukmejian, whose eight years as governor had ignited the biggest prison building boom in the history of America and almost certainly the entire world. During his tenure, and that of his Republican successor, Pete Wilson, the state of California would spend $10 billion, including interest, on new prison construction.

Prior to 1984, California had twelve state prisons. From 1984 to 1994, it would build sixteen more, with five additional state-of-the-art institutions under construction and funded, or partially funded, by 1994.

"The message has been clear," said Deukmejian "Commit these crimes and you will go to jail." And once in California's prisons, the Duke might have added, you will suffer. When, for example, one prisoner at Pelican Bay protested being locked in a suffocatingly small prison cell twenty-three hours a day for months on end by spreading his feces over his body and refusing to bathe, he was plunged into bath water so scalding it peeled away his skin. Discipline, according to a report by Human Rights Watch and the ACLU, also consisted of hog-tied prisoners being forced to lap up their food like pigs. During the mid- to late 1990s, eight guards at Corcoran State Prison were accused of arranging fights between prisoners for "amusement and blood sport." Nor was that all.

"Since 1989," wrote the *Los Angeles Times* in a 1998 investigative report, "thirty-nine inmates [in California prisons] have been shot to death and more than 200 seriously wounded by guards firing bullets [from high-powered rifles] to stop fistfights and melees—a practice unheard of in other states."

9

THE NEW YELLOW PRESS

IN APRIL OF 1993, MIKE REYNOLDS took his second trip to Sacramento, this time accompanied by the chief of police of Fresno, the sheriff of Fresno County, and four hundred fifty sign-carrying volunteers who'd forked over $15 apiece for the privilege of riding along with him on one of his "crime buster" buses.

The excursion had been heavily promoted on Ray Appleton's radio talk show, the first of several such shows that would have an enormous influence on Mike Reynolds's proposed three strikes law, both statewide and nationally.

By 1992, right-wing talk shows such as Appleton's were beginning to flourish and dominate the discussion of politics on the commercial radio airways. Local broadcasters like Appleton, and national ones like Rush Limbaugh, were soon to not only dominate AM talk radio, but *be* AM talk radio.

In the crucial year and a half to come, they'd emerge as the great champions of Mike Reynolds and his still gestating crusade. They were he, after all, and he they. And it was *they*—the yellow press of the airways—who would provide the stage, the backdrop, the cheerleading, and the drumbeat for Reynolds's message that the criminal justice system had been rendered impotent by "weird little ducks," as Mike Reynolds put it, busy defending criminals, not victims, and "making all the decisions for the rest of us."

If talk radio was primed for Mike Reynolds, he was more than prepared for it. In fact, he was a media natural: an articulate, grieving father able to render the horrific tale of his daughter's random murder with compelling drama, able to describe it for exactly what it was: everyone's worst nightmare.

Reynolds painted his own portrait as Gary Cooper in *High Noon*, calling on his town folks not to forsake him, his dead daughter, and, by extension, themselves. He perfected the pithy sound bite, as he did the headline-generating gesture. At a news conference announcing the capture of Douglas Walker, Reynolds hugged Detective Doug Stokes and handed him a framed picture of Kimber along with a note that read: "I know you have kids of your own. I hope you have room for one more."

At Walker's sentencing, Reynolds declared that, as far as he was concerned, "Mr. Walker has given up his dues card in the human race." Later, he noted disgustedly that Walker would "be getting out of prison about the same time my daughter's funeral is paid for."

The state of California, he pointed out, was "the one unindicted perpetrator in [his] daughter's murder." His description of Joe Davis was straight out of a Willie Horton campaign ad. Davis, he said, was "a socially destructive machine" who was "the most dangerous type of killer, because he looked human, but was not human."

10

TOUGH LOVE

SUE REAMS AND HER BOY

SUE REAMS WAS NINETEEN WHEN SHE MET Shane's father in Sacramento in the late 1960s. She wasn't just nineteen; she was a *young* nineteen—a willowy, naïve, five foot-eight brunette from a sheltered background in northern California. Her soon-to-be-husband, Johnnie Alulo (not his real name), was her polar opposite. A native Hawaiian stationed in Sacramento while serving in the Air Force, Alulo seemed hip and exotic to Sue Reams, with his curly black hair and tan skin and the self-assurance of someone making his way in the world. She was shy, he was outgoing and charming, with just that touch of bad-boy wildness some young women find so attractive. When Alulo asked her to marry him and move to Hawaii, she jumped at the chance. It was to be love and romance in the soft breezes of the South Pacific.

But it didn't turn out that way. Visions of sweet ukulele nights with Johnnie quickly gave way to a reality of being home alone while Johnnie was out chasing other skirts. Shane was born in 1969, but Sue Reams soon found out that Johnnie already had a child out of wedlock, with another on the way. He also "held an assumption" says Sue Reams, "that's common to some native Hawaiians that the more I hit you, the more I love you." And if that was the case, Sue Reams was receiving a lot more love than she was willing to accept.

After two years in Hawaii, she left Johnnie and moved with Shane into her grandmother's home on a tree-lined street in San Jose, California. Then she filed for divorce. Two years later, when Shane was four, she married Wayne Reams, a dispatcher for a trucking company and a part-time student at San Jose State. He was a nice guy and a good father to Shane, whom he'd help with homework and take to Little League games and soccer matches.

Wayne and Sue had two daughters together, and Shane, she recalls, "grew up a nice, gentle, obedient kid, helpful around the house, very calm, never involved in fights." Then he turned twelve and visited his grandparents in Hawaii. That summer Shane "experimented" with marijuana, returning home to what he'd later describe as "the turning point of his life": Martin Murphy Junior High School in suburban San Jose, where drugs were plentiful. He began smoking pot daily and using LSD and PCP. Shane grew to love drugs, and soon he started to change. He'd promise to do things, and then not do them. His grades began to fall—precipitously. He'd leave home without so much as a nod, and Sue would have no idea where to find him. He gravitated to a whole new set of friends, replacing Little League baseball with a new activity: breaking and entering to support his drug habit.

Sue Reams became so alarmed she sent Shane to live with Johnnie in Hawaii. Shane arrived in desperate need of his father's love and intent on proving that he was more Johnnie's son than the five other kids his father now had with his new wife.

Later, Shane would describe Johnnie as "emotionless, controlling, angry, jealous, violent and more of an overseeing order-giver than a father." But at the time, all he saw was the respect and fear his father sparked in everyone —reactions that left Shane awe-struck and utterly fascinated with Johnnie's bad-boy persona.

Shane's early schooling in how to be like dad began the first time he watched Johnnie and his uncle smoke crack right in front of him and his cousin. To his smoking of weed and dropping of chemicals, Shane, now fourteen, added a new touch: dealing drugs for daddy. But this wasn't enough to get him what he craved from Johnnie. So Shane began stealing his father's drugs and the money he received from their sale, "using every avenue to get [Johnnie's] attention"— hoping that his father would find out, give him a fatherly talk, and tell him that "he wanted something better for [his son] than what he'd had."

Instead, when Johnnie found out, he picked up a garden hose and beat his son mercilessly, while his uncle broke a 2 × 4 over his back. Shane fled, sold what was left of his father's drugs, and bought a one-way ticket home to his mother.

By then, the family had moved to Salt Lake City, where Wayne had found a job. Shane started working as a part-time grocery clerk. His family's move to Utah, as Shane Reams tells it, was tearing hard at the fabric of his mother's marriage. She was living in a strange place with no friends and hated her new surroundings. His return, and his addiction, "only added to the drama." For Sue Reams, however, her son's addiction *was* the drama.

It was about that time that Sue and Wayne heard about "tough love." "Tough love," they learned at group meetings, was a philosophy of parenting that involved "taking a stand." If your kids are refusing to behave and getting into trouble, went the philosophy, you call the police on them. If your kids are doing drugs, you call the police on them. If your kids are doing poorly in school and won't do their work, you kick them out of the house, leaving a note on the door, saying, "you can go to a youth shelter, but you cannot come into this house and continue your behavior."

So Sue and Wayne took a stand and kicked Shane out of the house when he wouldn't obey their rules. Then they learned that Shane had been arrested in San Jose for sleeping in the van of a former neighbor without the permission of the owners. The neighbor refused to press charges, but by then a desperate Sue Reams had become a tough love true believer. So when the San Jose police called and told her to send them a plane ticket so that they could ship Shane home, she told them to forget it, because she had no intention of sending any ticket. "Just keep him there," she told them.

Spending a few weeks or even months in jail, Sue believed, would scare Shane straight. She had no idea that because he was a minor, he'd be declared a ward of the state and placed in a California Youth Authority (CYA) camp until he was twenty-one.

Once Sue Reams understood Shane was going to remain in a CYA prison, she began having doubts about tough love. The first time she visited him at a CYA camp in northern California, the weather was cold and the experience frightening. She understood for the first time the ramifications of her decision. She saw how her son had to line up when he was told, and eat and sleep when he was told. And when she stopped looking around and stared into his face, she saw how hardened it had become, and how the teenager in him had died a rapid, premature death.

In fact, the change in Shane that had alarmed Sue Reams became obvious when he paroled out of CYA at twenty-one. He began smoking and selling rock cocaine. The bad decisions dictated by his addiction were now only underscored by his years in prison. He no longer knew "how to live in society," he later recalled, "how to hold a job, to relate to his family. [His] value on the outside had been somehow diminished."

"In the free world, one makes conscious decisions regarding responsibilities," he'd explain. "In prison, there are no responsibilities. You're told when, where, and how to do everything. What I'd learned in CYA since I was sixteen was the survival technique of all those [who are] locked up and surrounded by the predators and the weak. You were either/or; there was no in between. You took what you wanted." Those, recalls Shane Reams, "were the coping skills [he] brought home."

Sue and Wayne had moved once again, this time from Salt Lake to Irvine, a fast-growing suburban city in Orange County. Shane joined them there, got a job, made some friends, and started dating. And then, once again, he was suddenly gone, leaving in his wake another neighbor complaining of being burglarized.

Sue Reams didn't know which was worse, her anger and despair or her disappointment and utter frustration. It was always neighbors Shane stole from, always people she knew. Now he was again putting her in a humiliating position with her friends and neighbors. "Shane did it," she told her neighbor. "Call the police." And the neighbor called the police. A week or two later, Shane, who was on the run, phoned her.

"Listen," Sue Reams told her son. "You've got to let me pick you up and take you to the police. You can't keep running, you need to resolve things." The status quo, for her, was untenable. Shane was taking her car and driving under the influence. She was frightened that he might hurt himself or someone else. She was worried he might overdose. The only way to end it, she convinced Shane and herself, was for Shane to turn himself in. The police or courts might get him some help, she reasoned.

And that's what Sue Reams kept telling herself as she drove Shane to the police station. "If he does the right thing, he'll get some help. If he does the right thing, he'll get some rehabilitation." But Shane knew better, knew he was walking right back through that revolving door. But he didn't care. He was tired of lying to his family, his girlfriend, and most of all, to himself. I'm not addicted, he'd insist when he answered "the call to the streets." All he wanted was to smoke a little crack with people like himself, people who wanted to get high, feel good, and socialize.

But once that high started to evaporate, the hard truth would wash over him: that he'd do "*anything* to get drugs—even if it meant doing a crime [he] knew would send [him] to prison." But then prison was the only place he knew how to operate, the only place he knew how to *be*, so why not turn himself in? Subsequently, he plea-bargained to two felony residential burglaries and ended up serving eighteen months in state prison, where he received absolutely no help at all.

In California's prisons at that time, nobody did. The war on drugs was raging, and the Golden State was leading the way. In 1980, just 7.5 percent of California's twenty-three thousand inmates had been incarcerated for drug offenses. By 1999, California had one hundred fifty-eight thousand inmates, and 25 percent of the men and almost 35 percent of the women were imprisoned solely for drug offenses.

The state's prisoner recidivism rate, meanwhile, hovered at about 65 percent throughout the late '80s and the '90s. In 1997, to take one base year, about 17 percent of the state's former inmates were sent back to prison for committing new crimes. A staggering 51 percent went back for violating parole—mostly for testing dirty for drugs. Meanwhile, national studies were pegging the percentage of prison inmates with serious alcohol or substance problems at between 75 and 85 percent. Crime and drug addiction—the two were inseparable in an America whose only answer since the early '80s had been to lock up addicts, release them, and lock them up again when they inevitably either committed another crime to feed their untreated habits or tested dirty for drugs. No one, it seemed, was looking for any other answer.

That icon of right-wing criminal justice and proselytizer of state-sponsored tough love, then UCLA professor James Q. Wilson, questioned the very notion of rehabilitation: "Empty the prisons in California," he said, "and ask yourself: What are these people going to do? They are not going to give up crime." In short, once an addict and a criminal, always an addict and a criminal.

Consequently, until very late in the 1990s, 99 percent of California's prisoners received not only no rehabilitation treatment but no guidance to help them reenter the outside world. The most California was willing to do for its prisoners was to give them $200 "gate money" when they were released.

"Two hundred dollars isn't much," as ex-prisoner and former heroin addict Ricardo Hinojosa once pointed out. "Not when you have to buy shoes, socks, underwear, and a jacket, pay for your transportation home, and look for a place to live. By the time you show up at the local parole office, you've got $10 or $15 left. And they pretty much tell you, 'good luck.' In the 1990s there were only about forty-two beds in a place like San Diego County for paroled prisoners, and shelters, particularly in cold weather, were always filled. So if you didn't have family, there was really no place to go. Some dope at that point was certain to take the chill off your back."

Dumped cold back into the community, released prisoners were expected to figure out the rest. By the time Shane Reams was once again released, he had figured out nothing at all.

11

"WEIRD DUCKS AND BLIND FOOLS"

THE FIRST HURDLE FOR THE THREE STRIKES BILL was the state assembly's Public Safety Commission. Its five members would determine whether the Jones bill would even be allowed onto the assembly floor for a vote. Public Safety, like the assembly as a whole, was then controlled by the Democrats, who, over the past two decades, had been a bit more thoughtful and a bit less punitive than the Republicans in their approach to crime. But just a bit.

The Public Safety Committee, however, was more liberal than the body as a whole. Five of its seven members were Democrats, and two were from liberal San Francisco Bay Area districts—Tom Bates from Berkeley and Barbara Lee from Oakland. When Mike Reynolds spoke of them, he nearly choked with contempt. "They were not just liberals," Reynolds would say, bestowing on them his ultimate political insult, "but ultraliberals." "Never, never," he'd point out with genuine incomprehension and disgust, had

Bates "voted to enhance penalties for any crime—ever." As for Lee, well, she "was about of the same persuasion."

Barbara Lee certainly was of a different persuasion from Mike Reynolds, particularly when it came to an understanding of who America's criminal justice system served, and who it did not.

An African American who'd been elected to the state assembly from Oakland in 1990, Lee was a political child of the '60s—a passionate feminist and civil rights and anti-war activist. Born in El Paso, Lee had grown up hearing stories of her father's humiliations both in Jim Crow Texas and while serving as an army officer in America's then-segregated armed forces. And she never forgot them.

In 1972, while chair of Mills College's Black Student Union, she invited Shirley Chisholm to speak on campus. Chisholm was not only a liberal New York congresswoman but also the first African American woman ever to be elected to Congress. Equally important, she was mounting a serious (although highly improbable) campaign to replace Richard Nixon as president. Lee quickly joined her campaign and then went to work for the fiery, black, Bay Area revolutionary turned respected congressional leader Ron Dellums.

Now she was sitting on the Public Safety Committee, a champion of social justice but a realistic legislator, being asked to consider this three strikes bill. She knew what it would mean for tens of thousands of poor, disproportionately black men who could not even *conceive* of any way out of their doomed lives.

Her assembly colleagues, she would later bitterly complain, were constantly shooting down proposals for medical benefits and child care, for education, job training, and drug rehabilitation, but always seemed to vote for spending more to lock people up. This three strikes bill was perhaps the very worst product of that mind-set. And as far as Lee, Bates, and John Burton—the legendary liberal chairman of the powerful assembly Rules Committee—were concerned, it wasn't going to make it past Public Safety without serious amendments.

And indeed, the bill was something to behold. It mandated that after a third strike conviction, a defendant *had* to be sentenced to prison for twenty-five years to life and serve at least twenty-five of those years.

Washington state voters had passed a similar ballot initiative only months earlier, and Jones's proposal seemed like the same law. But it wasn't.

There were forty "serious" crimes listed in the Jones bill, and indeed, most of them *were* serious. They included such acts as murder, oral copulation by force, lewd or lascivious acts on a child under the age of fourteen, rape, the infliction of great bodily harm, and armed robbery.

But there were also several provisions that made it very different from the three strikes law of Washington state—or any other state that would subsequently enact such a statute. One centered around the nonviolent property crime of burglary of an inhabited dwelling house or trailer, "residential burglary," a crime which accounts for a large portion of felony convictions.

"Residential burglary runs the gamut from breaking into someone's bedroom in the middle of the night and raping his watch dog," as San Diego Public Defender Gary Nichols would tell it, "to someone walking into your open attached garage and taking a ninety-eight-cent screwdriver. If he then takes a hammer from a garage down the street five minutes later, he's now committed two residential burglaries. Once convicted, he's facing twenty-five years to life in prison under three strikes if he's ever involved in another crime. He can get a permanent job, marry, and have a family. And twenty years later if he gets a quarter of a gram of coke to help celebrate his tenth anniversary while the kids are away at grandma's, and he gets popped, that's it. He could well be off to jail for life."

There weren't many burglary victims who would share Gary Nichols's sympathy for the long-ago residential burglar gone almost good, of course. Residential burglary is a bad crime—an invasion of the home that is close to an invasion of the person. In fact, in California and many other states a person is allowed to use lethal force to repel an intruder. Yet it has not been included on the list of first and second strikes ("strikes prior") in any other state, or in the federal government's three strikes law.

"The reason that residential burglary is a problematical prior [conviction]," Alex Ricciardulli, a Los Angeles deputy public defender specializing in three strikes appeals, would later point out, "is because it is different than almost all the others on the list of felonies that count as strikes prior in California. There are only two other priors on that list that do not involve *express* violence: child molesting and selling drugs to minors. Residential burglary and these two other crimes do involve a *risk* of violence. If anyone catches a person committing a child molestation or selling drugs to kids, violence can easily result, especially if a kid's parent finds out."

In the eyes of many people, in fact, the sexual molestation of a child is an unforgivably violent act in and of itself. It's not in the same league with residential burglary. As Ricciardulli points out, "there's no question residential burglary is a less aggravated crime than child molesting or selling drugs to children. In fact, when compared to all the other ones on the three strikes 'serious felony' list, it is the least aggravated.

"In addition, while residential burglary has a long tradition of being considered a 'heinous felony' in the common law, the definition was widely expanded in California in 1983. Previously, residential burglary was the burglary of a residence *at night*. But as of '83, California does not have a nighttime requirement. The day/night difference has made California's law much more all-encompassing."

In short, the triggering mechanism in Washington and other three strike states for the law to click in was the commission of *violent* crimes. Under the proposed bill, defendants in California who had been convicted of residential burglary—but had *never* been convicted of a violent crime—would be subject to a third-strike, twenty-five-years-to-life prosecution, with residential burglary convictions counting as their first and second strikes.

"There are over five hundred crimes in California classified as felonies," pointed out California Superior Court Judge LaDoris H. Cordell in the documentary film about California's three strikes law, "The Legacy." "They range from murder and violent assault to writing a bad check, second conviction of shoplifting, or possession of a small amount of drugs. If someone had two strikes and is convicted of another felony, like possession of a small amount of cocaine [or petty theft], the punishment must be twenty-five years to life. That's the three strikes law."

This provision allowing *any one* of over five hundred felonies to count as a third strike, along with inclusion of residential burglaries as a prior strike, was what made the Jones bill so radical, wide-reaching, and powerful.

Moreover—and this was the real kicker—district attorneys would also be able to prosecute misdemeanors as well as felonies as third strikes because of an existing Deukmejian-era law permitting DAs to "enhance" a misdemeanor to a felony if a suspect had previously been convicted of a similar crime. A petty theft of a $10 pair of sunglasses, for example, or a pound of meat from a supermarket, or a six-pack of Bud from a 7–11, could be "enhanced" and prosecuted as a felony if the defendant had been convicted and jailed for a prior petty theft or any other theft-related crime.

Petty crimes in such situations are known as "wobblers." Depending on a local DA's policy, or on a deputy DA's mood on a particular day, the charge can wobble one way or the other— falling on the misdemeanor side or on the felony side. Once raised to a felony, a "wobbler" can then be counted as a "strike" for anyone with one or more prior "violent or serious felonies."

"The beauty of three strikes, and of Mike's thinking on it, was that it was simple enough both for the public to support, and for the criminals to understand," Bill Jones would later say. "They had three chances, and after they committed two of those, serious or violent, for the third one, almost anything could possibly send them [to prison] for twenty-five years to life."

Previous nonviolent convictions, in other words, would count as strikes when a judge was sentencing a defendant; and in many cases those convictions could date back to the age of sixteen and could have occurred decades ago. ("We ultimately decided to focus on sixteen- and seventeen-year-olds," said Reynolds, "people old enough to drive a car, old enough to know right from wrong.") The law would thus apply retroactively to the over two hundred seventy thousand Californians already convicted of one of the "violent or serious" felonies designated in the bill, and to the forty thousand convicted of two.

No suspending of sentences or granting of probation would be allowed, and those convicted would have to serve their time in state prison rather than a county jail.

That was for the *third* strikes. Second strikes would have their consequences, too. The sentence for a second strike would be automatically doubled. A crime that would normally get an offender a five-year prison term would instead automatically get ten years, 80 percent of which would have to be served before he or she could be paroled.

"The second 'strike,'" Mike Reynolds would later proudly proclaim, "the second strike was the true genius of this law. What it did was double their time and make them serve 80 percent of their time. It locked them up during the most prolific years of their criminal career. During the time when they would have or easily could have committed very violent crimes."

"Why didn't we feel we should wait until someone has a third 'serious' or violent conviction?" asked Reynolds rhetorically. "Well, number one, if you don't know who a person is by the time they've had two 'serious or violent convictions,' I'd suggest you're a bad judge of character. The person who should get a chance is that person's next victim. The question was [how] could we get an adequate number to really sweep the criminal element off the streets?"

And "sweeping" people off the street was exactly what Reynolds and the law's other authors had in mind. They even considered changing that verb to a noun and calling their law

"The Street Sweeper" because, as Mike Reynolds later explained, "this law would get the criminal garbage off the streets. We thought long and hard about that one."

They'd also thought hard about how to keep their bill untouched by human hands other than their own, deliberately dismissing and leaving unsolicited the expertise of criminologists, social scientists, and drug abuse experts. Deliberately discarded as well was the growing body of empirical evidence showing that new medications help stabilize mentally ill drug addicts, as do residential drug treatment programs that stress altering criminal values and healing the psychological scars that lead to drug and alcohol addiction and criminal behavior.

For the preceding decade, a legion of get-tough, maximum-minimum sentencing laws had swept through the American Congress and the nation's state legislatures like a tornado. Like them, this bill eviscerated a judge's ability to examine the unique circumstances of each case, the individuality of each defendant, and his or her prospects for redemption, and robbed the judge of the right to then craft a reasoned sentence suitable to both the crime and the person convicted. What made this bill unique were the stakes involved—twenty-five-to-life. Cesare Beccaria's seminal dictum from the Age of Enlightenment that the punishment should fit the crime, fast becoming an archaic relic of American jurisprudence, would be plunged ever deeper into the depths of irrelevance.

Unmentioned as well was the fact that the law would give prosecutors a bigger sledgehammer with which to threaten suspects during plea bargaining. Fearful of being sentenced to twenty-five years to life in prison for a petty crime, or for one they did not commit, they would accept a relatively harsh sentence rather than risk an imposed harsher sentence. A new policy, with heavy racial and class overtones bolstered by the war on drugs, was being proposed to replace rehabilitation: the radical notion of preventive detention. The underlying rationale was that a petty criminal *might* commit a more serious crime in the future, and therefore should be taken off the streets for decades, or for the rest of his life.

As Gary Nichols noted, the proposed law targeted not only people living a life of crime, but also people who'd done crimes when young but had been holding jobs for years or decades, and then were occasionally lured back to their old drug-using or alcohol-abusing ways. Sending them to prison for life seemed an extraordinary punishment for a petty crime or simple drug possession—a violation of the Eighth Amendment to the U.S. Constitution, which barred "cruel and unusual punishment."

But Mike Reynolds—like tens of millions of his fellow Californians and fellow Americans—either did not see or did not care about all these fine distinctions. Nor did he or they see themselves as extremists. They felt themselves instead to be under siege, victimized by bad seeds like Joe Davis and sold out by elected officials.

Most angrily dismissed or could not comprehend the complex link between crime and childhood abuse and economic, social, and cultural poverty. The likelihood of such kids finding family and status in gangs, thrills in a thrill-seeking culture, violence in a culture that glorified violence, and solace in drugs and the values of the street was simply alien to their consciousness.

As long as it's "easier to pick up a gun than a book," Mike Reynolds would later explain, "easier to do crime than get an honest-to-God job, the course of least resistance is the one that's going to carry the day."

And if you believed that it was all that simple, then obviously it meant little to you that from the early '80s to the mid-'90s, the proportion of children under the age of six living in poverty had risen nationally by 12 percent, while in California the rate of poverty had shot up by 24 percent, so that one in three of the state's young children was living in poverty. And it would also matter little that in 1994, California tied with Louisiana for last place in the nation in student reading scores.

Mike Reynolds exemplified Americans for whom none of that mattered. He understood one part of the crime equation—meaningful punishment—but seemed unwilling to go beyond himself to compute the rest of it. He understood and had empathy for people like himself of whatever color. But all others he understood only through a very narrow prism. And when he found people wanting—as he would anyone with a criminal history, or anyone who might question his assumptions or his goals, they too lost their humanity.

"Whenever I spoke to people in Fresno" (about the three strikes law), wrote Reynolds in his coauthored book, *Three Strikes and You're Out!*, "the question I was most asked was, 'How can anybody not vote for this?' [But in Sacramento], I was [to find] these weird little ducks [Lee, Bates, etc.] that didn't believe in what we were trying to do. Not only that, but these weird little ducks had their fingers on the voting buttons."

And who *were* these weird ducks other than blind fools who could not see that crime was tearing at the very fabric of America, and destroying its neighborhoods?

As Catherine Campbell wrote in her review of Reynolds's *Three Strikes and You're Out!*, "terms like 'predator' and 'moral poverty' mask a profound ignorance of the lives and experience of those who are doomed to live out their youths in our ghettos, slums and prisons. The criminal justice system cannot make us or our children safe, but it can, sadly, become the legitimization of our class and racial hatreds."

Mike Reynolds and his like-minded supporters could not *bear* that kind of talk. What they wanted was more of the all-out war on crime and drugs that their representatives in Sacramento and Washington had been eagerly giving them since the early '80s. The Jones three strikes bill was simply deploying heavier artillery and carrying those wars to their logical conclusion. Eventually, the pragmatic Public Safety Committee, realizing how volatile an issue crime was continuing to be, agreed to allow the bill to reach the floor, but in a modified version that resembled Washington state's three violent felonies law. Reynolds, however, would have none of it. The modified proposal, he felt, was "a goddamn lie," a "slap in the face . . . nothing more than the old habitual-offender law that had been on the books since 1982," combined with "a little enhancing of sentences." In reaction to Reynolds's intractability, the committee voted not to send the bill to the full assembly—a move that effectively killed it until at least January of 1994.

- - - -

Mike Reynolds blamed his defeat not just on the "ultraliberals" but on bad timing. "Unfortunately," said Reynolds, "news-wise, every once in a while there's a day that you shouldn't [try to get publicity]. And this happened to be on the day of April 20, 1993. It happened to be the day that the Feds decided to torch [the Branch Davidians in] Waco, Texas. That, of course, superseded any news that they ran on our behalf. Our [news stories about the bill] were right behind the pet obituary that day. Nevertheless, we went up there and made the biggest statement we could."

Vincent Schiraldi, head of the Justice Policy Institute, a progressive think tank adamantly opposed to Reynolds's proposed law, saw it differently. "They got Bill Jones to carry [the bill] and it went nowhere. Largely because it was a dog, it was a bad piece of legislation. None of the legislators were going to promote it. Even Jones didn't push it that hard."

Indeed, "the first time it came around," recalled California legislative analyst Jeff Long, "we didn't do any fiscal assessment because it didn't pass the so-called giggle test. It wasn't worth the effort, because this thing wasn't going to go anywhere, it was so patently stupid."

- - - -

Back in Fresno, Mike Reynolds plotted to sidestep the legislature altogether and place his version of the bill on the next statewide ballot. California voters had had the initiative and the referendum since the early twentieth century, when the state's high-minded, good-government Progressives had amended the state constitution to break the iron grip the railroad robber barons had on the California legislature. The amendment enabled voters to bypass the assembly and senate entirely, and pass laws by an initiative.

The initiative process was little used, however, until 1964, when California voters approved a ballot initiative that repealed a state law banning racial discrimination in housing (the courts later ruled the initiative unconstitutional). Then, in 1978, two conservative antitax crusaders, Howard Jarvis and Paul Gann, caught the mood of California homeowners and placed an initiative on the ballot that called for the radical lowering of California's property taxes. Known as Proposition 13, it proved wildly popular with a frustrated electorate whose property taxes were spiraling out of control in California's then red-hot real estate market.

Failing to respond to homeowners' pleas for tax relief was a singular display of ideological arrogance on the part of the liberal governor, Jerry Brown, and the Democratically controlled state legislature. They acted as if elderly Californians could just sell their homes and move into apartments if they couldn't afford their taxes, and open up the housing stock to younger people. The result of California's Democratic leaders so completely misreading the will of the middle class was that Proposition 13 passed overwhelming and was hailed as a great populist victory for California's middle (and voting) class, one that heralded the coming triumphs of conservative, tax-hating Republicans across the nation.

Rarely mentioned, however, was that two-thirds of the windfall tax savings from Proposition 13 went to corporations and businesses, or that with taxes so greatly reduced, the social service network and the public school and university system that had once been glories of the Golden State would begin a dramatic decline from which they have not recovered.

Proposition 13 was followed by another citizen-driven change in the law, this one precipitated by the killing of thirteen-year-old Cari Lightner by a drunk driver. Her grief-stricken mother, Candy Lightner, founded a group called "Mothers Against Drunk Driving," or MADD. What Jarvis and Gann had done for property taxes, Lightner and MADD did for drunk-driving laws: garner widespread public support for change. In this case the change lowered the level of alcohol drivers could have in their systems before being declared legally drunk. The only difference was that while Jarvis and Gann did it through a ballot initiative, Lightner did it through the legislative process.

Both the antitax and anti–drunk driver movements, however, "were able to take lapses in the law, personal tragedy, drama, and broad but unfocused public concern and create a powerful whirlwind," as Bruce Cain, a U.C. Berkeley professor specializing in California politics, later pointed out to the *Los Angeles Times*. "[Those whirlwinds] were strong enough to overcome politics as usual: A girl killed by a drunk driver. Elderly people losing their homes because they could not pay property taxes. These were issues that were lying there, waiting to be dramatized." Mike Reynolds knew in his gut his three strikes law was just waiting there as well.

- - - -

Beyond sensing that their law would be more popular with the public than with the legislature—where compromise is the order of things and the heart of democracy—Reynolds and his backers also understood that a ballot initiative was an insurance policy because of a special feature of the initiative law. A bill passed by the legislature and signed into law by the governor can be amended or repealed by the legislature by a simple majority vote plus the governor's signature. An initiative that amends California's constitution, however, can only be amended by a *two-thirds* vote of the legislature, plus the governor's signature, and the legislature can amend or repeal an initiative *statute* only with another voter-approved statute—extremely difficult barriers to overcome when dealing with uncontroversial laws, but nearly impossible with a tough, seemingly straightforward but politically charged law-and-order bill.

Having made up his mind to pursue his three strikes law on both the legislative and initiative tracks, Mike Reynolds spoke with his wife, Sharon. She told him that she wanted no part of a public life, but would totally support any course of action he chose. She too wanted revenge for her daughter's murder. And with that, Mike Reynolds plunged ahead.

ERWIN CHEMERINSKY

Outside the United States Supreme Court: "If fifty years to life for two petty thefts wasn't a violation of the United States Constitution's Eighth Amendment prohibition against cruel and unusual punishment, what was?"

KIMBER REYNOLDS

The driver pulled on Kimber's purse. When Kimber pulled back, he put a .357 Magnum to her head and pulled the trigger.

MIKE REYNOLDS

He announced to the world that he was going to continue to grieve and then he was going to "kick some ass."

DAN LUNGREN
He craved the big prize: the governorship of California.

SHANE REAMS UP TO BAT

He replaced Little League baseball with a new activity: breaking and entering to support his drug habit.

SHANE AND SUE REAMS

Shane Reams faced twenty-five years to life in state prison, a place designed to be cold and impersonal, to break a man so he never wants to come back, to make his life as miserable as possible.

MARC AND POLLY KLAAS

"The search for Polly was about bringing that little girl home," said Marc Klaas. "It was the most desperate time any parent can experience."

RICHARD ALLEN DAVIS

"Mr. Davis," intoned the judge, "this is always a traumatic and emotional decision for a judge. You made it very easy today by your conduct." He then sentenced Richard Allen Davis to death.

PHOTO JOHN STOREY, COURTESY GETTY IMAGES

MARC KLAAS WITH POLLY'S FRIENDS

The FBI pursued the theory that Polly had run away with a boyfriend. But Polly didn't *have* a boyfriend. She hung out with giggling girlfriends, listened to music, and played board games.

STEVE COOLEY

Being sworn in as Los Angeles district attorney. "I always felt that unless used judiciously, the [three strikes law] could result in injustice. . . . My fears were well founded."

PART THREE

THE POSTER CHILD AND WILLIE HORTON

12

RIGHT OUT OF HER OWN BEDROOM

RICHARD ALLEN DAVIS'S SURREPTITIOUS ENTRANCE into twelve-year-old Polly Klaas's house was one of those twists of fate that mock the notion of a loving God.

Polly was up a little late on that balmy October night in 1993—it was already close to 10:40—but she was hosting a slumber party for her two best girlfriends, Kate and Gillian. All three were happily engrossed in a board game, oblivious to the fact that Davis had just sneaked into Klaas's two-bedroom bungalow through an unlocked back door.

Shortly before, the thirty-nine-year-old Davis had smoked a joint and downed a couple of quarts of beer at Wickersham Park, about a block from Polly's Petaluma, California, home. Because of its proximity to a local Greyhound station in the middle of town, the park had become a gathering spot for many of the town's homeless, and for the passing-through down-and-outs such as Richard Allen Davis.

Now there he stood, dressed in black, in Polly's bedroom—a

big man with a prison-weight-lifting physique, pale white skin set off by the dull blues and faded reds of jail-house tattoos, coarse, graying black hair swept back in a leonine mane, face shaped by a saggy beard and thick, dark eyebrows over menacing eyes. There he stood, an unholy visitation, holding a butcher knife.

He told them he was there to rob the place, and that he'd slit their throats if they didn't do exactly as he said. Using white cloth strips, Davis then tied the hands of Polly, Kate and Gillian behind their backs, gagged them, put pillow cases over their heads, and told them to get down on the floor and count to one thousand.

It was at this point that what looked like a crude, bold home robbery took a turn that made that crime trivial by comparison. Ignoring the household valuables he'd asked about, Davis scooped up the four-foot-ten-inch, eighty-pound Polly, carried her down the hall, past the bedroom where her mother and younger sister lay sleeping, and disappeared into the night.

- - - -

Petaluma is a charming northern California city of about forty-five thousand, with beautifully maintained Victorian homes, antique shops, upscale stores, and coffeehouses, radiating the small-town aura of a Norman Rockwell lithograph. So much so, in fact, that in 1984, the living embodiment of that image—Ronald Reagan—had used Petaluma as the scenic backdrop in his "Morning in America" presidential campaign commercials. Earlier, the film director George Lucas had done the same, choosing Petaluma as the setting for his ode to the '50s, *American Graffiti*.

Davis had visited Petaluma just a few weeks before abducting Polly. Cruising north from his room in a vine-covered San Mateo "transitional living" shelter called the Turning Point, he'd driven his '79 white Pinto through Petaluma en route to visit his sister, who was then living on the Coyote Valley Indian Reservation about seventy miles further north.

Just ninety days before his October trip, Richard Allen Davis had been paroled from a state prison in San Luis Obispo with the breezy-sounding name of the California Men's Colony (CMC), after serving half of a sixteen-year sentence for kidnapping and robbery. But names can be deceptive. As lawyer and journalist Jeffrey Toobin later pointed out in the *New Yorker*, CMC was not only California's biggest prison, but "the last stop for many of the state's worst criminals. The part of the prison in which Davis lived had about thirty-five hundred inmates and almost a third of them were doing life sentences."

As Davis himself tells it, he was born in June 1954, the third of five children, "half American Indian, Paiute and Shoshone, . . . and half white," in Nevada. His "family," he says, "was not the 'group-hugging, emotion-showing' [sort] that normal kids probably have." His mother had had two boys before meeting his father, whom his father "never knew about and [whom she] kept hidden from him."

"One Saturday morning," Davis later wrote, "she dressed the two boys up and they left the house. When my mother came back later that day, the two boys were not with her. . . . As my grandmother said, 'Probably like cats, [she'd] tied [them] up in a sack and tossed [them] into the water.' Nobody ever found out, and nobody ever pressed her about it. That was life."

His mother, that "gutter-snipe dog bitch," and his father were alcoholics who divorced when he was eleven. His longshoreman father, Robert R. Davis, was awarded custody "because," as Davis tells it, his father "proved her [to be] unfit and immoral," a woman, remembers Richard Allen Davis, whom he "saw . . . in the backseats with other men," who fed her children dog food and beat them with "barber straps because the hangers were leaving marks."

His parents' divorce appears to have been the defining moment in Richard Allen Davis's young life. "I don't think," he would later write, "that people can open their minds to see how I started looking at life at a young age. I will tell you that a choice was made . . . at about 11, 12 years old, maybe the sweet age of 13, 'not to care anymore.' . . . [The] cards one is shuffled out [sic] . . . start from the moment they drop from the womb. . . . Then as other happenings follow into their life's [sic] pattern . . . one finds one self [sic] at the 'crossroads.' "

The crossroads in Richard Allen Davis's life seems to have appeared the day he was packing to leave his mother's home. "My father said it was time to grow up," Davis recalls, "and he gave me the large trunk to go pack up my sisters' and my clothes. As I was in my sisters' room trying to get their clothes, my mother and grandmother were in the hallway yelling at me. . . . This was when my mother informed me that I had been born a 'blue baby,' and if the doctor had had any sense he would have let things be, and that . . . I was a 'bad seed,' because the best part of 'me' had been left on the sheets."

Robert R. Davis was hardly the model father, either. Davis and his two sisters went to live with their father "up in the redwoods," where Robert R. Davis—who frequently farmed out his five children to either his or his ex-wife's parents—soon announced to his son that he would have to take care of himself and his sisters. "I have to work," he said. "You'll have food; if you run low, there are guns, and you know where the fishing poles are." His mother, who had "all visitation rights," never wrote, called or visited.

Soon Richard Allen Davis's behavior turned bizarre. Life was all downhill at that point, for Richard Allen Davis and for the pets in his neighborhood as well. He soaked cats with gasoline and then set them ablaze, neighbor Ruth Baron told *People* magazine, and "used dogs as targets for knife-throwing practice."

At the age of twelve, he was arrested for stealing checks from his neighbors' mailboxes. Then he dropped out of school in the ninth grade and began getting seriously drunk. Throughout his teens and early twenties he made all the wrong moves and said all the wrong things as he was constantly arrested for petty theft, residential burglary, dealing in stolen property, public drunkenness, and disorderly conduct. After being booked, he'd invariably confess to crimes the police hadn't even asked about.

In 1974, at twenty-one, he was sentenced to his first stretch in state prison—six months to fifteen years for attempted burglary. But Richard Allen Davis's criminal record up until then had consisted of relatively minor raps. It was when he was released from prison at age twenty-two that Davis's pathological behavior really began kicking in.

In 1976, he spotted a woman at a suburban San Francisco BART (Bay Area Rapid Transit) station, and, as he later told it, "had the feeling she wanted something done to her." When the woman walked into the station's parking lot, he snuck up behind her and, at knifepoint, ordered her into the passenger seat of her car. He then drove her, a twenty-six-year-old legal secretary named Frances Mays, to an abandoned area. "At that point," Mays later told Jeffrey Toobin, "he exposed himself and said, 'I'm going to count to three—you know what I want you to do.'"

Mays knew what she *didn't* want to do, so she grabbed the knife, leaped out of the car, and started screaming. A passing car stopped. It turned out to be Mays's lucky day. Inside was a California Highway Patrol officer, driving his wife to work, who arrested Davis at gunpoint.

While in jail, Davis tried to hang himself and was sent to Napa State Hospital for psychiatric observation. About three months later, he escaped from the hospital and, over the course of the next five days, broke into a nearby house and smashed a woman in the head with a fireplace poker; stole drugs, a shotgun, and ammunition from an animal shelter; and unsuccessfully attempted to kidnap another woman at gunpoint. Finally, he broke into an unoccupied house and was re-arrested after being found hiding, gun in hand, in a backyard.

He was tried in Napa County for kidnapping, two assaults, receiving stolen property, and being in possession of a gun, and was sentenced to six years in prison under the new "determinate" sentencing law. After that, only a blind fool could fail to see that Richard Allen Davis was an incorrigible, dangerous criminal who needed to be kept in prison for as long as possible.

But once he served his full sentence, his parole board had no option but to set him free. This was due to California's 1977 Uniform Determinate Sentencing Act, a "reform" that laid out rigid sentencing and release requirements for judges and parole boards. Each person convicted of a crime had to receive approximately the same sentence as someone convicted of a similar crime and had to be released after serving approximately the same number of years.

Prior to the law, judges had been able to sentence defendants to open-ended, "indeterminate" sentences, which allowed some convicts to be released on parole after a relatively short term, and others who'd committed the same crime to languish in prison for decades. A parole board could hold or release inmates based on its perception of whether or not they had been rehabilitated. But that system hadn't worked to anyone's satisfaction.

Conservatives felt that rehabilitation—the theoretical underpinning of indeterminate sentencing—was yet another insane liberal notion. And liberals thought that the system was arbitrary and unfair—keeping people who should have been released under lock and key while allowing others, with political connections or well-paid lawyers, to be released at the first opportunity.

So in 1977, they banded together and passed the Uniform Determinate Sentencing Act. "Rehabilitation" was stricken as the stated goal of imprisonment, replaced in the preamble to the new law with "punishment." Henceforth, punishment was to be the goal for judges when sentencing, while a parole board's discretion to release or hold a prisoner was eliminated except in capital crimes.

After being released, Davis went on a robbery spree. During one incident, he and his girlfriend, Sue Edwards, robbed an acquaintance of Edwards, threatening her with a gun and, according to Jeffrey Toobin, forcing her to withdraw $6,000 from her bank and give it to them. He was given the maximum sentence—sixteen years—and was released after serving eight. Thus it was that Richard Allen Davis, instead of being locked away for life, wound up brandishing a knife in Polly Klaas's bedroom.

13

ANOTHER PIERCING SCREAM

LIKE MIKE REYNOLDS, MARC KLAAS was asleep in his bedroom when the phone rang. And like Reynolds, he was forced out of his slumber by his wife's piercing scream with news of his daughter. "Polly's been kidnapped," she said. Grasping the receiver, Klaas heard Polly's stepfather, Allan Nichol, repeat the words: "Polly's been kidnapped and is still missing."

In full-fledged denial that such a thing could have occured, Klaas—who was divorced from Polly's mother and lived several miles away in Sausalito—swiftly drove up to Petaluma with his wife and a friend. Once they got there, Klaas was briefed by the local police and the FBI, rented a motel room, and waited.

He was immensely relieved to see the FBI agents. He knew enough to know that they were the Big Boys, the top of the line, and it was comforting to have them on his side. They had the experience in abductions-by-strangers that the Petaluma police lacked, as well as unlimited resources.

The Bureau had, in fact, investigated nearly a dozen stranger abductions in the Bay Area over the previous decade. Unfortunately, none of those investigations had saved any of the kids, but Klaas would not learn that until later.

Klaas himself was in desperate shape. Unable to sleep, his back was aching, he was chain smoking Marlboro Lights, and he was on his way to losing thirty pounds through nervous exhaustion, sweating so profusely that he later had to throw away a pair of sneakers because of their stench. But he had no option but to sit in that motel room and wait. And then wait some more. When the phone finally rang, it was the Petaluma police asking him to come to the station house.

- - - -

In sharp contrast to the bald, portly, and otherwise nondescript Mike Reynolds, Marc Klaas was a handsome, intense man who resembled a leaner, more delicately featured version of the actor Alex Baldwin.

Both Reynolds and Klaas were quintessential Californians, but each was emblematic of a very different region of the state. Reynolds was inland, Central Valley, small-town, '50s California to his core. Marc Klaas was Haight-Ashbury circa 1968.

His father, Joe Klaas, had lived a life straight out of a Warner Bros. World War II propaganda movie. A dramatic-looking man with a head of gray-white curls and a silver beard, Joe Klaas had been raised in the Seattle area and was attending the University of Washington when World War II broke out in Europe. Quitting school, he joined England's Royal Air Force and fought as a Spitfire pilot in the famous American Eagle Squadron before being shot down over North Africa. He spent the remaining years of the war as a German POW, seeing, as he later told it, "Allied prisoners gunned down not fifty feet from him," escaping and being recaptured, and then being taken "on a forced death march" in a freezing European winter that, "in two days, killed twenty-seven hundred of the ten thousand POWs being moved."

After his service in World War II, he earned a BA in public relations and an MA in creative writing from the University of Washington. He worked as an AP correspondent, a radio talk show host, and a station manager, "published eight or nine books," and had lived a good many years in San Francisco. He was, in short, a tough act for any son to follow. And Marc Klaas did not respond well to the challenge.

Marc grew up to be a bright, verbally fluid man with a retentive mind. But at the time of his daughter's kidnapping, he had done very little with his life. At nineteen, he'd opposed a Vietnam War that his war-hero father supported, but had joined the army anyway, both to avoid the draft and to please Joe Klaas.

He spent what he would later describe as a miserable three years as a medic, "serving against everything [he] believed in." Following his discharge, Marc Klaas never really got a handle on what he wanted to do with the rest of his life. Like a brother who had died of alcoholism, Marc Klaas developed a drinking problem and a fondness for marijuana.

By his own description, he'd always been "pig-headed," always the first guy in line to question authority. So he plugged right into the then pulsating Bay Area counterculture, took an obligatory "hippie trip around the world," returned, drove a cab, and then found a niche as a bellhop working in what he describes as "piece-of-crap" jobs.

While taking a few courses at City College in San Francisco, he met Polly's mother, Eve, who came from South Orange, New Jersey. Her family was well-to-do, her father a high ranking executive at AT&T. She'd come to the Bay Area with her first husband, who was about to enter law school there, and when their marriage fell apart, Klaas "stepped up," he recalls, and "caught Eve on the rebound."

Their marriage produced Polly, their only child together, who was born in January of 1981 in San Francisco. Two and a half years later, Marc Klaas moved out and Eve initiated divorce proceedings. The settlement was amiable; Eve got physical custody of Polly, and Marc Klaas got weekend visitation rights and unlimited access to his daughter.

After Klaas began dating his current wife, Violet Cheer, they moved into a condo in the quaint tourist town of Sausalito, where Polly vacationed and spent many of the holidays. She spoke on the phone with her father almost daily.

Eve, meanwhile, married an architect named Allan Nichol, with whom she had a daughter, Anne. Polly never got along with her stepfather, partly because she resented being constantly uprooted as Nichol moved from job to job in one small northern California town after another.

When Eve and Allan Nichol separated, Eve moved to Petaluma with Polly and Annie. Polly liked Petaluma and began to blossom, joining a contemporary theater group and her junior high school band.

Meanwhile, a job that Marc Klaas really wanted was offered to him: the chance to run the Hertz rent-a-car franchise at the luxurious Fairmont Hotel in San Francisco. With his new marriage also doing well, Klaas was truly happy. Until the evening of October 1, 1993.

- - - -

He arrived at the police station consumed by a feeling of dread that was exacerbated by his being told to wait outside the station house. The longer Klaas waited, the darker were his thoughts, until he became absolutely convinced that the police were going to tell him Polly was dead.

Finally, an FBI agent stepped outside. There was no news of Polly, he said. The reason they'd asked him to the station house was to administer a polygraph exam—a common practice when a child of divorced parents is abducted. But there was no way that was going to happen that day, he told Klaas, because he was obviously far too agitated and emotionally distraught for the test to have any accuracy.

Then he did something, as Marc Klaas tells it, that was rare for a cop, and particularly an FBI agent. Perhaps he was reacting to the pain in Klaas's face, perhaps he was just playing good cop. But suddenly he put his arm around Klaas and told him that he should go back to the motel where he'd been staying, get some sleep, and try to refocus his attitude. He had to be the general in charge of the effort to bring Polly home. There was never a time, he added, that his child needed him more than she needed him now.

Meanwhile, a massive local effort to help find Polly had geared up, and Klaas was quickly contacted by several people who knew just how wretched he was feeling. One was a man named David Collins, whose son Kevin had been kidnapped several years before. Another was a woman whose three-year-old daughter had also disappeared about that time. But they were little comfort because neither of their children had ever been found. Meanwhile, Eve Nichol cried out their despair. "I have a daughter out there," she said, "without shoes."

The first several weeks following Polly's kidnapping, the FBI pursued the theory that Polly had run away with her boyfriend. But Polly didn't *have* a boyfriend, and never had. She was, as Marc Klaas would point out with mounting frustration, "a twelve-year-old prepubescent child." She hung out with giggling girlfriends who loved nothing more than endlessly listening to the boy-group music that twelve-year-old girls love. When that unlikely theory collapsed, the FBI began to postulate that the entire incident was a plot contrived by *Polly* and her twelve-year-old girlfriends. "If they believed *that*," thought Marc Klaas, "no wonder they wanted me to take a polygraph."

Eventually, however, Klaas did take and pass the FBI polygraph, and sat through a series of grueling interrogations. He told the agents things he'd never told anyone. He told them *everything*. And then he told the agents all about his brothers, who knew people, as he later put it, "who'd never make the A-list social register." But none of it, as it turned out, was relevant.

14

"GUNS DON'T KILL PEOPLE"

WITH TELEVISION CAMERAS ROLLING, reporters scribbling away, and Sharon standing at his side silently holding a framed picture of Kimber, Mike Reynolds held a joint news conference with the National Rifle Association (NRA). The purpose was to announce the powerful gun-advocacy group's support for Reynolds's campaign to have his three strikes law placed on the November 1994 ballot.

Placing an initiative on a statewide California ballot can have an enormous political payoff, but it's also a massive undertaking. In 1994, three hundred and sixty five thousand valid signatures had to be gathered for an initiative to qualify, which in reality meant about six hundred thousand, given that tens of thousands are inevitably stricken as invalid.

Because getting that number of signatures solely through the efforts of volunteers is a near impossibility, political firms specializing in gathering signatures, and in shaping and promoting an issue, had long ago developed into an innovative cottage industry in California. In the process they'd turned a populist ideal into a special interest tool for any organization with enough money to pay professional signature gatherers a buck or two a signature to qualify an initiative for a place on the ballot. But they didn't work for initiatives they thought were losers.

The first thing Reynolds had needed, therefore, was some proof that the three strikes law would garner public support and inspire the kind of contributions that would make money for a campaign consulting firm. All of this required start-up money Mike Reynolds didn't have.

So he began to seek financial support from organizations with a clear interest in the legislation. Among them were the NRA and the California Correctional Peace Officers Association (CCPOA)—the latter an extraordinarily powerful public employee union that represented the state's twenty-five thousand prison guards.

For decades, the NRA had enjoyed enormous success in blocking gun-control legislation by generously supporting friendly political candidates and pointedly warning others that they'd better tow the NRA line. The NRA line was simple: *All* gun control legislation had to be fought, because *any* law in any way limiting the rights of gun owners would eventually lead to the abolition of the sacred right of Americans to own guns, leaving the public defenseless against a tyrannical government or deadly criminal.

The NRA membership took this line of reasoning *very* seriously, and was consequently taken *very* seriously by politicians as well. By the early '90s, however, the organization's clout—while still powerful in much of the country—was on the wane among many California voters who were both worried about and weary of gun-related violence. A 1992 *Los Angeles Times* poll (conducted prior to LA's incendiary post–Rodney King riot) found that an extraordinary 15 percent of the respondents in LA County and 13 percent of all Southern Californians reported that they, or a household member, had been the victim of a crime or an act of violence involving a firearm. Almost 30 percent believed that gun crimes in their communities occurred "frequently," and almost 40 percent responded that they occurred "occasionally." The poll also quoted people like thirty-one-year-old hospital orderly Julio Rojas, who sometimes carried a .22 caliber pistol to protect himself when he went out at night. If carrying a gun could save his life, he told the *Times*, then he didn't care if it was a felony, one "that you never get punished for anyway."

But many Californians weren't interested in Rojas's solution, or in reacting to gun crime by passing laws permitting even more guns for "self-protection." Unlike Texans, they didn't want people bizarrely packing concealed weapons to church on Sunday morning. They wanted sensible gun laws, and many in the state were starting to understand that the NRA was a huge impediment to that.

What the NRA needed in the Golden State was an image makeover and to be, as Mike Reynolds later put it, "proactive rather than reactive." And a three strikes campaign was a perfect way to change the conversation, take the focus off the easy availability of guns and shift all responsibility to those using them.

The NRA had accomplished all those things in Washington state, the home of the nation's first "Three Strikes, You're Out" law. In 1992, a group called Washington Citizens for Justice couldn't even gather enough signatures to have their proposed three strikes initiative placed on the ballot. To the rescue rode the NRA, donating $90,000 to the same campaign the following year. The result was the passage of the then-toughest law in the nation that special-interest money could buy, and the birth of the three strikes movement.

Wanting to repeat its triumph in the nation's most populous state, the NRA was among the very first organizations to support and finance Reynolds's three strikes proposal.

Because of Mike Reynolds's passion to reduce crime, one would have thought he'd have little use for the likes of the NRA. But a like-minded agenda and an infusion of cash can make for strange bedfellows, or in the case of Mike Reynolds, some convoluted logic. "Look," he said, "my daughter was murdered with a .357 Magnum. They placed it in her ear. What I want is that kind of conduct stopped. So let's talk about some of the [gun control] proposals. . . .

"Banning cheap handguns won't be effective. That would just put more reliable guns out on the street. . . .

"As for assault weapons, it depends on what's an assault weapon—you can get around a clip-size ban by taping two clips together and reversing them—and you've walked around a law with nothing but a piece of tape. So while it may feel good, is it making things safer? . . .

"Machine guns are against the law in California [yet] I just had an opportunity to buy one. So the question is, have laws been effective in stopping machine guns? . . . And the answer is they have not. . . . Drugs are illegal, and has it stopped them? Hell no it hasn't. It's a supply and demand thing."

In other words, Reynolds seemed to be saying—and in language remarkably similar to that of the state's law-and-order, pro-gun governor, Pete Wilson, and its attorney general, Dan Lungren—that *no* gun control was better than some gun control, because no gun control law could ever be perfect.

Never mind the blood-soaked horror the people in America's ghettos faced on a daily basis because of the easy availability of cheap handguns. Mike Reynolds and his middle-class family would almost certainly never experience another handgun crime, nor would almost anyone in their world. Forget about the fact that one generation of locked-up criminals will only be replaced by the next generation, and that the guns will still be there to be fired at the next generation of victims. And never mind the parents, who, as one teacher in LA's teeming immigrant ghetto of Pico Union put it, "come around the corner to get their kids from school and walk right by a shooting victim, or witness a shooting, but don't go to the cops because they don't trust the police." But then, Mike Reynolds could hardly oppose the NRA. Not after its initial contribution of $40,000 launched his three strikes campaign and saved his fledgling ballot initiative.

15

THE PRINCE OF "J" STREET

DON NOVEY COMES ON BOARD

IF THE NRA HAD WORK TO DO ON ITS IMAGE, Don Novey was a man who had *his* image down pat. An engaging smile rarely left the face of the president of the California Correctional Peace Officers Association. Nor did the twinkle in his eyes. At fifty, Novey's P.R. persona was that of the quaint, self-effacing, down-home country boy reluctantly forced to set all those wrongheaded big-city sophisticates straight. His only desire, he liked to say with wide-eyed sincerity, was to help California continue on "the great historic trail of the Golden State—the melting pot of this civilization."

But beneath the folksy facade lay an iron will that enabled Novey to take a weak collection of law enforcement employee associations and transform them into a public employee colossus with disturbingly disproportionate policy-making power.

Squat and unimpressive looking, Novey's trademark affectation was his hat, which rarely left his balding head. He kept six or seven different styles in the back of his car, but seemed to favor his snap-brim, which he'd wear Bogie-style—pushed back, just right, off his forehead.

A "fifth-generation Polish American" from Sacramento, Novey himself was the son of a corrections officer and, like Mike Reynolds, was a man with nothing in his background to indicate that he'd one day become one of the shrewdest kingmakers in California politics. He had graduated from tiny American River College, served in army intelligence during the late '60s, and then gone on to work as a guard at Folsom Prison.

In 1980, he became president of CCPOA, added California Youth Authority supervisors and parole officers to his prison guards, and built up CCPOA's membership from about fifty-six hundred to nearly twenty-five thousand. At the same time, he won unprecedented pay and benefits for a membership whose jobs required nothing more than a high school diploma, six weeks of training, and a high tolerance for human misery. Before Novey, the top salary for a corrections officer was $21,000; by 1994, it had risen to over $44,000. With benefits included, the total package was $53,000—$10,000 more than that of the average California schoolteacher.

Using his membership's nearly $8 million a year in dues, and its offices in Bakersfield, Indio, Rancho Cucamonga, Fresno, suburban Sacramento, and downtown Sacramento, Novey maximized his political influence. He played a pivotal role in creating "Crime Victims United," which was supported almost entirely by CCPOA, and became its creature. What Don Novey wanted, "Crime Victims United" wanted, and vice versa. He gave twice as much in political contributions as did the California Teachers Association, which had ten times CCPOA's membership. The tactic paid off so handsomely that Novey was able to boast—and with absolute truth—that his union had "won thirty-eight out of forty-four bills introduced under the last three governors."

Novey not only rewarded his political water-carriers, he spanked those who dared defy him. John Vasconcellos was a good example. Vasconcellos was a Bay Area liberal who was then the highly respected chairman of the assembly's powerful Ways and Means Committee. Vasconcellos had ardently opposed California's extraordinary, decade-long prison-building boom. Not surprisingly, CCPOA was among its very fiercest champions. Although Vasconcellos's seat was one of the most secure in the assembly, Novey decided to donate over $75,000 to his opponent, who had little chance of winning, during the 1992 election. His message was directed more to other politicians than to Vasconcellos—a reminder that Don Novey *wanted* that construction to proceed and did not *appreciate* Vasconcellos signing a ballot argument against a prison-bond initiative in 1990. Vasconcellos still stuck to his principles following Novey's brash public warning, and won the election. But he went to great pains to make sure that his opposition to the state's new prison construction, and his opposition to self-serving criminal justice laws, could not be construed as criticism of Don Novey, his union, or his prison guards.

By that time, Novey was already speaking of making and influencing public policy as if he were a popular, well-entrenched governor with his hands firmly on the levers of power, able to deliver whatever he fancied. And why not? Candidates for governor were stumbling all over themselves to get Novey's endorsement and some serious campaign money. They had come to understand that a nod from him could mean the difference between victory and defeat.

Democrat Dianne Feinstein (now California's senior U.S. senator) found that out in 1990, when she was running for governor. Novey gave almost $1 million to her Republican opponent, Pete Wilson, who went on to win in an extremely close election.

"Di-Fi gave me a plaque even though I didn't endorse her," Novey said mockingly of Feinstein during a 1994 interview at CCPOA's headquarters in a spacious, modern, glass and wood structure about ten minutes outside downtown Sacramento. "It reads 'A Woman's Place is in Her CCPOA.' " "Di-Fi's daughter was working for us at the time—we have sixteen attorneys working for us right down the hallway here. And that's just *here*. We've got twenty-four total protecting our employees' rights."

CCPOA's contribution to Wilson's campaign was second only to that of the Republican National Committee. In the following, nonelection, years of 1991–92, CCPOA contributed over $1 million to legislative political campaigns and gave $91,000 to Governor Wilson. Wilson then raised the salaries and benefits of CCPOA's members, while instituting a pay freeze on all other state employees.

- - - -

Initially Don Novey was reluctant to use his union's money to support three strikes legislation, feeling, he told Reynolds, that the timing was a little off, that he had other fish to fry, and that Reynolds should wait a year or so. But the law resonated so deeply in his gut, as well as his head, that he soon came around.

"Supporting three strikes" as he'd later say, "was the only right thing to do; it would get 'career criminals' off the street, people who were the dregs of society, [who] prey on their fellow citizens."

Of course, the fact that it was also good for business—*his* business—didn't hurt at all. Warehousing ever increasing numbers of prisoners for vastly longer periods of time meant hiring more corrections officers, which, in turn, meant more union dues and even more political influence for CCPOA.

So the California Correctional Peace Officers Association would wind up contributing over $100,000 to the three strikes campaign, just as the NRA would contribute at least $130,000—becoming Mike Reynolds's financial angels early on, when it counted most.

Nevertheless, that money did not immediately flow to Reynolds in one lump sum; it came in stages. And while those early contributions kept his campaign alive, his bill remained bottled up in committee in the assembly; and his would-be ballot initiative had garnered only twenty thousand signatures after two hard weeks of trying. What was lacking—*really* lacking—was that white-hot spark that would propel Mike Reynolds's three strikes law over the top. He needed something big. Something dramatic.

16

POLLY KLAAS

AMERICA'S CHILD

EVEN IN THAT CRIME-OBSESSED AGE—when local television news had become the broadcast version of the supermarket tabloids, every police car chase was aired live, and SWAT teams dressed like over-the-top Ninja Turtles were routinely filmed knocking down doors with guns drawn to make petty drug busts—even with all that, most crimes in America went unnoticed by the press.

That was not the case with Polly Klaas. Klaas was an innocent. A sweet-faced, twelve-year-old suburban white kid—"America's Child," as *People* magazine would later dub her. Her surreal abduction tapped into every parent's deepest fear and into the public's thirst for twenty-four-hour-a-day soap operas.

The residents of Petaluma, for their part, would not let go of her story or of hopes that somehow, somewhere, she was waiting to be rescued. The morning after Polly's abduction, for example, a local printer named Bill Rhodes became the center of the remarkable efforts of the citizens of Petaluma to find Polly—"a dynamic guy," remembers Marc Klaas, "who began printing up flyers and asking people to come and help search for Polly. For two days after the abduction, about six hundred people showed up at his shop. And the media reported it all—the people searching in the surrounding woods and fields, putting up flyers, placing them on automobiles, searching under the bridges, and looking everywhere."

"The Coast Guard had three hundred forty-one cadets searching for Polly that first day," remembered Joe Klaas. "Navy Seals searched the entire delta of the Napa River, which runs through Petaluma. It was," he added with his own special brand of hyperbole, "the biggest missing child search since the Lindbergh baby." By the third day after Polly's kidnapping, over fifty FBI agents and local cops, two to three hundred search-and-rescue personnel, and over one thousand volunteers had joined the search.

Meanwhile, according to the Santa Rosa, California, *Press Democrat*, "more than one hundred thousand flyers bearing Polly's photo and a sketch of the kidnapper [taken from descriptions provided by Kate and Gillian] were being mailed and distributed." In addition, videos of Polly dancing, of Polly acting on stage, of Polly playing at home, were being distributed all over town.

"The search for Polly was about bringing that little girl home," Marc Klaas later recalled. "Every ounce of my energy was invested in it. It was the most desperate time any parent can experience. Getting up and not knowing. Hopefully whoever took her, took her just for companionship. If enough people were looking and were aware, then hopefully we could bring her home alive. That's what the two-month search for Polly was completely and totally about. It drew an enormous amount of attention. The president of the United States got involved, political people in California. It just became almost the event *du jour*."

But as the weeks wore on, Polly's story began to wane in the big-city press, turning into that most contemptible of things in any newsroom—old news. Then, suddenly, it got that extra splash of juice that would make it hot tabloid fodder again: the involvement of a celebrity.

The luminous young actress and Petaluma native Winona Ryder, whose star was then ascending, offered a $200,000 reward for Klaas's return. "My greatest wish right now," said Ryder, "[is] to meet her in person and to hug her." It was a headline story anyone could write: "Hollywood star is touched by kidnapped hometown girl, puts up money to save her."

And predictably, the tabs and even the straight media ate it up. Polly's story was featured on E! Entertainment, "MTV News," and "America's Most Wanted," which did five shows on her. She became the first missing child whose story was carried on the Internet. On at least half a dozen occasions, her story made the front page of the *Los Angeles Times*. She was featured in *People* magazine. *New Yorker* reporter Jeffrey Toobin did a lengthy profile centering around Richard Allen Davis and Polly's kidnapping.

Joe Klaas, who had majored in public relations, told the journalists flat out, "we're going to use you to find Polly." "Everybody else was afraid of the media," remembers Klaas, "and had been trying to keep reporters at arm's length. I said, 'no way, take me to them.'" Joe Klaas understood that in a story like this, the media not only wanted to draw every drop of titillating sensationalism and ratings-rich melodrama out of it—but they also wanted to *help*. Joe Klaas was right. After all, did not a story such as this touch the hearts of even the most jaded of the self-serving jackals of the press?

For his part, Marc Klaas began doing dozens of interviews, all in an effort to keep his daughter's story alive. He and his supporters formed the Polly Klaas Foundation and applied for nonprofit status, which it received a phenomenal twenty-three days after applying—yet another story.

About six weeks after Polly's abduction, however, there came a stunning development. A woman claimed in a civil law suit that Bill Rhodes, who was playing a major role in the search for Polly, had molested her twenty years ago, when she was nine. That was followed by revelations that in 1968, Rhodes had been convicted of indecent exposure, and that same year had been acquitted of allegations that he had held three girls at knifepoint and sexually molested them. As ugly, as *grotesque*, as that information was, it caused yet another wave of publicity about the case, another reminder that twelve-year-old Polly Klaas had been abducted and was still missing. But none of it seemed to matter.

- - - -

About an hour after abducting Polly, Richard Allen Davis drove down a rural private road about twenty miles from Petaluma, just off Highway 12. At the road's end was a single house surrounded by one hundred eighty-eight acres, occupied by Dana Jaffee and her twelve-year-old daughter.

A chef at one of the local resorts in Sonoma County, Jaffee had arrived home that night at about 11 o'clock, passing nobody on the private road. Inside, she chatted for about ten minutes with her daughter's eighteen-year-old babysitter, who then said her good-byes and left.

Driving down the road in her jeep, the babysitter noticed a Pinto stuck in a ditch at the side of the road, and was startled a moment later to see a sweaty, wild-eyed man frantically flagging her down. Quickly speeding past him, she stopped at the bottom of the hill, found a phone, and called Jaffee. "There is a wild man on your property," she told her, "you should get out of your house."

Jaffee instead called the sheriff's department. Just after midnight, two deputies in separate squad cars arrived. They found Davis leaning against his Pinto, calmly smoking a cigarette. "What are you doing here?" they asked Davis. "Sightseeing," he replied. The next thirty-eight minutes were a tale of incompetence, indifference, and missed opportunities.

First, the deputies were unaware that Polly's kidnapping had even occurred. The Petaluma police had broadcast an APB alert, but the Sonoma County sheriff's dispatcher decided not to notify his patrol cars, fearing that the press would be listening in, monitoring the calls.

That was black-comedy joke number one.

The deputies then ran a license plate check on Davis's car. When they discovered they'd run the wrong plate number, they decided to ignore their mistake and not rerun the number.

Nor did they run a criminal history on Davis, because law-and-order Attorney General Dan Lungren had earlier decided not to spend his discretionary funds on the kind of new communications equipment that would have enabled the deputies to get the information, opting instead to buy a fleet of Cherokee sport vehicles for high-ranking officials in the AG's office.

Finally, they searched the car, and amidst the clutter discovered the tools of abduction—duct tape and ties—and a partially consumed six-pack of beer. Unaware of the kidnapping, they simply gave Davis a field sobriety test, which he passed. Then the officers helped Davis push his car out of the ditch, and sent him on his way. He turned south. They turned north.

All the while there was no sign of Polly Klaas.

Two months later, Dana Jaffee took an early morning walk near the spot where Davis had parked his Pinto, looked down, and spotted a condom. Close by were duct tape, a dark, large-sized sweatshirt, a pillowcase with makeup smudges, a pair of tights, and white cloth strips like those used to bind the hands of Kate and Gillian.

Jaffee called the sheriff, and when a deputy arrived, reminded him of the man who'd been questioned just before midnight on October 1. After that, it was simply a matter of tracking Richard Allen Davis down. He was arrested on November 30, 1993. It took six days and a palm print that matched the one in Polly's bedroom for him to finally confess.

Davis then led police to Polly's rotting body, which he'd stashed beneath a pile of plywood at an abandoned sawmill. She was dead from strangulation, probably raped, and killed before the sheriff's deputies had even arrived on the scene. Five days passed before Marc Klaas was summoned to the Petaluma police station and given the news. Next to him, as Klaas later told it, an FBI agent and a Petaluma cop stood weeping.

Polly's life was now officially extinguished. As for Richard Allen Davis, well he—as he told his public defender in a jailhouse interview—was too drunk and too high to remember much of what had happened, but he was feeling "very disgusted with himself."

17

HAPPILY SHAKING FATE'S
SORRY HAND

THE SAME DAY THAT MARC KLAAS learned that Polly was dead, Mike Reynolds returned to his three strikes committee headquarters to find the phones ringing off the hook. "The hand of fate," Reynolds later said, "had struck." The Klaas family's unspeakable loss was Mike Reynolds's indispensable gain, given to him by Richard Allen Davis with one riveting, high profile, cold-blooded act of kidnapping and murder—an act so incendiary that it caused tens of thousands of people throughout California to place themselves outside the insularity of their own daily lives and say, "this is intolerable, something *must* be done."

And there was Mike Reynolds, waiting in the wings with the answer. And ready to respond to the deluge of calls flooding in as talk show hosts in the Bay Area, led by KGO's Ron Owens, started giving out the three strikes committee's 800 number—800 C-O-N-V-I-C-T—and urging listeners to call in, pick up petitions for qualifying the three strikes bill for the November ballot, and get them signed by voters.

As of October 1, 1993, Mike Reynolds had just twenty thousand of the almost three hundred eight-five thousand signatures he'd need to qualify his three strikes law for the November 1994 ballot. Three strikes appeared dead. Then the public's rage found an outlet.

Between December 11 and December 21, claims Mike Reynolds, his committee would receive eighty thousand calls. They came from places like Ukiah, Redding, and Yuba City in the state's far north, and from as far south as San Diego, near the Mexican border. There were so many that they overloaded the San Joaquin Valley's 800 system, causing the phone company to temporarily shut down the three strikes campaign's lines.

Bay Area talk show host Ron Owens placed calls to both Joe Klaas and Mike Reynolds almost immediately upon hearing of Polly's death. Owens's talk show was a solid ratings gatherer in the Bay Area, despite his self-righteously proclaimed commonsense, middle-of-the-road politics, which were really only middle-of-the-road in comparison to the right-wing screamers who had curiously come to dominate talk radio in that most liberal of major American cities, San Francisco.

"I'm about to do a live, remote broadcast from a Petaluma shopping mall," Owens told Reynolds and Klaas, "and intend to distribute three strikes petitions. Why don't you come up here?"

Although it was the first he'd ever heard of three strikes, Joe Klaas quickly agreed. As for Reynolds, he immediately bought a toothbrush and disposable razor, rented a car, stuffed it with three thousand petitions paid for by the NRA, and zoomed to Petaluma. Both men were stunned when they arrived. Hundreds of people were snaking around the shopping mall, patiently waiting in line to sign petitions and pick up others to copy and distribute.

It was unbelievable. It was big. As big as that Lindbergh baby kidnapping in the '30s. They turned the Petaluma search center for Polly into a local headquarters for the distribution of three strikes petitions. Down in the Bay Area, a retiree named Skip House set up shop with two of his friends at a BART train station, and later claimed to have gathered twelve thousand signatures, which, with cameras rolling from the ABC newsmagazine "20/20," he then presented to Reynolds.

"People were really into this Polly Klaas case," recalled Owens in the PBS documentary "The Legacy." "They really understood how this affected their own lives. We had to move quickly to make sure that we didn't lose that momentum if we were going to do anything about 'Three Strikes and You're Out.' So we put together the show real fast, and didn't know what to expect. The public response just astounded me. There were people coming from San Jose. I mean we are talking about people coming eighty, ninety miles just to sign a petition. That's the chord that 'three strikes and you're out' [struck] in people."

Then others got on the bandwagon. Over the next tumultuous weeks, President Clinton invited Reynolds to the White House and would soon recommend a federal "three strikes and you're out" law for anyone convicted of three violent felonies.

Not to be outdone, U.S. Senate Republican leader Bob Dole announced his own federal proposal: "Three strikes and you're in—for life."

Meanwhile, Reynolds appeared on CNN's "Crossfire," as Owens and Ray Appleton continued promoting his ballot initiative on their shows. In a matter of weeks, Richard Allen Davis had become the three strikes campaign's poster-boy monster, and Polly its poster-girl martyred angel. "Davis was a three strikes offender," recalls Vincent Schiraldi, the head of the Justice Policy Institute in Washington, D.C., and a vocal opponent of three strikes. "And several of his strikes were violent. Folks looked at him and said, 'What is this guy doing on our streets?' And that rage immediately had a vehicle. 'What can I do about it [they asked themselves]?' 'I could sign this damn petition.' And they couldn't print those petitions fast enough."

The memorial service for Polly was a media event. Three days after the Ron Owens show, on the rainy Thursday evening of December 9, about fifteen hundred people gathered in and around Petaluma's St. Vincent de Paul's Church for a memorial service for Polly Klaas. Standing by the flower-strewn altar (backlit by George Lucas) was Joan Baez, who sang "Amazing Grace," and Linda Ronstadt, who performed a powerful rendition of "Somewhere Out There"—the unofficial theme song of those who'd been involved in the search for Polly.

- - - -

In a newspaper in Munich, Germany, a headline read, "America Cries: Polly Is Dead." Polly's death, declared the *Los Angeles Times*, "had bruised the psyche of a nation." Nearby, CNN and local television stations were broadcasting the service live as a message of condolence from President Clinton was read.

As the memorial proceeded, the transcendental spiritualist Ram Dass spoke, the police officer who had coaxed the confession out of Davis read a poem, and Senator Dianne Feinstein and Governor Pete Wilson eulogized Polly Klaas.

Both, as Marc Klaas would later recall, "took the opportunity to pitch": Feinstein a ban on assault weapons, and Wilson passage of a three strikes law. "It was mind boggling," Klaas later thought, "my little girl was dead and here were these politicians launching campaigns at her memorial service."

But in his eulogy, Wilson seemed to reach beyond mere political calculation when he powerfully summed up what people all over the country were feeling: "We cannot call ourselves a civilized society, if our children aren't safe even in their own bedrooms."

Meanwhile, down in Los Angeles, "John and Ken," two bombastic afternoon radio talk show hosts, began to turn up the heat. They aired on the then highest-rated all-talk station in southern California, KFI—the Los Angeles home of the skilled, radio-savvy parrot of the Republican talking point, Rush Limbaugh, and of Laura Schlessinger, the pseudopsychologist famous for her homophobia, imperious condescension, and verbal slaps upside the head to her call-in listeners.

Like many radio talk shows in the '90s, John Kobylt and Ken Chiampou's show was more about feigned indignation, angry-white-man venting, and stirring it up to get ratings than it was about politics. But whatever politics the two did espouse was instinctive, gut level, smoldering, and contemptuous of any kind of nuanced understanding of complex issues. They focused, as Kobylt once put it, on "the stuff you yell at the TV screen in bed when you're watching at home. That's what we do. It's the first impulse. Raw, unedited, and unfiltered."

"It was such an easy call," Kobylt later explained in "The Legacy." "You had a dead twelve-year-old girl strangled. Maybe sexually abused. And you had this beast, this monster, Richard Allen Davis, that we caught how many times before? How many times was he arrested and convicted and then released to prey upon this little girl? Who is going to be against a law that was going to put this guy away forever, who?"

As Mike Reynolds later described them, John and Ken were a "chain saw," "guys who knew how to make things rock and roll." And rock and roll they did.

When Reynolds was interviewed on their show, he mentioned "the gang of three" in the state assembly—Burton, Bates, and Lee—and how they'd thwarted his three strikes bill in the Public Safety Committee. On air, John and Ken decided to phone them to find out why they were keeping the bill bottled up in committee.

Then they performed one of their specialty acts: injecting themselves into the story. Hourly, on air, they began announcing the phone number of one of the three and urging listeners to join them in calling. "We generated so many calls that we basically shut down their offices in Sacramento," recalled Kobylt. "The switchboard, [we] just shut it down. We shut down some of the offices of the assembly members themselves. They couldn't make a call out, they couldn't get any business done." They did this day after day for weeks.

"People actually called my office, and accused me [of being] responsible for the tragic death of Polly Klaas," recalled Barbara Lee. "And it got very scary because people believed that. They [had listened to] these talk shows pumping up that kind of rhetoric throughout the state."

Right about then, Michael Huffington rolled into the picture. Huffington was a one-term Santa Barbara Republican congressman married at the time to the outspoken author, newspaper columnist, and political gadfly Arianna Huffington.

A puffed-up, bland empty suit whose pockets were stuffed with his daddy's Texas oil money and his head with his wife's political ambitions, Huffington would prove ready to spend a stunning $30 million in his bid to unseat California's Democratic U.S. senator, Dianne Feinstein.

While his credentials were limited, his timing was perfect. Nineteen ninety-four was a disastrous year for Democrats, who lost both houses of Congress to Newt Gingrich and his Contract With America.

Huffington, for no reason other than the right-wing drift of the political winds, and those thirty million bucks, came within a hair of defeating the tough, tenacious Feinstein—who during the campaign moved about as far to the right as she could on issues like crime and corporate welfare without being jailed for impersonating a California Democrat.

"Huffington didn't have much in the way of issues," as Mike Reynolds later pointed out, "[but] three strikes seemed like one that he might be able to get a little bit of mileage from." Huffington, of course, was banking on getting a *lot* of mileage out of the issue.

In the weeks and months following Polly Klaas's murder, as the popularity and visibility of the three strikes initiative, now known as Proposition 184, began to soar, Huffington's contributions to it would soar as well, eventually amounting to $350,000 of the over $1.6 million that Reynolds would raise. (In contrast, the "No on Proposition 184" campaign received less than $28,000 in contributions, with $10,000 of that coming from just one donor, the California Teachers Association.) For his $350,000, Huffington was named cochair of the three strikes campaign.

If Polly Klaas's murder had reignited the "Three Strikes and You're Out" campaign and placed it center stage, it would be Huffington's $350,000, the NRA's combined donation of more than $90,000, and CCPOA's contribution of $101,000 that would pay for the show. Two organizations with self-serving political agendas and a political nonentity looking to buy his way into the U.S. Senate had latched on to Mike Reynolds's cause for their own ends, while Mike Reynolds used the tragic death of a young stranger to touch his funders' highly selective bleeding hearts and milk them for every penny he could.

- - - -

Although the national publicity generated by the Klaas murder gave a boost to Reynolds's campaign, support was not universal. As some form of a three strikes law began to appear inevitable, four other bills with milder provisions targeted at repeat offenders were proposed in the state legislature. One was by the California District Attorneys Association. Initially, the DAs didn't like Reynolds's bill because they feared it would limit their ability to maneuver and plea bargain—a practice which saved them enormous amounts of time and effort and allowed them to avoid costly trials. Later, the association would change its position when it realized that the law actually *strengthened* their already strong prosecutorial powers. All they had to do was threaten a crushing three strikes life sentence, and most defendants would leap at whatever was offered by way of a deal.

LA County's then district attorney, Gil Garcetti, also had misgivings, and trekked up to Sacramento to lobby for a law more focused on violent criminals. "I do believe in the 'three strikes' principle," Garcetti told a news conference that June, "but it should be reserved for the violent repeat offender. If it is not, the civil courts will have to close down, because criminal cases will take precedence."

Instead, said Garcetti, he supported the most viable alternative legislation to the Reynolds-Jones proposal—the Rainey Bill, which was named after Richard Rainey, the conservative Republican assemblyman and former Contra Costa sheriff who'd introduced it. His bill was modeled after Washington state's three *violent* strikes law. Unlike Reynolds's proposal, it did *not* include third strike prosecutions for nonviolent petty crimes, or for residential burglaries—the crime for which so many petty criminals had gotten their first and second strikes—or the mandatory doubling of a sentence for a second strike.

It was still a very tough law, but at least it had a certain rational proportionality to it, and a crude logic that many people saw as justice. It seemed to resemble a compromise, except to Mike Reynolds and his staunch, mainly Republican, allies, who knew they had political momentum, popular support, and the Democrats on the ropes.

Like Garcetti, Joe and Marc Klaas came to have misgivings about the Reynolds version of three strikes, but only later, after the discovery of Polly Klaas's body, when Mike Reynolds contacted Marc Klaas and asked for his support. "He didn't know a whole lot about the situation," Reynolds discovered, "but he knew we'd been through a similar situation, and I think he wanted to support whatever could be done to prevent this from ever happening again." The two men immediately bonded. "Our daughters had been murdered," says Marc Klaas. "We were very angry guys, and we wanted to do something about it."

Marc Klaas proceeded to campaign hard for the Jones-Reynolds bill. At one rally he told an audience: "I am not going to let my daughter's death be in vain. There are an awful lot of bad men on the street, and what I am trying to do in California as a father, is to push this 1, 2, 3 strikes and you're out legislation to get these bad men off the streets, and get them off the streets for good."

Joe Klaas, however, had been looking into Reynolds's three strikes law with a cooler eye and from another perspective. Sometime in February of '94, Joe Klaas, who was rooted in the liberal tradition of politics and investigative reporting, talked to a reporter in Petaluma who told him about some of the more draconian provisions of the Jones-Reynolds law. Afterward, Klaas decided to read the proposal for himself. And, as he did, he asked himself some hard questions: "What the hell is this business about serious and/or violent felons, and what's a serious felony?" Klaas then "looked up 'serious felonies' in a law book and didn't like what [he] was seeing, because it included nonviolent crimes."

Joe Klaas then spoke with someone in the Legislative Analyst's Office who explained that the bill included not only nonviolent felonies, but "wobblers" as well. Klaas was horrified. "This isn't what everybody thinks it is," he thought. "Nobody's ever mentioning these nonviolent crimes."

When Joe Klaas told his son about Mike Reynolds's "sleeper" provisions, Marc Klaas went "through the goddamn roof." He was livid, not at Reynolds's lie of omission, but at his father, who he believed was "going soft on crime."

A few days later, however, Marc Klaas had cooled down and thought it over. There *were* some strange provisions that had been included in the law—so strange that he concluded that what was driving Mike Reynolds was "passion, not reason." Reynolds and supporters like Dan Lungren were repeating the same mantra over and over. "Polly Klaas, violent crime; Polly Klaas, violent crime. But they weren't saying 'shoplift a beer and go to jail for life.'"

Joe Klaas was particularly disturbed by the inclusion of burglaries of unoccupied homes as a strike. Mike Reynolds might be driving around saying that Polly had been kidnapped by a residential burglar or that his daughter Kimber had been killed by a purse snatcher—but that was just sophistry as far as Joe Klaas was concerned. "Polly was kidnapped by . . . a kidnapper," he pointed out, "Kimber [killed] by an armed robber. You don't have to put half the population of the state in prison to get at people like Davis. All you have to do is get at people like Davis."

Marc Klaas, who had always respected his father's "integrity and ability to see through a lot of crap," began to realize that he had less in common with Mike Reynolds than he'd thought. He himself had "engaged in some of the things that under Reynolds's bill would get a man thrown in jail for the rest of his life."

"How much of the population can you put behind bars?" he asked himself. "How much money can we spend?" Sixteen new state prisons had been built over the past ten years, he'd learned. California's prisons were overflowing, with half of the inmates incarcerated for nonviolent crimes, and nearly 20 percent solely for drug crimes.

Those priorities were wrong, Klaas felt. The focus instead should be on the truly violent offenders—on "pedophiles and psychopaths who need to be taken out of society, [and] not on people born into poverty and recycled into the prison system for their entire lives."

Despite the opposition of Joe and Marc Klaas to the Reynolds-Jones proposal, not many others were willing to publicly agree with them, or to engage Reynolds and his supporters in formal debates. In fact, the Klaases and just a few others formed the entire cadre. They debated Reynolds, Dan Lungren, and Bill Jones, but it was a very lopsided contest.

Reynolds and his allies now had huge amounts of money rolling into their war chest, and the support of almost every radio talk show host and on-the-record politician in the state. They had money to charter planes and rent campaign Winnebagos to chauffeur them up and down the length of California and to pay for huge support rallies and massive mailings.

The opposition, the "No on [Proposition] 184" group, had, by comparison, only a minuscule amount of money and less than minuscule popular support. "I am hoping we raise enough money so that I can get reimbursed [for my services]," the group's political consultant, Leo McElroy, told the *Los Angeles Times*.

Nevertheless, Joe and Marc Klaas toured the state, pointing out the flaws that they saw in Mike Reynolds's law, while Marc Klaas signed the argument against Proposition 184 in the official voter pamphlet guide. He also charged that Reynolds's political supporters were involved in a "cynical, insensitive attempt" to use crime and three strikes to win the upcoming election, and with one single line dramatically summed up his opposition: "I've had my stereo stolen and I've had my daughter murdered," he said, "and I know the difference."

Meanwhile, one of Richard Rainey's staff members had contacted Joe Klaas and asked him to support Rainey's milder version of a three strikes bill—which they wanted to name after Polly. Joe Klaas readily agreed, and both he and Marc begin working for its passage. One day, they jointly spoke before a retirees' organization and, together, convinced them to endorse the Rainey bill. Flush with their success, the Klaases sped over to Rainey's assembly office to tell them the good news.

They just managed to make it before the office closed. Not that it mattered. Rainey had just withdrawn his bill. "Why?" an incredulous Joe Klaas asked. "Because," replied a staff aide, "Governor Wilson asked him to." Wilson, who before Polly Klaas's highly publicized death had wanted nothing to do with a Reynolds's bill he viewed as a sure loser, had subsequently become an ardent supporter. A huge political payoff was his for the taking, and Pete Wilson, being no fool, acted decisively, announcing that he wanted *only* Reynolds's genuine, original bill to pass, without one word altered or one comma moved. Bowing to the wishes of his powerful Republican Party leader, Richard Rainey proceeded to simply fold his tent.

Joe and Marc Klaas had changed their minds far too late to impact either the state legislature or popular opinion. By not fully evaluating the Jones-Reynolds three strikes bill before supporting it, they had let a genie out the bottle that refused to be stuffed back in. "They were used," says former California state senator Tom Hayden, "and then marginalized by [Governor] Wilson and the three strikes forces that wanted the most extreme version of the law to pass. It was tragic to see this father and grandfather dropped and shunned after Polly's death had been exploited to the hilt. Politicians in Sacramento knew better, but they also knew that if they supported Joe Klaas's [new position], they would be attacked as soft on crime." The only viable attempt to modify Mike Reynolds's law was now dead in the water.

- - - -

As Bill Jones reintroduced his three strikes bill in March of 1994, Mike Reynolds appeared before the state assembly's Public Safety Committee accompanied by eleven television cameras, including those of CNN and "20/20." As the cameras rolled, the bill barreled through the Public Safety Committee on a seven to one vote, and then, almost by acclamation, through the assembly and senate.

Polly Klaas's murder had put Mike Reynolds in the catbird seat and he was playing it for all it was worth. When Art Torres, a Democratic state senator from Los Angeles, sought to amend the bill to include money for crime prevention, Mike Reynolds, private citizen, put his foot down and said, no, absolutely not. Although it is extraordinarily rare for a spectator to be permitted to speak during a legislative debate, Reynolds simply stood up, walked to an open mike, and, as if he were Assembly Speaker, said: "When *we* start adding amendments, it's going to open a Pandora's box. It will also demonstrate to me, at least, the inability of the legislature to act in a responsible way." The November elections, he reminded them in a startlingly unveiled warning that spoke volumes, was just eight months away.

As the amendment was publicly killed, Art Torres left his seat, approached Reynolds, whispered in his ear, smiled, and shook his hand. It wouldn't do to antagonize Mike Reynolds, and it wasn't hard to understand why.

Polls were showing 80 percent approval for Jones's three

strikes bill, and Reynolds had already gathered more signatures than he needed to qualify *his* three strikes initiative for the November ballot. A lot of legislators were up for reelection in what was shaping up to be a disastrous year for anyone considered a "liberal."

- - - -

White, liberal Democrats had been tagged as coddlers of criminals ever since the early 1960s, when some had seemed to masochistically enjoy being mau-maued by angry black militants and were all too ready to explain away vicious black street crime as a justifiable manifestation of black rage. It was one of the biggest mistakes they ever made. Ever since, Democrats had been vulnerable to attack by Republicans on the issue of crime.

George Bush the elder had clobbered Michael Dukakis in the 1988 presidential race with a TV campaign ad featuring a frightening photo of Willie Horton, an African American convict with a long record of violent crimes, who'd been released from prison on a weekend pass and promptly committed a murder. Dukakis had been governor of Massachusetts at the time, the ad's voiceover announced, and was therefore responsible for Horton's release.

Dukakis then played into his Republican-engineered image of weak, liberal criminal stooge by stammering a near incoherent answer to a question put to him during a presidential debate, asking what he'd hypothetically want to do to someone who raped his wife.

That had been the last nail in the coffin, not only for the very few liberals still perceived as making excuses for black crime, but for any kind of thoughtful approach to crime in general. The

Democrats determined they would never again be Willie Hortonized. They were not just going to be tough, they were going to be tougher than all those law-and-order Republicans.

Bill Clinton and his "New Democrats" went on to break new ground for a modern-day Democratic administration with their policies. Under his leadership, the broadest expansion of the federal death penalty in the nation's history was enacted; a law was passed allowing immigrants to be deported without ever seeing the evidence against them; and the tightest restrictions on appeals since Lincoln suspended habeas corpus (the right of prisoners to appeal their convictions) were enacted into law. They were not going to be caught with their pants dangling around their ankles, as Michael Dukakis had.

And with Polly Klaas's death, Bill Clinton's crime strategy had melded as one with that of California's Democrats.

It wasn't simply that the public had a legitimate fear of crime; it was also the fact that people's fears were being pumped up and exploited by groups and organizations with a special interest in hyping crime and fear. The NRA, CCPOA, and the prison construction industry were obvious examples. But as veteran *Los Angeles Times* reporter Beth Shuster would later point out in a brilliant three-part series entitled "Living in Fear," they were just the tip of the iceberg. "Police stoke fear," wrote Shuster, ". . . to prime their budget, politicians . . . manipulate it to win votes. News organizations amplify fear by ratcheting up their crime coverage . . . security companies, theft-detection manufacturers and others tap into deeply held fears and end up turning a profit."

"In some respects, the merger of profit and political advantage has turned the crime business into the domestic equivalent of what President Dwight Eisenhower once described as the 'military industrial complex.' "

But while crime was *the* center-stage political issue in 1994, it was also emblematic of something far larger: the codification of "liberal" as a dirty word, the emergence of right-wing talk radio as a major political force, and the realignment of American politics, so that henceforth the game would be played with the conservatives playing offense.

At the center of it all stood Rush Limbaugh, that slick master of the half-truth, brilliantly using his network of six hundred fifty stations as a hub to stoke the pent-up frustrations of tens of millions of Americans who'd collectively decided that crime and everything else wrong with the nation was the fault of '60s libertines like Bill and Hillary Clinton.

"In 1980," Hendrik Hertzberg pointed out in the *New Yorker*, "only seventy-five stations in the United States used the all-talk format, and most of them were politically anodyne." As the 1990s came to a close, there were at least thirteen hundred talk-radio stations, "the vast majority of which [were] relentlessly right-wing."

Limbaugh and hundreds of other powerful right-wing talk show hosts would move into relentless attack mode, dominating the political discourse, framing the issues, and defining the nomenclature while proudly serving as strong-arm mouthpieces for the most regressive elements of the Republican Party. Together, they would lift Newt Gingrich and his Contract With America on their backs and carry both to triumph; even as the Democratic Speaker of the U.S. House of Representatives lost his congressional seat, Republicans captured both houses of Congress for the first time in decades, and Democrats found themselves having to defend their positions on virtually every issue. Crime was simply first among them.

For California's Democratic politicians, therefore, three strikes was no longer the issue. Nor was Polly Klaas's murder. The issue was their political survival; their task was to counter all those campaign mailers and thirty-second sound bites painting them as people who couldn't care less about *your* twelve-year-old being abducted and murdered. It didn't matter that the Department of Corrections was projecting that housing and caring for a prisoner serving a twenty-five-years-to-life sentence would cost the taxpayers of California a minimum of $600,000 (in 1994 money).

"When education or health care or transportation issues were debated," Assemblywoman Barbara Lee later pointed out in "The Legacy," "what would drive the debate and determine the outcome was always its cost. But on three strikes, the attitude was 'forget about how much it costs, we've got to do it.' "

"Every goddamn politician in California," recalled Marc Klaas, "was saying that [Reynolds'] three strikes bill was the deal. Whether they believed in it or not, whether they were supportive of it prior to Polly's [killing] or not, this avalanche was so powerful and had so much public support based solely on my daughter's situation, that there was no turning it back and no stopping it."

Thus it was that Mike Reynolds's unaltered law was passed by a state legislature and signed into law by a governor representing over thirty million Californians. As strategized by Reynolds's group, no professional analytical input was permitted or given by criminologists and other social scientists, no hearings to receive their expert opinions were held. It was a complete triumph of fear, emotion, and political cowardice over reason.

The avalanche in the state legislature that year wasn't limited to Reynolds's three strikes law. Far from it. That same legislative session would see the passage of a bill requiring that inmates convicted of a violent crime serve at least 85 percent of their sentence (as opposed to the previous 50 percent good-time requirement). Another bill allowed fourteen- and fifteen-year-olds to be tried as adults; a third limited the insanity defense; and a fourth set up a detailed system of tracking registered sex offenders.

More tough-on-crime legislation would pass in 1994, one veteran state senator told the *Los Angeles Times*, than in any other year in his two decades in the state legislature. Willie Brown, the liberal Assembly Speaker and lifelong scorner of the futile political gesture, best summed up the steamroller that had become three strikes in an admonition to his fellow liberal legislators: "Better get the hell out of the way." He advised his Democratic colleagues to vote for whatever version of the bill Republican governor Pete Wilson wanted. Then he invited Mike Reynolds to appear on his new television show.

Marc Klaas and Mike Reynolds saw the state legislature's actions with equal cynicism. "They didn't get out of the way," said Klaas; "they jumped on the train." "The second time we went up there," said Reynolds, "those suckers saluted."

18

CHECKING THE WEATHER VANE

SO THERE STOOD MIKE REYNOLDS wearing his American flag tie, basking in the glow of his triumph as Governor Pete Wilson signed his—signed *Mike Reynolds's*—three strikes bill into law on a sunny Los Angeles photo-op day in March of 1994. Flanking him, announcing the new California order, were some stern-faced, well-tailored LAPD law enforcers and the state's most powerful jailer, Don Novey.

"Three strikes and you're out," said Wilson to Reynolds as California listened in, "will finally put an end to revolving door justice. To [you] Mike, it is the most meaningful possible memorial to your own lovely daughter, Kimber, and to all the children of other grieving parents."

Just one year earlier, when Pete Wilson had gone to a Fresno fund-raiser to collect $100,000 from his San Joaquin Valley agribusiness supporters, his poll ratings had been the lowest of any California governor's in thirty years. Only 17 percent of Californians approved of his handling of the state's severe recession. But by early '94, his numbers had begun spiking upward.

Short, flaxen-haired, and baby-faced at sixty, Wilson, whose handlers over-spun him as a tough, can-do ex-marine, was a thirty year political veteran who'd been a state assemblyman, the mayor of San Diego, and then a U.S. senator before resigning his Senate seat to successfully run for governor in 1990. He was pragmatic, and therefore was described by lazy reporters as a "moderate." (Sidney Blumenthal, writing in the *New Yorker*, put it less charitably, once describing Wilson as a "man who could not locate his motives.")

Nevertheless, Wilson would handily win a second term, defeating the hapless Democrat Kathleen Brown. For Pete Wilson was nothing if not a smart politician, desperate to be reelected and willing to do whatever it took to make that happen. "There's a lot of Nixon in Pete," *Los Angeles Times* political columnist George Skelton once quoted a Wilson political ally as saying. Indeed, in Wilson's eulogy to Richard Nixon, he quoted the man himself: "It was his heart that taught us the great lesson of Richard Nixon's life. Never give up. 'Never give up. Never, ever, give up.' "

With polls showing that a significant number of white and African American Californians were feeling overwhelmed by all the Mexicans surging into the Golden State for the privilege of doing donkey work for subsistence wages, Wilson decided to run television campaign ads with infrared shots of a Mexican mob rushing across the border into the blackness of the Southern California night. They were as falsely alarmist and deliberately divisive as Bush's Willie Horton attack ads. But they got Wilson a jump in the polls and probably contributed to his reelection.

(Later, however, they would also spur a historic rise in voter registration among Mexican Americans and produce a politically devastating backlash against the Republican Party within the ranks of Latino voters.)

With the discovery of Polly Klaas's body, Wilson had made the smart move and become a strong, pivotal advocate of Mike Reynolds's law. But to be fair to Pete Wilson, with 1994 being crime-fighting time in California, he wasn't the only politician clinging like Velcro to the law. So were Dan Lungren, Dianne Feinstein, Michael Huffington, and seemingly every candidate running that year. The state legislature and Wilson's Democratic opponent, Kathleen Brown, were falling over each other to prove their bad-ass bona fides. In fact, Brown, the politically liberal daughter of former two-term Democratic governor Pat Brown and sister of former two-term Democratic governor Jerry Brown, was running to the right of Wilson on crime. Brown charged that Wilson was allowing dangerous parole violators to walk the streets of California; and she got into a fierce debate with Wilson over which of them more strongly supported a proposed *one*-strike law for sex crimes (a law that was enacted in late 1994). "Brown's latest ads," pointed out the *Los Angeles Times*, "all contain some version of this litany: 'I support the one strike law against rapists, three strikes law against felons, and, as governor, I will enforce the death penalty.' "

Meanwhile, the crime rate, which had begun dropping in California in 1993, declined by another 7.5 percent in the first six months of 1994. The historic drop in crime in California and much of the nation had already begun without the aid of three strikes laws. But few people noticed.

- - - -

Following the signing ceremony, Mike Reynolds beckoned reporters and camera operators to accompany him as he walked into an LA police station to submit a symbolic handful of petitions for the upcoming November ballot initiative. The LAPD officers, however, wouldn't accept them. "It's too political," they told him. ("I mean," said Reynolds later with self-righteous incredulity, "this is a crime issue, where's the politics here?")

Then Mike Reynolds boarded a Queen Air plane on loan from a Fresno department store, flew to his hometown, and then went on to Sacramento for more ceremonies. Across the state, meanwhile, the eight hundred forty thousand petition signatures that Reynolds's organization had collected were being submitted en masse.

That November, Mike Reynolds got all that he could have hoped for. Seventy-two percent of California voters cast a ballot in favor of Proposition 184. The Republicans, too, got what they wanted. "It was sweet fruit for the GOP," wrote George Skelton. "Republican candidates allied [themselves] with a compelling issue, and it helped draw to the polls right-leaning occasional voters who otherwise might have stayed at home."

It would now take a two-thirds vote of both state houses and a governor's signature to amend Mike Reynolds's law.

PART FOUR

ROCKS THE SIZE OF PEAS

19

LOOKING EAST, LOOKING WEST

BY THE BEGINNING OF 1996, Shane Reams was trying hard to stay straight. He was living with his family and holding down a job at a warehouse, regularly reporting to his parole officer, testing clean for drugs, and trying to establish a relationship with his son, A.J. (not his real name) who was now five years old. Or at least that was the way he'd later tell it.

But he was also falling into his old pattern. Three weeks clean, one week of bingeing—staying high and living on the street.

On February 9, he once again got that itch that never stayed scratched. At about 6:15 in the evening he wound up standing on a corner adjacent to a small, dark alley in a residential neighborhood that was known, according to Santa Ana police, as "a very high-crime and very high-narcotics area."

Santa Ana police officer Ruben Ibarra, meanwhile, was driving a "plain," or undercover, van, playing the buyer in a "buy and bust" that he and his fellow undercover cops were trying to make happen. Cruising around a corner, he spotted two men standing idly by, talking. One was Shane Reams. The other was a guy Reams sometimes got high with named Robert Lee Cox.

Ibarra was part of Santa Ana's fifteen-member "Community-Oriented Policing Task Force," known as C.O.P. As he drove by, two other unmarked police cars simultaneously parked about a hundred yards away on different side streets, ready to pounce.

It was already dark when Ibarra swung by again, caught Cox's eye, and pulled up parallel to him.

"Hey, what's happening?" asked Cox.

"Give me twenty of rock," Ibarra replied. Cox moved closer to the car window, flashed a clear plastic container, removed the lid, and revealed two white rocks of crack, both the size of peas. He handed one of the rocks to Ibarra, who reached into his left front pocket, forked over a marked $20 bill, and then took off. Moments later, he pulled a mobile police radio from behind his seat and announced that he'd made the buy. Six officers in three police cars swiftly converged at the corner and made the arrest.

Accounts of what happened next differ wildly. According to Ibarra, during the buy Reams had been "constantly looking to his left and right, east and west, three times each way," serving as a spotter for any cops who might roll onto the scene. At one point he'd even "yelled" to Cox to "hurry up [and] give him one." Cox, it seemed, had been taking too long to remove one of the rocks, because, as Ibarra later testified, "his fingers were bigger than the container itself." "I'm *trying* to hurry up and give him one," Cox then allegedly shouted back. "Hold on!"

Shane Reams's story, however—a story that would remain unshakable—was far different. After a long day sucking on a crack pipe, he and Robert Cox had been walking the streets, looking for a safe place to get high, when a van pulled up and asked if they had any rocks. Shane continued walking because he "didn't have any dope." But Cox had some rocks, and stopped. "I may have been looking back and forth while I was standing there," says Reams, "but not as a lookout. Those streets were a hotbed of gangs and cops. I never said 'hurry up, give him one.' I did say 'hurry up,' but only because I saw car lights coming and couldn't tell if it was the cops, gangbangers, [or nothing.]"

In any case, as Cox turned away from the officers, he dropped the container (and presumably the other rock of cocaine, which was never found), and meandered over in Shane's direction.

It took about thirty seconds for the cops to rush them both and to tell Shane he too was "going down" for being Cox's lookout, even though Shane had no drugs on him. The entire incident, from the time Cox had approached the van to the time of the arrest, took less than a minute and a half.

The private attorney Sue Reams hired for her son told her not to worry. Even though the Orange County DA had decided to try Shane on a third strike, a third strike prosecution wasn't going to go anywhere, she said. Shane might have to do a little time, but he would probably be home in a couple of months. The lawyer had been recommended by a friend who'd used her on a drunk-driving case. The choice proved a grave mistake.

Shane went to trial that May as a codefendant with Robert Cox, accused of aiding and abetting Cox's sale of the crack. "Why can't their cases be separated?" Sue Reams kept asking Shane's attorney. "Why are they being tried together?" The attorney's answer was a verbal shrug.

During the trial, Sue Reams realized that Cox's experienced public defender was doing a better job than was Shane's private attorney. Sue and Wayne, in fact, had had to drag her over to the site of the crime the night before the trial, and mark off how far Shane had been from his codefendant—because she certainly wasn't going to do it on her own.

Neither the second pea-sized rock nor the marked $20 bill was ever found. Not on Cox, or Shane, or anywhere else. The small clear container *was* found. But any kid, as Cox's lawyer pointed out, could have thrown a similar container away at any time after extracting the candy that it originally held. And during the trial, Cox never admitted that Shane was playing lookout, even though the prosecution had unsuccessfully tried to make a deal with Cox to finger Shane.

The prosecution, in short, had no proof that Shane was a lookout, other than Ibarra testifying that he had been. Ibarra was the only cop who witnessed the deal. It essentially came down to the word of Officer Ibarra (a veteran of the LAPD—soon to become infamous for setting up people and planting evidence during the Rampart scandal) versus that of two crackheads. The only "action" Reams had taken (a vital element in obtaining a conviction for aiding and abetting) was his alleged "looks back and forth."

But it took less than a day—four or five hours—to try the case. About 4:30 that afternoon the case was given to the jury. At 4:45 they came back with a verdict: guilty. Under the law, juries are not permitted to know that a defendant is being charged under the three strikes law. So they never knew that Shane was facing twenty-five years to life in prison for being an alleged lookout on the sale of a $20 rock of cocaine to an undercover cop.

The next day Robert Cox, who did not have strike priors, was sentenced to four years in prison, of which he wound up serving two. Three or four months later Shane was sentenced on a third-strike conviction to twenty-five-to-life.

20

SAY HELLO TO HITLER, DAHMER, AND BUNDY

"FUCK YOU," SHOUTED MARC KLAAS as he was hustled out of a San Jose, California, courtroom packed with reporters and stunned spectators on a September day in 1996. Unlike the routine sentencing of Shane Reams, the sentencing of Richard Allen Davis for the rape and murder of Polly Klaas had turned into a circus with Davis as ringmaster, using the opportunity, as Joe Klaas put it, to "pierce my son through the heart."

At the start of Davis's trial five months earlier, recalls Klaas, prosecutor Greg Jacobs had briefed the Klaas family on the rules of the game. They were to remain civil in their dealings in the courtroom and avoid any emotional outburst. Violation would result in their being removed from the courtroom and kept out.

Marc Klaas, however, wanted to see Richard Allen Davis, that "punk," that "monster," dead, and he had lobbied publicly—and with understandably strident outrage—for Davis to receive the death penalty.

Davis, in contrast, had said little from the time of his video-taped confession thirty-four months earlier. In June, however, the jury had convicted him of ten felony counts, including murder, and had recommended the death penalty. After that, Davis had let Marc Klaas know exactly how he felt about *him*. He said nothing, but instead turned to Klaas, and using the middle fingers of both hands, flipped him the bird.

But that was a small thing compared to what had caused Marc Klaas's outburst as he was physically ejected from the hushed atmosphere of the courtroom. Moments earlier, as the representative of the Klaas family, Marc Klaas had addressed Richard Allen Davis. "Mr. Davis," he said, "when you get to where you're going, say hello to Hitler, to Jeffrey Dahmer, and to [Ted] Bundy."

Santa Clara County Superior Court Judge Thomas C. Hastings then turned to Davis, who had not taken the stand in his own defense, and asked if he had anything to say before sentencing. Marc Klaas couldn't believe it—the judge was giving Davis the last word! Richard Allen Davis made the most of it.

Reading from an unfocused and seemingly never ending statement, he apologized to Polly's mother, the absent Eve Nichol, and then zeroed in on Marc Klaas. "I would like to state for the record that the main reason I know that I did not attempt any lewd act that night was because of a statement the young girl [Polly] made to me while [I was] walking her up the embankment: 'just don't do me like my dad.' I have to pay my dues," Davis said to Marc Klaas, "and so should you."

With that, Marc's mother gasped, and began, as Marc Klaas put it, "to emanate strange sounds." Looking her way, Klaas feared she might be having a heart attack before his very eyes. Not ten feet away from him, thought Klaas, Davis was killing another member of his family. That was when Marc Klaas snapped, lunged at his daughter's heavily guarded executioner, and was forced out of the courtroom.

After things had settled down, Judge Hastings turned and addressed Richard Allen Davis. "Mr. Davis," he intoned, "this is always a traumatic and emotional decision for a judge. You made it very easy today by your conduct." He then sentenced Richard Allen Davis to death.*

* As of September 2003, Davis remains on death row pending the outcome of his appeal of verdict and sentence.

21

PIZZA FACE

LIFE IS TOUGH FOR POOR-BOY Chicanos in San Diego's teeming Barrio Logan, especially if, like Jesus Romero, you have acne scars so bad your street name is "Pizza Face." Dark-haired, pock-marked, and as skinny as he was awkward, the thirty-four-year-old Romero was meek, unhardened, and deferential—the kind of guy who, when sent to prison for some harebrained screwup, would sit in the corner trying not to be noticed. Sort of like Shane Reams. And as it had been for Shane Reams, 1994 was a bad year for Jesus Romero.

Early one morning in June of '94, he and a friend had been walking down a barrio street when a cop stopped to check them out. Romero, according to the officer, began wiping his face with a paper napkin. The cop asked what he was doing. "I'm wiping my face, I'm sweating," he replied, tossing the napkin to the ground. When the officer retrieved it, he found two small rocks of cocaine—a feather-light thirteen one-hundredths of a gram.

Like Shane Reams, who had simply stood on a corner and moved his head back and forth, Jesus Romero, caught possessing a minuscule amount of cocaine, was immediately plunged deep into the whirlwind of California's three strikes law, where he too would wind up facing twenty-five years to life in prison.

The similarities with Reams didn't end there. Of five drug-related previous convictions, none were for crimes of violence. But two had been for residential burglaries, giving him two strikes at the time of his arrest. One of those convictions had been for *attempted* burglary; the other conviction was eight years old.

Like Shane, Romero had been in and out of prison, in his case, three times. One big difference between their cases, however, was that Romero didn't want to roll the dice and go to trial. Jesus Romero had been caught red-handed with the evidence. Deputy Public Defender Michael Butler was consequently pushing hard for a deal. Any deal.

But the timing was bad. The San Diego DA's office, now armed with the three strikes law, held all the cards and intended to play them. Jesus Romero was a sure conviction; why should they deal? So they refused to offer Romero *any* kind of plea agreement. None. Period. As in LA and many other California counties, the policy of the San Diego DA's office at the time was to refuse to negotiate a three strikes prosecution unless they had a case they might lose.

Indeed, the San Diego DA, as public defender Butler later put it, "wasn't offering jack shit. This guy had two qualifying priors." Butler remembers a deputy district attorney telling him, "The law mandates that the three strikes law be applied in this case, our office policy is that we're not going to strike any strikes, and the court has no power to do so. Sorry, that's the way it is."

For cops, prosecutors, prison guards, and defense attorneys, deeply felt compassion has to be sparingly ladled out if they wish to do their jobs and not go home and drink themselves to death. But after their first meeting, Butler felt deep pity for Jesus Romero. Here was a guy, he thought, who was unsuccessfully battling a serious drug addiction while living an unsuccessful life on *any* level—social, romantic, on the job, and on the street. He was a loser any way you cut it, struggling just to get through the day.

Michael Butler knew what it was like to struggle. He was legally blind and couldn't see well enough to read or write. He had to have all his information read to him before he could formulate a case and dictate a reply.

Butler was the son of left-wing Irish American parents who he "didn't think could bear even the thought of his becoming a prosecutor." And like his family, Butler knew where he stood: with the little guy against an all-powerful, increasingly unforgiving government.

A public defender for six years when he first spoke to Romero, Butler had a hard time getting him to understand that twenty-five-to-life was his likely fate. At each subsequent meeting, Butler could *feel* the sadness radiating out of Jesus Romero. But it was an odd kind of sadness. Not the sort of deep dread he'd experienced from other clients to whom he'd brought life-destroying bad news, but the resignation of someone who'd never had any good luck in life and had long ago given up expecting any.

- - - -

Michael Butler hadn't been surprised when the three strikes law passed. Over the years he'd watched as weight after weight had been placed on one side of the scale of justice, tilting it lopsidedly in favor of the police and prosecutors. It was tempting to think of three strikes as just another disadvantage to which he'd have to adjust. But it wasn't. It was qualitatively different—a "horrible statement" of where California and much of the country was continuing to head in its wars on crime and drugs.

And there seemed to him to be no countervailing force. Certainly not among the vast majority of California's judges—many of whom were former prosecutors appointed by two successive law-and-order Republican governors over a period of twelve years. Oh, they purported to be nonpolitical and nonideological, of course, but that was nonsense. A substantial number, in fact, were intensely political animals who saw the world as did Mike Reynolds, and were more than willing to check their compassion and sense of proportionality at the courtroom door, more than willing to serve as automated bank tellers reflexively dispensing sentences dictated by prosecutors using rigid sentencing guidelines like requests for cash.

But for other judges, the three strikes law had stretched the no-discretion-in-sentencing movement beyond tolerable limits and thus raised a compelling question: What was the point of even *having* a judge, if he or she had no power to intervene where there was an obvious injustice? Michael Butler understood the dilemma, understood it as clearly as he understood that he had no way to get justice for Jesus Romero except to lay his slim hopes on a judge he knew was experiencing such a dilemma.

- - - -

Around San Diego County Superior Court, how you viewed Judge William Mudd depended on where you stood. If you liked smart, independent judges who had no fear of offending the get-along, go-along judicial establishment, then Bill Mudd was your guy. If you didn't, then Mudd was short-fused, stubborn, and too prone to gut judgments.

Michael Butler was one who respected Mudd and thought that he had a conscience. And there was something else. From the first, William Mudd had never hid the fact that he thought the three strikes law was stupid, noting that a case such as Romero's "was worth about sixteen months [in prison] regardless of what the record is." In one case, in fact, Mudd had written what amounted to three single-spaced pages denouncing the law.

Knowing that, Butler decided to do an end run around the DA and "present a brief to Mudd stating the reasons why he, as a judge, clearly had the power and the right to strike strikes." As Butler suspected, Mudd was very receptive.

Perhaps, Michael Butler later thought, this was because William Mudd had "a real desire to do justice." Here, after all, "was a defendant who had no violence on his record, and no history of being a serious predator." Sure, a judge could look at Romero and legitimately think that this was a guy who might never be rehabilitated, who would go to prison, get out, and go back to getting high again—endlessly repeating the story of his life. But to give him the same sentence most murderers received was a mockery of justice.

The thing was, what *was* William Mudd, wood? Was he there just to rubber stamp anything the DA wanted, like some secretary? What self-respecting jurist would want to live, as Mudd himself put it, with a law that "basically castrates a judge"?

So Butler gave him a legal brief outlining the reasons why

Mudd had discretion to eliminate a strike and *not* send Romero to prison for a quarter of a century. And Mudd decided to eliminate not just one prior strike, but two (burglary and attempted burglary). Mudd's decision was a triumph for Michael Butler, but certainly not any sweetheart deal for his client. William Mudd may have had a heart, but it was not exactly bleeding for Jesus Romero, as Mudd made abundantly clear by giving Jesus Romero a sentence he would never have handed down before the three strikes law. Before the three strikes law, he might, as he said, have given Romero sixteen months in prison.

But that was then. Mudd by now had adjusted to reality and, instead of sixteen months, he sentenced Romero to three years for possession of those tiny rocks of crack, and an additional year for each of his three previous prison terms, giving him a grand total of six years behind bars. Still, in the new land of three strikes, Judge Mudd's sentence seemed akin to a lover's caress. Which is exactly how the San Diego DA saw it. He was outraged. In fact, after William Mudd handed down his sentence, the DA immediately filed an appeal, confident that Mudd's decision was such a blatant, showboating violation of the new three strikes law that an appeals court would swiftly overturn it.

And the DA's office was right. On January 10, 1996, a three-judge panel of the Fourth District Court of Appeal heard the case and wrote an opinion that, as Michael Butler characterized it, said that "Michael Butler was an idiot, William Mudd was a bigger idiot for listening to him," and that the three strikes as it currently existed was the greatest crime deterrent since those old Georgia chain gangs. The only way a judge could eliminate a strike, the court emphasized, was to first get the approval of the DA.

Five months later, however, the California Supreme Court got into the act. With six of its seven justices Republicans, the court was very conservative. In the years to come, it would uphold almost every aspect of the three strikes law. But it ruled unanimously in favor of Romero and Mudd's sentence. The disposition of a criminal charge, wrote one of the court's most conservative members, Justice Kathryn Mickle Werdegar, "is a judicial responsibility."

The first faint fissure in the three strikes law had appeared. The California Supreme Court had created a new bottom line: The decision on whether a defendant should be tried under the three strikes law would no longer be left solely in the hands of elected DAs; no longer left in the hands of full-blown political animals, many of whom would choose to have lung cancer over being accused of being "soft on crime". Now judges were back playing God, along with the DAs.

Mike Reynolds and the law's authors had struggled mightily to leave nothing to chance, to close all loopholes and insure that their law would withstand every constitutional test. And it had. But in any law the devil is in the details, and in this case, the Supreme Court ruled that the devil was not in what was in the law, but in what was not. The district attorney had argued that the three strikes statute should be interpreted to read that it prevented judges from exercising discretion in eliminating strikes. But the court ruled that if that was what the law's creators intended to do, they should have spelled it out in clear, unambiguous language, which they had not.

"The Supreme Court could have left its decision at that," says Gary Nichols, the appellate lawyer from the San Diego Public Defender's Office who took the case from Michael Butler and represented Romero on appeal. "They could have said simply, 'here are the words of the statute, and here's how we've interpreted those words.'

"Instead, they took it one step further, ruling that excluding judges from a serious role in sentencing violated the state's constitutional separation of powers doctrine. They didn't need to go there. They wanted to go there. In that sense, it was turf war, and the Court was protecting their fellow judges' turf. *That's* why they went there. It was obvious three minutes into my argument."

By pinning its ruling on constitutional grounds, the justices insured that their decision would stick. Reynolds's allies would have had to muster a two-thirds vote in the legislature to change the constitution and their own ballot initiative. Which would have been extremely difficult. You can intimidate a majority of politicians into voting your way by holding a Polly Klaas over their heads and threatening to declare them soft on crime if they don't do what you demand. Anyone in the public could understand Polly Klaas. But a two-thirds vote over the intricacies of a judicial turf war, well, how many members of the public cared about that?

If few voters were up in arms over the California Supreme Court's decision, the crime fighters certainly were. "I'm very concerned that what criminals can read into this is that they can somehow squirm their way out [of three strikes] in front of soft-on-crime judges," said Mike Reynolds.

Vowing to amend the law to restore its prior invulnerability, Governor Pete Wilson proclaimed that "we cannot tolerate a situation which permits judges who are philosophically unsympathetic . . . to three strikes to reduce the strong sentences that the voters intended to impose on habitual criminals." Bill Jones, meanwhile, called the ruling "over-judicial discretion," adding that he was disgusted by the decision.

Pete Wilson's promise to plug those loopholes was echoed by the assembly, which passed a bill by a vote of fifty-six to nineteen to do so. But when it hit the Senate, it took a different twist. Three Democrats and an Independent bottled up the legislation in the Criminal Procedures Committee, where it sat. And sat, until it died. The outraged sponsor of the assembly bill, Rob Hurtt, a Republican from the Orange County suburbs of Garden Grove, threatened to place it on the statewide ballot, vowing to make it tougher than even Mike Reynolds's law. But the public was unaroused and Hurtt, along with his promised ballot initiative, fell back into obscurity.

But Wilson, Jones, Reynolds, and Hurtt need not have worried. This was hardly the beginning of the end for three strikes. If anyone thought that the Supreme Court had any problems with the law other than protecting the prerogatives of their fellow judges, the justices quickly set the record straight.

The Court would soon rule that a judge's discretion to eliminate a strike when sentencing a defendant was *not* unlimited. The defendant's offense had to be "*outside the spirit*" of the three strikes law before a judge could eliminate it—in other words, a judge couldn't eliminate a strike in just any case. The Court warned that trial judges could not let "personal antipathy for the effect that the three strikes law would have on a defendant [guide them], while ignoring the defendant's background, the nature of the present offenses, and other individualized considerations."

Nevertheless, Gary Nichols would still consider the ruling the capstone of his career. "I've been a public defender for twenty years," Nichols would later say. "And I've saved more guys more time in prison with the *Romero* case than all the other cases I've handled throughout my career, or ever will handle in the future. There are thousands and thousands of people who have avoided serving a life term because of *Romero*. There are justices who before the ruling were keenly aware of the injustice they were being forced to perpetrate, and who now have a clear option: let the punishment fit the crime." In January of 1997, in another ruling, the California Supreme Court would also give judges "broad authority" to take petty crime wobblers filed by prosecutors as felonies and reduce them to misdemeanors.

But for many judges, the more things changed, the more they remained the same. Writing in the *Duquesne Law Review*, Los Angeles County Deputy Public Defender Alex Ricciardulli pointed out in 2003 that approximately one half of the defendants serving life sentences under three strikes were in jail for nonserious current offenses, and that that percentage "has not changed significantly before or after *Romero* was issued."

Moreover, the sentences handed down when a third strike *was* eliminated were nothing for defendants to rejoice over. LA County Superior Court Judge William Pounders, in a display of astounding hubris, boasted: "I think the best example of a case in which . . . I eliminated a strike [was for] a man who was charged with going into a grocery store and taking four cans of instant coffee. That was a felony. It was petty theft with a prior. . . . He had two very serious prior strikes, but they were twenty years old. And in the last twenty years, he had basically rehabilitated himself. I felt that twenty-five-years to life for stealing four cans of coffee was excessive, so I eliminated a strike. I offered, and the defense accepted, twelve years [in prison]—which essentially is three years for every can of coffee he stole—and everyone seemed satisfied with it; even the prosecutor agreed that the discretion was appropriately exercised."

22

ANOTHER REYNOLDS BILL

"TEN, TWENTY, LIFE"

MIKE REYNOLDS'S MIND WAS RACING at 9:30 A.M. on a May morning in 1998 as he tooled through a deserted downtown Fresno, revved up on his usual daily doses of Diet Coke. As he turned onto a commercial strip where there were some signs of life, the subject, as always, was crime. "This is Route 41, probably *the* artery of Fresno," he said. "It's perceived as a crime belt, but when these little punks have wheels they go all over. They don't go downtown anymore because there's nobody there to rob and mug. I get a kick out of this black comedian who said there's two kinds of malls, the ones where white people shop and the ones where white people used to shop."

After breakfast, Reynolds drove over to the Daily Planet, the restaurant where his daughter was gunned down, and introduced his guest to the owner—a middle-aged woman looking harassed as she prepared for a new workday. When the guest returned from the restroom, Mike Reynolds was fuming. The owner, he said on their way back to his van, had just told him that it'd been six years since Kimber's death, that all this attention was hurting her business, and that he should stop bringing people around on tours, and instead, "get a life."

"Sure it's hurt her business," said Reynolds bitterly. "But it's wrecked our lives. 'When will this be over?' she asked me. I told her it will be over when my daughter comes back."

- - - -

At about one o'clock, Reynolds arrived back at his rambling house. Since the passage of his three strikes law, Reynolds had been spearheading the implementation of another of the nation's toughest criminal justice laws: "Ten, Twenty, Life," which became law in January 1998. Under its provisions anyone over the age of fourteen who pulls a gun in the commission of a crime now has extra, mandatory, decades-long prison time tacked onto the original sentence.

In his living room he put on a thirty-second "Ten, Twenty, Life" video. It was a cautionary tale, explained Reynolds—who wrote the video and got professional volunteers to produce it—designed to inform people of the new consequences of using a gun in a criminal act. The video featured Alan Autry, who played "Bubba," one of the lead cops in the TV series "In the Heat of the Night."

With the piercing wail of a police siren in the background, Bubba suddenly appears in front of several police cars with their cherry-tops flashing: "California has just begun enforcing the toughest law in the land on criminals who use guns," he intones. "So if you know a punk with a gun who thinks he's tough, let him know this law is tougher. If you're fourteen years or older and you pull a gun to commit a crime, you're going to get an extra ten years. If you pull the trigger, you're going to get an extra twenty.

And if you shoot someone, you're going to spend the rest of your life in prison." Then the background voice of an announcer fades in: " 'Ten, Twenty, Life,' the law is here," he says to the clanging vibrations of a jail cell door slamming shut.

That evening, Mike Reynolds hustled into a meeting of Leadership Fresno. In a large room with the look of a small, spotless gym, clumps of businesspeople and bureaucrats chatted away, trying to network, as Reynolds entered.

Missing not a single beat, he began promoting his latest project—a $500 million ballot initiative to build new "juvenile [jail] facilities" in California, in order to lock up ever growing numbers of California's young people.

He buttonholed a Fresno County supervisor and pitched the bond initiative. "The county pays one fourth [for the proposed jails]," Reynolds told him, and "the state pays three-fourths." Was that three-quarters "for bricks and mortar"? asked the thin, elderly supervisor. "Bricks and mortar," nodded Reynolds. The supervisor was dubious. The state, he said, was always voting to build something and then leaving the financially strapped counties to operate them, and therefore he didn't have a "comfort level" with such programs.

"Oh, I know, we're already second swamp water," Reynolds replied, retreating as it became obvious that the supervisor's support wasn't there, at least for the moment. Before leaving, however, Reynolds got a commitment from the superintendent of public schools for San Joaquin Valley to place copies of his "Ten, Twenty, Life" videos in all the district's classes. "Every kid in the Valley will know about this law," said Reynolds.

Arriving home, he picked up his wife and continued on to a Republican fund-raiser. With Pete Wilson term-limited out, Attorney General Dan Lungren was already running hard for governor in the upcoming election and Reynolds was supporting Dave Stirling, Lungren's chief deputy, who was running for the Republican nomination for the AG's post.

At the fund-raiser, about a hundred people were sitting at round, linen-draped dining tables, watching the emcee for the evening—a farm growers' attorney named Ron Barsamian—speaking at a podium. He began by noting what a great job Stirling had done when he served as general counsel for the Agricultural Labor Relations Board. Before Stirling, said Barsamian, the ALRB "was completely staffed by the most biased, [liberal] people ever, excluding," he said to nervous laughter, "the SS during the war years."

"But by the time Dave left," he continued, "the ALRB had the fewest hearings in its entire history. . . . So we don't have to wonder if Dave Stirling is going to do a good job as attorney general. We saw what he did in a really bad agency, and with a really bad [farm workers' rights] law."

"Now," he finished up, "I have the real pleasure to introduce Mike Reynolds . . . the driving force behind the three strikes law—a happy side effect [of which] for a lot of the communities here in the San Joaquin Valley has been the growth industry it's created in the building of prisons. . . . Mike, on behalf of my children, thank you."

Having been called upon, Reynolds, who'd been seated with Stirling's wife, Stephanie, at a table of seven or eight, strode to the podium and gave the invocation: "Let us remember that God's work here on earth is truly our own. May we come together to unify our efforts to elect Dave Stirling. . . . This Valley has worked hard to reduce crimes with laws like three strikes and 'Ten, Twenty, Life.' We also know the future success of these laws is in the fragile hands of our next attorney general. . . . amen."

Following the pledge of allegiance, great slabs of prime rib were served as Stephanie Stirling chatted with Sharon and Mike Reynolds and several other couples. Tall, thin, blond and well spoken, Stirling was perfectly poised as she participated in the tedious small talk required of politicians' wives: "We live in Walnut Grove in the Delta. . . . I'm a northern Californian and I've kind of made Dave one. . . . It's a nice retreat from Sacramento."

"I ran into Willie Brown on an elevator in Sacramento," interjected Mike Reynolds. "And I pretended I didn't know him. There's one thing worse than knowing who he is, and that's not knowing who he is. . . . You know something? For two cents, I would have given him a fifty cent tip."

"He's a fun person," replied Stephanie Stirling, "if you can put the rest of it aside." The conversation then shifted to—what else—crime and punishment. "You know," said Sharon Reynolds, a quiet, unassuming woman who remained as bitter as her husband over her daughter's death, "in Canada they have home sentencing—child molesters and rapists serve time in their homes."

"None of those monitoring bracelets," added Mike; "they're just hoping they'll stay home, and if they [don't] they're sentenced to more time at home."

"More time at home," echoed Sharon Reynolds, adding to general laughter at the table: "You can't go out of your room, now, for twenty years."

"Isn't that insane?" Stirling replied.

"They serve one-sixth of their time," replied Mike Reynolds, "one-sixth! Their prisons are like motels. We complain about cable TV and weight rooms and a law library [in American prisons], but there they get everything but room service."

"The real person we're afraid of," Mike Reynolds continued, "is [Democratic nominee and eventual winner for attorney general] Bill Lockyer. He's very scary. When Dave takes this nomination, I've got some scripted commercials to run against Lockyer. If they can be of any help to you," he told Stephanie Stirling, "let me know . . . they're real smokers."

"He [Lockyer] sleeps apparently four hours a night; the rest of the time he's politicking," said Stephanie Stirling. "People like that make me nervous."

"He's not married, is he?" someone at the table asked. "He's *not?*" replied Mike Reynolds in that knowing way of people who think they've just been handed a juicy piece of gossip. "I can get into this discussion, but I'm not going to," said Stirling with a rueful little laugh. "There have been many interesting stories, let's just put it that way."

And with that, Mike Reynolds summed up where his suffering over his irreplaceable loss had, and had not, taken him. "I had dinner with [liberal Democratic state senator] John Vasconcellos," he told Stirling. "And he said he'll always oppose three strikes, and that [he] can always find what is perceived as being an unjust case, and someone who is the victim of [such] a law. Well," said Mike Reynolds in real, uncomprehending exasperation, "supposing . . . we executed a person who was actually innocent? Does that mean that we should do away with the death penalty?"

As for that other hometown boy, Ray Appleton, well, he has had no second thoughts about his role in passing California's three strikes law. "Second thoughts?" he said, when interviewed years later. "Oh, God, no. Are you kidding me? No, this has been great fun! I even did some work over in England where I was asked to speak to their lower house and then their upper house about helping them—or commenting—on their two strikes law for rapists, which was strictly cut out from our project here in Fresno. So, this is great fun! I mean, this thing has gone from beyond Fresno, obviously it's gone national and international. For a long time, I had to champion this on English radio, because people over there thought it was extremely draconian, but they got it, and now they're happy campers."

23

JEAN VALJEAN REDUX

GREGORY TAYLOR WAS A YOUNG MAN in his early twenties when he snatched a purse from a bewildered woman standing on a sidewalk. The mugging, which occurred in the early '80s, netted him ten dollars, the woman's bus pass, and what would become his first strike. His second arrest, for an unarmed, failed attempt at a street robbery, netted him nothing other than strike number two.

Taylor had grown up in south Los Angeles, that vast swath that once housed one of the nation's strongest, most successful black middle classes; that had produced two of the bloodiest American insurrections of the twentieth century; and that had been the home turf to that voice of the '92 riot—those gangsta-glorifyin', cop-hatin', in-your-face "Niggas with Attitude Straight Out of Compton."

The early '80s were the dawn of a disastrous time for south LA, a time when the economy was about to collapse as the opening rounds of sweatshop globalization were fired into the gut of blue-collar America. Unemployment among the area's men was approaching 45 percent, crack wars were about to fully flower, and the Bloods and Crips were gearing up to kill each other— and any innocent bystanders who happened to get in the way—in astounding numbers. By the mid-'80s, in fact, gang killings were numbering over three hundred a year in the city, and close to seven hundred countywide.

Gregory Taylor had joined the Crips at the tender age of fourteen, and by what would have been his senior year in high school, he was doing time in the California Youth Authority.

But the tall, thin Taylor was no wild-eyed, violence-prone Bad Nigger looking to get his respect in the 'hood. He was a young wannabe thug. And as the years passed, violence, or at least violence that resulted in an arrest, disappeared from Taylor's life, replaced by that hyperactive God of the '80s, crack cocaine, and by the cooler poison of an earlier hipster-cum-hippie era, heroin.

In '92 Taylor got caught short with some coke and picked up a conviction for possession. Later, he was arrested for a parole violation, arrested, that is, for failing to report to his parole officer as scheduled. The missed appointment was deliberate. What was the point of going, after all, when he knew he'd only test dirty?

He'd try hard to stay straight, working for a while in the cheap goods garment stalls and flower shops that surround LA's skid row. When there was some construction work available, he'd do that. But then he'd get that urge, get that jittery, metallic ache in his body, and become overwhelmed by a desperate, unrelenting desire for relief. So he'd gather up what money he could, score some dope, find a fleabag, skid row hotel room, and shoot up and bliss out. Then he'd crawl back out to the streets.

The romance of Woody Guthrie's hitting the hobo rails, of Jack Kerouac's *On the Road*, and of the cute, weekend hippie corner beggars declaring the Age of Aquarius was long gone when the reality of Ronald Reagan's recession hit in the early '80s and people living on the street became part of big-city America's civic furniture. By the mid-'90s they were half a million strong—with women and children accounting for about a third of them. If they're noticed at all today, it's with a mixture of annoyed disgust at their dank, greasy-clothed, visually polluting presence, and steely contempt for their weak character.

In LA, Gregory Taylor was one of an estimated fifty to eighty-five thousand men and women who roam the streets homeless on any given day. On the eastern fringes of downtown Los Angeles, like an unwelcoming sentinel as you approach the central city, stands what is often their sole alternative to the streets—Los Angeles County's mammoth Twin Towers Correctional Facility. Through the doors of that banal, brown behemoth of postmodern architecture, one hundred sixty-five thousand prisoners flow in, and are disgorged, every year.

Many of those, like Gregory Taylor, who have no place else to go, join the skid row shadow world of crazed, kinetic crackheads, washed-out winos, puncture-ridden junkies, and the untreated mentally ill with their dazed, dreamy looks of incomprehension. At dusk, like freaks in a Fellini movie, they crawl into large, beige cardboard boxes that seemingly appear out of nowhere, lining the streets for blocks on end—freestanding hotel rooms of last resort.

Gregory Taylor was luckier than most, as Associated Press reporter Martha Bellisle pointed out in her definitive profile of Taylor, because he had a family that cared about him. He had eight brothers, including the major league outfielder Dwight Taylor, and a strict, God-fearing, church-going mother, who over the years had drifted from nursing to welfare under the weight of rearing the nine boys she'd given birth to in seventeen years. But nothing—not his older brother Dwight's attempt to take him under his wing, not his preachifyin' minister aunts proclaiming the glory of Jesus, not his mother proclaiming the wrath of God—could turn Gregory Taylor away from his heroin-induced flights to nirvana.

Then, in the late '80s, he was befriended by a Franciscan priest, the Reverend Allan McCoy, who ministered at nearby St. Joseph's Catholic Church. Taylor would frequently wait outside the church rectory in the early morning, hoping to catch McCoy as he stepped out to start his workday, and hit him up for a favor or two. And sometimes McCoy would respond by giving him sandwiches, spotting him some cash for a hotel room, or driving him to visit his mother. Sometimes, he'd even permitted Taylor to sleep overnight at the church.

In return, Taylor did chores in and around the church. McCoy later told Bellisle that he came to view Taylor "as a peaceful man, a man who helped out down at the center with the feeding of the street people." In time, Taylor came to regard McCoy as something of a surrogate father. Nothing much changed over the course of the nine years they knew each other. Not until Taylor had passed his thirty-fifth birthday. Not until the morning of July 11, 1997—the morning that changed his life, and transported Gregory Taylor from purgatory to hell.

It was sometime between 4:00 and 4:30 that morning, and he'd gotten hungry. Hungry enough to head for the back door of St. Joseph's and try to pry open the screen covering it with a four-by-four construction board. On the other side was the church's kitchen pantry, and the food he craved. That's all he wanted, just a little food. Or at least Gregory Taylor swears to this day that

that was all he wanted. It certainly was exactly what he told the two security guards who, instead of jacking up Taylor and telling him to wait the two hours until the pantry opened, decided to go for the big bust of a man who had nothing—nothing but an appetite. So they crouched in the shadows, keen to nail the perp in action. Which they did, for attempted burglary. Strike three.

Dale Cutler first read Gregory Taylor's court file that same summer. At fifty-six, Cutler was an eight-year veteran Los Angeles County deputy district attorney who'd been a county probation officer for the preceding twenty-three years. In that capacity he'd worked testing probationers for drugs after they'd pissed into a cup, and with teenagers in a California Youth Authority prison. Those long years in the criminal justice system hadn't exactly made Cutler cynical or jaded, but they had taught him, as he later put it, "to know bullshit when [he] heard bullshit."

Cutler was working downtown as a grunt in one of the general trial pools that handle run-of-the-mill cases when he drew Taylor's to prosecute, just two days before it was set for trial.

Looking over the file, he noted that Taylor was going to be charged with attempted burglary and that it would be handled as a third strike. But he thought little of it. As a trial lawyer, his focus wasn't on the justice of the third strike filing, which, in any case, was a decision that had already been made by head deputy Susan Spears. It was on the prosecution itself. True, it was a marginal crime, but "reasonable minds," as he'd later say, "could have gone either way on the decision."

In fact, once he read Taylor's file, Dale Cutler's prosecutorial mind took hold, and Gregory Taylor morphed from Rev. McCoy's peaceful, homeless man with a drug problem—from a man so hapless and depleted of drive or cunning he'd been living in skid row degradation for at least the past nine years—into a conniving cat burglar out to steal the church's "icons and other things of value."

Taylor's position that "he was attempting to break in and steal food," Cutler would maintain, was simply "not tenable." "He could have waited until the hour that [the priests] got up," Cutler argued, "because they fed him all the time. If he had waited another hour or two, they would have fed him. Or, if he'd had the munchies so bad that he couldn't have waited an hour, there was a doorbell on the rectory that he could have rung." Cutler was certain that had Taylor simply rung that bell and awakened McCoy at 4:00 or 4:30 in the morning, "the Father, who is just a wonderful person, would have [gotten up] and fed him."

Therefore, Cutler reasoned, Gregory Taylor "wasn't really looking for food." He had just "said that to the security guards at the time as an explanation of why he was [breaking in]." But that explanation "wasn't a logical position because he had so many other options."

For those who were later incredulous that Taylor was being prosecuted for a third strike, Cutler's worst-case scenario seemed a convoluted, deliberate distortion of the facts—the prosecutorial equivalent of Mr. Johnnie's mantra in the O.J. trial that "if it doesn't fit you must acquit"—argued by a robotic deputy DA.

Dale Cutler, of course, did not see himself, or the extraordinary punishment that his office was demanding, in that way. Cutler viewed himself as a *prosecutor*, as one of a breed. A breed whose members "wore the white hat," who could "make the decision of who and who not to prosecute, [and] didn't have to represent people [they] knew were guilty and had done crimes," as did those whoring defense attorneys. "And, at the same time, as a prosecutor, "if [he] saw some injustice being done [he] could say, no, we won't go ahead, this isn't right." For Dale Cutler, Gregory Taylor didn't fit into that latter category.

He and Taylor had been raised in two different worlds, and like Mike Reynolds, Dale Cutler saw things as very clear and very simple. He'd grown up in the then almost exclusively white and conservative suburban San Fernando Valley—LA's Queens, New York, circa 1958. His family had then moved to New Zealand for a year and a half, and when they returned had settled in Denver, Colorado, where Cutler spent his high school years. After graduating, he'd served in the Marine Corps, gone to college, and put himself through law school while working as a probation officer. He'd pushed hard all his life for everything he got, done it within the system by, as Bill Clinton used to say, "following the rules and working hard"—unlike parasitic street lice like Gregory Taylor, for whom Cutler had "very little sympathy."

As he saw it, Taylor "had been in and out of jail, not just for drug related offenses, but for other crimes against people. He had a robbery and a burglary on his record," and had "been preying on society for a number of years. And every time he got out, he'd get himself into trouble again, and usually end up hurting someone." The three strikes law, in Cutler's mind, was written precisely for guys like Taylor—"for career criminals."

"Taylor gets out [of prison], and then continually commits these types of crime. It obviously was not a crime of violence, but at the same time it certainly was a burglary."

That Gregory Taylor's pitiful, failed attempt to pry himself into the pantry of St. Joseph's was to be tried as a third strike was not in the least bit unusual in Los Angeles. On one hand, it was a city with a police force led by black chiefs of police from 1992 to

2002; a city that had been led by a liberal black mayor for the twenty years between 1972 and 1992; a city with the largest chapter of the ACLU in the nation; and a city with a liberal political establishment generally in the forefront on issues such as gay rights, living wage ordinances, and affirmative action. On the other hand, its criminal justice system in many ways resembled that of Texas at its redneck worst, that is, Texas then governed by George W. Bush—a man who smiled his little half-smile when he boasted during the 2000 presidential elections of how the Lone Star State was the nation's leader by far in executions, and who was positively convinced that no Texan on *his* watch had ever been executed who didn't deserve it.

In LA, the district attorney's office was the product of a get-along, go-along criminal justice system that had long ago discarded the God of justice for the tight clamp of control. The DA back in 1997 was Gil Garcetti, the mildly liberal Democrat who'd spoken out against the Reynolds-Jones three strikes bill back in 1994.

Thin, rosy-cheeked, white-haired and aristocratic-looking, Garcetti was a well-placed, decades-long veteran of the DA's office. When he was elected in 1992, it was as the only viable alternative to his predecessor—another white-haired man—the stout, noble-headed Ira Reiner.

Reiner looked just as he should—solid, squint-eyed, stern, and B-movie-star handsome. But he'd lost favor with the electorate after a series of defeats in the high-profile cases that ambitious DAs—that is to say, almost all DAs—live for.

His culminating defeat was that loss of losses (before O.J.): the debacle in Simi Valley—the stunning, riot-causing acquittal of the four LAPD officers who had so methodically whacked Rodney King's kidneys, arms, legs and head fifty-six times with their solid aluminum, two-foot-long Monadnock PR-24 batons. The loss of that case was particularly galling, and especially inept, given that the prosecution had all the proof it could have wished for in George Holliday's world famous video of the beating.

With little chance of winning reelection, Reiner ceded his '92 run for DA to Garcetti in midcampaign. But not before Reiner had announced his new policy to deal with the very real, pressing problem of gang violence. His plan was sort of an attitudinal precursor to Reynolds's three strikes law. Henceforth, he said, his office would no longer plea-bargain with gang members. His deputies would "use each occasion that a gang member was arrested for a crime, no matter how minor, as a means to remove him from the streets for as long as possible."

It was the kind of simple solution to a complex problem that people like to hear. Who, after all, could argue against taking gang members off the streets? And who among those with viable political careers was crazy enough to challenge Reiner when he suggested that the current generation of gang members should simply be "written off"? Who would be stupid enough to challenge *that* statement come next election?

Since there were very few white gang members, other than scattered skinheads, the pivotal, white, middle-class voters of LA knew exactly whom he was talking about, and it wasn't *their* kids.

But then why bother to sort them out? Many black and Latino working- or middle-class voters were far more fearful of gang violence than were whites—and had far more reason to be, given their closer proximity to the violence. But many of them also had the mixed feelings of the impoverished immigrants doing LA's sweat labor for coolie wages, or those of the single mother raising five kids in Watts. It was *their* kids who were most likely to be in some way involved with gangs. Of course those parents wanted protection from the gangs that were either victimizing their children or socializing them into a culture of crime and violence. But they didn't want that protection to focus almost exclusively on locking up tens of thousands of their children and leaving them to rot in prison while their younger brothers and sisters stepped up to take their places, and nothing—nothing but the faces—ever changed.

When Gil Garcetti replaced Reiner, he continued the same brand of ineptitude. His office lost the first Menendez brothers trial, a murder case against the rapper then known as Snoop Doggy Dogg, and, of course, O.J.'s "trial of the century," with Johnnie Cochran outfoxing the either petulant or near-hysterical Marcia Clark.

"In New York," former NYPD sergeant and Temple University professor James Fyfe once said, "the cops hold the door for the DAs. In LA, it's the other way around." This had been true for forty years before Garcetti became DA, but Garcetti gave the police department what amounted to carte blanche. The LAPD rarely sent cases of criminal acts by its officers to the DA for prosecution. But even among the few presumably strong cases the LAPD did send, only 8 percent resulted in prosecutions, as opposed to 70 percent brought against the general public, from 1995 to 2000. And among the one hundred cases of criminal use of excessive force by officers, only one was prosecuted—as a plea bargain misdemeanor.

At the same time, the intensification of the wars on drugs and crime by state and national law enforcement; LA's headline-grabbing gang violence (which made the crime rate appear to be going up, when, in fact, it was going down); and the loss of the O.J. case, had all contributed to a new "us and them," "win-at-any-cost" mentality in the DA's office.

As Charles L. Lindner, the former president of the Los Angeles Criminal Bar Association wrote in the *Los Angeles Times:* "Two decades ago, prosecutors and defense [attorneys] regularly socialized [not far from LA's behemoth downtown courthouse] at Little Joe's Restaurant in Chinatown. [However] this [kind] of critical relationship has deteriorated, especially in LA County. . . . Deputy district attorneys are [now] trained and encouraged to have a near paranoid distrust of defense council. Prosecutors who have left Garcetti's office to join the defense ranks are considered to have 'gone over to the dark side.' " Such was the mentality of the Los Angeles district attorney's office when Gregory Taylor was prosecuted in 1997.

- - - -

Although Garcetti had publicly opposed Mike Reynolds's three strikes law in '94, he now abandoned his opposition to an all-encompassing three strikes law because it had suddenly become politically risky. He stepped boldly forward to announce that he now intended to use the three strikes law to pluck gang members off the streets and prosecute them to the maximum extent of the law. If thousands of men and women with long-ago or no gang experience also got caught up in his new policy, well what was really the difference? The public had spoken, had it not?

- - - -

It was incredible, really, the farce that was being played out with a straight face in the courtroom of Superior Court Judge James Dunn. Kafkaesque, black comedy, comedy of the absurd—pick your description of reality that day as Gregory Taylor went on trial.

Dale Cutler had his rap down cold, arguing that a break-in was a break-in, and that it made no difference if Taylor had been after food or after those icons. Not, of course, that the evidence *supported* Taylor's sob-sister story of hunger, in any case. *Truly* egregious, moreover, as Cutler portrayed it, was Taylor's action in "betray[ing] the trust of a priest who'd defended him for many, many years. Nine years of doing good for a man, and that's how he [was] repaid for his kindness." No matter that McCoy had told the court that he "knew the defendant to be a peaceful man, and that it would not be just or merciful to impose such a sentence on a good person who made mistakes."

Judge Dunn must have bought Cutler's damning characterization, for when public defender Graciela Martinez argued that the most Taylor had been guilty of was trespassing, and that he couldn't have committed burglary because he believed he had tacit permission to take some food, Judge Dunn would have none of it. There was not enough evidence for the jury to even consider that point of law, he declared, and he would not allow it to do so. Not being permitted to consider that argument, the jury soon found Gregory Taylor guilty.

When the time came for sentencing, Judge Dunn declared that it was obvious that the jury thought Taylor was out to steal those icons, otherwise, why would it have found him guilty? And then, ignoring Rev. McCoy's opposition to the three strikes law—and to a third strike sentence for Taylor—he sent him off to prison for twenty-five-to-life. As for the jury, several of its members asked to be permitted to plead for a lighter sentence for Taylor before the judge, but Dunn would have none of *that* either.

Taylor's case was subsequently heard by the Second District Court of Appeal in April 1999. Two of the three judges on the panel agreed with James Dunn. Dunn had acted properly, they said, when he refused to tell the jury that it could find Taylor guilty of simple trespassing, not just of attempted burglary, if they believed that he thought he had permission to enter the church. Taylor, wrote Justice Fred Woods, "may have honestly believed that the priests had consented to his taking their food by their prior acts of charity. But such . . . belief, does not equate to an honest and good-faith belief that he had consent to forcibly enter the church . . . to get food, and [to] damage the door in the process."

With undertones of incredulity, Judge Earl Johnson wrote in dissent that Taylor should not have been prosecuted for a third strike, and that the jury should have been allowed to hear his good-faith argument: "A hungry, homeless man is sent away for twenty-five years to life for trying to break into a church so he could eat some food he thought the church would be glad for him to have—a defense that the jury wasn't [even] allowed to consider."

AP reporter Martha Bellisle's profile of Taylor ran on the front page of the *Los Angeles Times* under the subtitle "Justice: Attempt to break into church kitchen constituted third strike for modern day Jean Valjean." The reference to Valjean had come from Justice Johnson. But in *Les Misérables*, Valjean actually wound up with a better deal for stealing that loaf of bread for his starving family:

nineteen years in a French penal colony. Taylor would have to do at least twenty-five. And he never even got the bread.

When questioned by CNN about Taylor's third strike prosecution, Garcetti replied that it was "his duty to protect the community. [And that] if [his] lawyers believed that a person had earned the right to be in prison the rest of his life because he is a continuing danger to the community, then [so be it, he] would back them."

In the following year, 1998, 79 percent of LA County's third strike prosecutions would be for nonviolent crimes, and two-thirds of *those* cases would be for nonserious third strikes. The most common third strike prosecution was for drug offenses, which accounted for 33 percent of the total.

As for Gregory Taylor, he's now doing his time at Corcoran State Prison, up in Mike Reynolds's San Joaquin Valley. But Gregory Taylor's fate was, of course, only the subtext of the real story. The real story was that during the 1990s, California had produced a law straight out of Victor Hugo's nineteenth-century nightmare; a man of mean ambition like Gil Garcetti; a self-justifying functionary like Dale Cutler; a hanging judge like James Dunn; and an appeals court for whom contorted semantics were more important than the rest of a man's life.

- - - -

In 1995, Marc Klaas attended the premier of *Little Women* starring Winona Ryder, a film dedicated to the memory of Polly. Afterwards, reported the *Los Angeles Times*, "as Klaas crossed the street, a woman pressed against a barrier and extended a notebook and pen for an autograph." Sometimes people still approach, and thank him for doing so much to get California's three strikes law enacted. Sometimes he tries to set them straight, to tell them he *opposed* the goddamn law; sometimes he doesn't even bother.

Meanwhile, he and his wife, Violet, had started their own lobbying organization called the Klaas Kids Foundation, focusing on preventing crimes against children. The Foundation has helped pass a *two*-strike life-in-prison law in Wisconsin for anyone convicted a second time of sexually molesting a child. It also helped pass another Wisconsin law, mandating the lifetime monitoring of child molesters. Klaas also lobbied for laws requiring background checks of little league coaches, teachers, scoutmasters and others who have "unsupervised access to children."

"My advice to parents," he told the *Los Angeles Times*, "is to raise your children as if there is a registered sex offender living in your neighborhood."

While Marc Klaas sought a measure of nobility in his daughter's death, Attorney General Dan Lungren was getting applause before an approving crowd at Sacramento's Comstock Club, demonstrating what had catapulted him into the Republican nomination for governor of California. Major crimes, he told his audience, had dropped 12 percent statewide in the first nine months of 1996 and continued to drop in '97. If elected governor, Lungren promised, he intended to see that trend continue.

Despite the stunning drop in the crime rate that both California and the nation had experienced over the preceding four years, Lungren was campaigning as if crime were still the all-encompassing issue it was in 1994. And with a lot of confidence.

Lungren condemned the state's decade long multibillion dollar prison construction boom as still inadequate. He vowed if elected to build yet more prisons and jails—despite a $3.6 billion annual corrections budget that had already risen from 2 percent to 8 percent of the state's overall spending during the '80s and '90s. He promised in addition to fight a "zero tolerance" drug war resembling "World War II, not Vietnam," and passionately opposed the state's 1996 medical marijuana law.

As California's attorney general, he'd also assisted in drafting the Republican contribution to the '96 federal Anti-Terrorism Bill, which dramatically cut time and resources federal prisoners have to file appeals of their convictions, and which limited the grounds for appeal to only incompetence of counsel. (New evidence proving a convicted prisoner's innocence can now no longer be considered.) As governor, he told the audience, he'd see to it that California enacted the same limits for California's prisoners. But that was all background noise to the cornerstone of his campaign, the touchstone of his crime fighting crusade: Mike Reynolds's three strikes law and Lungren's unswerving contention that it had been the most effective crime-fighting tool since the ancient tribal chiefs of Arabia had conceived of cutting off the hands of thieves.

From Lungren's perspective, the success of three strikes could be measured by the over thirty-five thousand inmates (almost one-quarter of California's 1998 prison population) who had been sentenced to prison on second and third strikes.

Peter Greenwood, the head of the Criminal Justice Program at the RAND Institute, on the other hand, was dubious about the law's impact. "Nobody believes that three strikes is having the impact Lungren claims. Crime has been going down significantly almost everywhere in the county, and it isn't a three strikes law that's responsible for bringing crime down in all those states that don't have such a law. All the theory and numbers are running against these assertions, but he [Lungren] never agrees to debate one of the twenty people who make their living analyzing this stuff."

"So, all the public was exposed to when it came to this law," said Greenwood, as the campaign progressed, "was the rhetoric of politicians and what they're learning watching television. And that's the principal criticism I have of Lungren: that he's behaving like a politician about things like three strikes, rather than as the leader of an agency [the Attorney General's office] that can do the analysis and educate the public."

Everything Greenwood said was true. But it was also true that between 1993 and 1999, California had experienced the steepest drop in violent crime—41.8 percent—of any state in the Union. New York came close with a 40.9 percent drop (a statistical dead heat); Massachusetts's crime rate dropped 33.3 percent; Washington, D.C.'s, 31.4 percent—all without a three strikes law. Outside of California, the nation's overall crime rate dropped 19 percent.

Many factors had contributed to the decrease in crime in California and throughout the nation: a strong national economy; low unemployment; a relatively small population in its prime crime-committing years; gang truces and gang workers who kept those truces in effect for many years; community policing; more cops with better equipment on the street; innovative new strategies for fighting street crime; and especially the end of the crack wars and the use of crack cocaine, which was responsible for a significant drop in homicides and robberies.

But according to a 1999 study by UC Berkeley professor and criminologist Frank Zimring, repeat offenders were still being arrested for new felonies at about the same rate as before the three strikes law.

"If California's crime decline [was because of] three strikes," said Zimring, "we would expect to see the drop in arrests concentrated among the [groups targeted by three strikes]. Instead, the decline is spread evenly—over the 90 percent of all potential offenders not affected by three strikes; and [over] the 10 percent who were. That sure doesn't look like a three strikes effect to us."

The study, reported the *Berkeleyan*, also found that "before three strikes, 44.8 percent of all felony arrests involved suspects with a felony conviction on their record . . . [and] after three strikes, that proportion remained essentially the same, 45.4 percent."

Zimring also found that "before three strikes went into effect, individuals with one or two strikes on their record were responsible for 13.9 percent of all adult felony arrests. . . . After the law went into effect, that number changed only slightly, to 12.8 percent of arrests."

Harsh punishment as a deterrent certainly works for some people. But it's also interesting that in 2001, the *New York Times* noted that "over the last twenty years, the homicide rate in states with the death penalty [such as California] has been 50 to 100 percent higher than the rate in states without it."

PART FIVE

THE COUNTERREVOLUTION
(SORT OF)

24

THE MORE COMMITTED
EXECUTIONER

IT'S A SUNNY MORNING IN AUGUST OF 1998, and Dan Lungren is already well into his campaign day, busy touring a factory in Torrance trailed by a local reporter and photographer, a CNN camera crew, and aides and plant executives. Lungren hustles from one spot to another, looking at aluminum frames, blue plastic chairs, and stacks of wooden tabletops all being pushed in repetitive loops on a conveyer belt.

As November approaches, Lungren is badly trailing his centrist Democratic opponent, Gray Davis, in the polls. Crime has been plunging, along with his hopes for another Johnnic One Note crime-buster campaign. The favorite flavor this election year is education, a subject about which Lungren has little to offer but platitudes.

Leading the group with Lungren is the president and CEO of the school furniture manufacturing plant, Bob Virtue, a balding, no-nonsense man in his late sixties. Behind them, Doug Virtue, Bob's son and the Virco Company's executive vice president, shouts the day's spin over the factory din: His father's been a big, long-time supporter of Lungren, because Lungren's been great for California business.

They emerge from the plant into a huge lobby festooned in red, white, and blue, where tables and chairs have been set up in front of a podium backdropped by a yellow and blue "Lungren for Governor" banner. About four hundred of Virco's employees file in—a captive luncheon audience for Lungren, courtesy of Robert Virtue.

Stepping to the podium, Virtue praises Lungren and then introduces Ruben Barrales, who's running for state treasurer. A dream Republican Latino candidate, Barrales has that high WASPish Harvard-Wall Street forehead, wavy brown hair, white baby-smooth skin set off by large blue eyes, and an engaging manner that allows him to deliver a rags-to-riches GOP speech with great charm in an English as flawless as his Spanish.

Then it's Lungren's turn. Discarding his text ("I read this audience, and it was not the kind of speech they would have wished to have," he'd later say), he talks instead about his life: how he's one of seven children ("How many of *you* are from a large family?"); and how on his first campaign, he walked door to door with his wife while wheeling a baby carriage. Near the end, he hauls out a hardy old campaign perennial—a funny, dead-on imitation of Richard Nixon—and then gamely tries to get a few laughs with dippy USC-Notre Dame football references that leave his mainly Latino immigrant audience bewildered.

One of the few issues he does mention is the low academic achievement of California's students. His solution, he tells these people struggling just to survive, is for *them*, as parents, to make their children's schools better. The audience, which had been subdued and somewhat dull-eyed when they entered, is not exactly jumping on the table with enthusiasm. But Lungren holds their attention through the skillful use of that prerequisite for any successful conservative hater of social welfare: make nothing sound like a great deal. The day sees Dan Lungren at his best—congenial and down-to-earth, when unchallenged.

Another campaign day not long after finds sixty-five people from the Greater San Fernando Chamber of Commerce and the Latin Business Association seated in a white plastic tent on a blistering San Fernando Valley summer day. Dan Lungren is working the predominantly white, small-homeowner crowd, pressing harder than he should have to as he again focuses on education.

"Some people say that if you're a Republican, you certainly can't be concerned about education," Lungren tells the audience. "I thought about that for a while . . . and I realized I've been a *parent* longer than I've been a politician . . . And to me, that is more important in getting insight about our schools than *any* meeting I could have with a teacher's union. . . ."

"What is needed in education," he continues, "is more local control of schools, higher standards, and the end of 'social promotion.' And after that—for those who need a second chance—a community college, where if they get a B or better average, they will be guaranteed a spot in the UC system or the highest levels of Cal State. That's my pledge," he concludes. He fails to mention, however, that similar policies have already been in existence in California for many years.

A brief Q and A follows. A large man wearing pince-nez glasses and a goatee tells Lungren that he (Lungren) has "a great opportunity to bring in a lion's share of the windfall from the tobacco [lawsuit settlement]." "The state of Minnesota settled for what?" he asks. "About $6 billion?"

"I'm not sure what it was," says Lungren, his charm evaporating as a hint of annoyance creeps into his voice, "but they got several billion dollars."

"I was wondering if [in] your negotiations with the tobacco industry . . . you have a plan to get the most you can for California?"

"We currently have a lawsuit against the biggest tobacco firms . . . and I have fifty-six or fifty-seven people working on it."

"You're battling the Evil Empire," says the man.

"They're not nearly as bad as the drug lords," Lungren replies, head down now and face slightly flushed. "I just wish," he says, "I *devoutly* wish that we were spending one tenth the time and energy on defeating drugs that we're spending on tobacco. . . . People can say what they want about using marijuana for medicinal purposes . . . but it sends a [wrong] message to our kids, and *I* am not going to stop the fight against drugs," he says to a ripple of applause. But even on *his* playing field—drugs, crime, and three strikes—Dan Lungren would not fare well.

Don Novey and his prison guards union, for example, had thrust their political muscle behind Democratic gubernatorial nominee Gray Davis, not the fiscally conservative, instinctively anti-union Lungren. Lungren, as he later told it, had refused to swear he'd be Don Novey's big-time sugar daddy, and consequently had paid the price—$2 million the union would contribute to Davis's campaign, not his.

The most heated and darkly comic moment of the campaign would come as the candidates answered questions about the death penalty during a major statewide debate. Lungren thought he owned the issue. Davis wanted to steal it away by proving his macho bona fides.

A thin, clenched, gray-haired political veteran, Davis acted as if every smile took a year off his life, and every political decision had been filtered through a cost-benefit analysis with him as the sole beneficiary. But no one ever accused Gray Davis of not being tough and shrewd. So when the debate was joined, he and Lungren began shouting that if elected governor, it was *he* who would insure the execution of the maximum number of inmates sitting on death row, and not his opponent. Having thus made sure Lungren would score no points against him on the issue of crime, Davis vowed to be the education governor and easily won the election with 58 percent of the vote.

As Pete Wilson had done, Gray Davis then repaid Don Novey by granting his union members a stunning 25 percent raise, just as he was gearing up for his 2002 reelection campaign. No matter that California was facing an unprecedented budget deficit of somewhere between $35 and $38 billion, or that most other state employees were getting no raises or were being laid off. Novey had delivered. Now it was Davis's turn.

The defeat of Dan Lungren would also prove no victory for those hoping to modify or overturn the three strikes law. "As long as you have me," Davis told a group of the law's active supporters, "you'll have a governor who believes in and supports three strikes."

25

LENNY, DRUG COURT, AND THREE STRIKES

"*RE-NNNNAALLLL-DO!* GRADUATING? I don't believe it! Let me look you up," says Santa Clara County Superior Court Judge Stephen V. Manley, shuffling some papers on his bench.

Manley, who is sitting in his small, packed, downtown San Jose courtroom, is a tall, charismatic, sixty-one-year-old man with thinning blond hair and a ruddy face dramatically set off by a black eye patch he wears over a left eye injured long ago. He's speaking not only to Renaldo, but to a captive audience of drug court defendants, whom he refers to as his "clients." It is judges like Stephen Manley and a ballot initiative known as Proposition 36 that provide the second modification of California's three strikes law.

"You don't have a single violation of probation," an avuncular, booming-voiced Manley tells Renaldo as the thin, shy man, wrapped in a hooded yellow windbreaker, takes a seat behind a long wooden desk. "You've done everything I've asked . . . just look at these reports!"

Off to Renaldo's left on this July morning in 2002 are sixteen shackled prisoners dressed in orange jumpsuits and seated in a sectioned-off area against the wall. To his rear sit the over fifty "clients" already on probation, who, following Renaldo, will appear before Manley.

Monday through Wednesday, the clientele is drawn from a wide spectrum of users and tends to be whiter, more upscale, and better educated—recreational users, accountants, college students, nurses, and lawyers—many of whom, before their arrests, had been leading functional lives while quietly struggling with their habits, or had simply been caught in the wrong place at the wrong time. Most of them, says Santa Clara County Public Defender Bernardo Saucedo, are "one-rock people—not those constantly in and out of the system—and are usually sent to AA programs, early intervention, or educational-type programs, not to residential facilities."

But today is Friday, a court day reserved mainly for those who've been diagnosed as mentally ill *and* seriously addicted. Many come from families with multi-generational histories of abuse, addiction, and degradation and are living lives of bad choices and perennial poverty. And they look it: black women with dreadlocks and strained faces; battered Mexican men in their fifties with the resigned slump and blank eyes of those who know their lives are already over; pasty, bloated white women with mangled hair, rotting teeth, and thigh-wide arms; a man who says he's dying of hepatitis C and wants to read a poem.

Renaldo, who continues to be effusively praised by Manley because he's just completed his treatment program, is now allowing a slight grin to spread across his face as the judge continues.

"All your reports are glowing. . . . What a wonderful way to start the day."

For almost a decade, Manley, the supervising judge of all felony drug cases in San Jose, has been a leader of California's Collaborative Justice (drug) Courts, which began in Alameda County in the early '90s. The courts spread as thoughtful judges saw that the old system of catch, punish, and release was a revolving door. In response, they turned to the rehabilitative approach of drug courts, which by 2002 numbered one hundred forty-six in California and about seven hundred nationwide.

The assumption underlying drug courts is that deputy DAs, public defenders, probation officers, and drug treatment professionals—working in unison and led by judges like Manley—can provide the resources, care, and follow-up needed to help addicts kick their habits and fix their lives. Since 1989, according to the National Association of Drug Court Professionals, "over 100,000 offenders [nationwide] have participated in the drug court system, and 71 percent of those have either completed their program or are actively participating in one"—an extraordinarily high percentage for a treatment in which false starts and relapses are, for many addicts, part of the process.

Drug courts like Manley's operate on the belief that drug addicts should be treated as people with a disease, not as criminals, and that hard-core users can be transformed in the therapeutic communities to which many of the courts' most difficult cases are sent. But until 2000, drug courts had been reaching just 5 percent of the Californians eligible, and only a handful of chronic addicts in the state's prisons.

Throughout most of the '80s and '90s, in fact, the perception within the criminal justice system was that drug treatment simply didn't work for hard cases like Jesus Romero, Shane Reams, Leandro Andrade, and other addicts moving in and out of prison. In 1998, as John Ratelle, the warden of California's R. J. Donovan Correctional Facility, put it, "I'd seen a lot of programs where inmates laid around all day, continued to use, manipulated untrained correctional counselors, got their day-for-day credit—and then got out and went back to drugs and crime." That was the attitude from the inside.

On the outside, however, therapeutic communities, or "TCs," had been meeting with success for decades. In the late 1950s, Charles Dederich, Sr., a self-destructive alcoholic and former salesman for Gulf Oil, started his own AA group in his small apartment in the LA beachfront town of Venice, California. It became the genesis of TCs.

Drug addicts soon joined the alcoholics at the meetings and stopped using drugs—something that was unheard of. People believed that alcoholics could clean up, but not junkies. The proof had been the notorious inability of the two federal hospitals then dealing with addicts to devise programs that worked.

Out of those Venice meetings grew a community known as Synanon. The group's fundamental philosophy was the same as AA's—when addict A helps addict B, addict A also gets better. Synanon differed from AA, however, in that people lived together, and in a confrontational atmosphere. If you thought someone was lying to the group or to themselves, you were bound to tell them so.

The original members of Synanon were a rough crew—chronic junkies, hookers, ex-cons. Many successfully cleaned up, although the group itself eventually disintegrated into a dangerous and scandal-plagued cult.

From Synanon, the TC concept grew into a movement within the rebellious counterculture of the '60s and '70s. An exploding rate of drug addiction had become a hallmark of the times, and the medical and psychiatric establishments—which had so utterly failed in the treatment of addiction and alcoholism over the preceding forty years—continued to be irrelevant.

In that vacuum, the therapeutic community movement flourished, using the early years of Synanon as a model. Its broad goal was far more ambitious than mere freedom from substance abuse; it was personal transformation through the development of self-reliance within a supportive, humane community, using as its tools group encounters, seminars, psychodrama, community rituals, and written and oral exercises. Each member progressed individually. Once recovered, the ex-member was obliged to be part of a wider social transformation. Out of the coalescing of all these features grew the now widely accepted and successful drug-treatment methods used by TCs such as Day Top, Phoenix House, Walden House, and the Amity Foundation.

But TCs, and drug treatment in general, failed to prove themselves in prison until 1990, when the California Department of Corrections started a pilot program at the R. J. Donovan Correctional Facility. It proved an eye opener for Donovan's warden, John Ratelle, who had been highly skeptical that any drug treatment for prisoners could work. In 1992, he ordered a surprise urine test of the prisoners in the program, which was run by the Amity Foundation. "I knew that I had two hundred guys with serious drug problems, all living together and not isolated from the main yard," recalls Ratelle. "So if they wanted to get drugs, they could. I assumed that 25 percent . . . would turn up dirty." But only one participant "was positive for drugs—marijuana. I was shocked. But I was very impressed. That was the single most important event in convincing me that [these kinds of] programs were really working."

The California Department of Corrections agreed with Ratelle and in 1999 began expanding the program, which, as of 2003, reaches eight thousand prisoners.

In November 2000, California voters approved the Substance Abuse and Crime Prevention Act, or Proposition 36, by 59 percent. The law mandated that nonviolent drug offenders be sentenced to drug treatment—as opposed to jail or prison—for possession or transportation of illegal drugs for personal use. Defendants would be given at least two shots at successfully completing a treatment program before a judge could re-sentence them under the state's otherwise unforgiving drug statutes. Had the law existed previously, Jesus Romero, whose third strike was for a low-level, nonviolent drug offense, might well have been sentenced to treatment instead of prison.

Prior to Proposition 36's passage, about thirty-six thousand Californians a year were being incarcerated for simple drug possession—more than in any *nation* in the world, on both an absolute and a per capita basis. In 1980, just 7.5 percent of California's twenty-three thousand inmates were doing time for drug offenses. By 1999, California had built twenty-two new prisons at a cost of about half a *billion* dollars each, the prison population had skyrocketed to a hundred fifty-eight thousand prisoners, and over 20 percent of the men and almost 35 percent of the women were being incarcerated for drug offenses.

As for those strikes, by 2000, almost five hundred eighty people had been sentenced under the law to twenty-five years to life in prison for "possession of a controlled substance;" others, like Renaldo, had gotten the same sentence for very minor drug crimes.

Manley, on the other hand, is encouraging in his approach as he continues to praise Renaldo while the others listen in, awaiting their turn for jail or salvation. The weight of the state is always there in Manley's courtroom, of course, insuring that his clients will comply. "Coerced treatment," in fact, is a crucial element of the drug court system, as it is of Proposition 36. "We do coerce and hold people accountable," says Manley. "But it's not adversarial. Judges are personally involved with each client [as part of a team], trying to get them clean and sober and to improve their lives in many other ways."

"And by the way, Re-nalll-do," Manley concludes as he's about to dismiss him, "don't forget that we're inviting you to come to our graduation on July 18, so we can celebrate together. OK?"

Then Stephen Manley, not exactly a teddy bear, walks down and around his bench, signals for Renaldo to stand up, meets him halfway, shakes his hand and gives him a hug.

- - - -

It's a dog day afternoon in July 2002 in San Jose, and probation officer Gary Giarretto is cruising along in a gray four-door Kojak Chevy. Giarretto is a slender, graceful man with a ponytail, low-slung beard, Bay Area hippie background, and a master's degree in marriage, child, and family counseling.

Hunched in the back is Bernardo Saucedo, a heavy-set Mexican American wearing a pencil-thin moustache and a summer suit. At fifty-two, Saucedo has spent about half his life as a public defender. He tells a story as an illustration of who he is and where he's coming from. One morning while he was talking to a deputy DA, a bailiff turned and suddenly slapped one of Bernie's clients hard on the side of the head. "The guy was throwing gang signs," the bailiff explained. "But there's no one in the courtroom to even be throwing signs *at*," Bernie told him. "The way you practice is the way you play," he added. "If you're willing to slap my client that hard here, what would you do in the back room?"

Seated next to Bernie is Ed Bervena, gray-haired, brown-skinned, and barrel-chested, looking at forty-five like a Hawaiian surfer a decade or two past his prime. Bervena's from San Jose, however, which makes him perfectly suited to be the third member of Judge Manley's team—the street guy. A recovering addict of fourteen years, Bervena was a barrio kid who had chalked up eighteen arrests and eighteen convictions in his heyday as a crackhead, before Manley got him into treatment and later gave him a job. Since 1999, he's been working with Gary and Bernie on Manley's team as a probation community worker.

Ed too has a take on the system. Each time Ed had been released from jail, a deputy whom he'd known in high school would process him out. "See you next time," he'd say to Ed, "see you next time." And with Ed, there always *was* a next time. He didn't know then how *not* to go back. Finally, one day he figured it out. Going to the jail to pick up one of the team's clients, he ran into that very same guard. "We still got a place here for you, Ed," he said. "Not anymore," shot back Bervena, who realized that the same system that had rolled him over eighteen times before Judge Manley had gotten him the help he needed was the same system that had produced that guard.

Ten minutes later they arrive at the Jacob's Center—a small

residential drug treatment facility on a quiet street not far from Manley's courthouse. Ed gets out of the car and drops into casual conversation in the driveway, when suddenly Lenny Wilson (not his real name)—a wiry, coal black African American with a thin, sharp face—arrives, zooming up on a Schwinn racing bike, screeching to a stop not an arm's length from Ed, and dismounting so quickly he looks like a pop-up toy.

"Yo, Ed," says Lenny as he turns and flashes a grin revealing nothing but gums, the result of having all his rotted teeth recently removed for a new set of dentures.

Nevertheless, the last words you'd use to describe the forty-five-year-old Lenny are "old" or "decrepit"—not when he's aglow with the kind of kinetic energy that a six-year-old boy exudes as he bounces himself off a sidewalk like a pink rubber ball.

Lenny occupies that space where Proposition 36 rubs up against California's three strikes law, and a drug defendant is sentenced under one or the other. Lenny was lucky. He'd landed in the court of Stephen Manley—a judge who believes fervently in drug treatment. If he'd been arrested solely for simple drug possession, that wouldn't have mattered. The DA would have been forced to place him in a drug treatment program under the provisions of Prop 36 in any case—notwithstanding the fact that he would otherwise have been eligible for a third-strike prosecution because of his twelve-page-long rap sheet. Among other things, it contained two burglaries in '76; arrests for multiple parole violations, trespassing, vandalism, and disturbing the peace; possession of cocaine in '86; petty theft with a prior in '88; and drug possession in '98.

But Lenny had gotten lippy during his arrest and picked up an additional misdemeanor charge for telling the cops who had stopped him for "no reason and outside of their jurisdiction" that he was going to "fuck their wives and kill their kids." Lenny laughs as he tells all this; it was, after all, just his usual brand of hyperbole. But had the DA decided to prosecute on *that* non-drug misdemeanor, and without a sympathetic judge, he could easily have received a third strike sentence.

"Prior to Prop 36, we [the Public Defender's Office] would have had to crawl on our hands and knees to convince the DA that Lenny was mentally ill and drug addicted," says Bernie Saucedo, "and that we needed to do something other than incarcerate him for the rest of his life under the three strikes law. But with Prop 36, we now have way more leverage."

Unlike Lenny, Tommy Lee Fryman and André René Floyd had neither a sympathetic judge nor good timing. Their drug possession arrests occurred *prior* to Prop 36's implementation date of July 1, 2001.

In 1998, Fryman was arrested in San Jose for being under the influence of cocaine. Tommy Lee was being strip-searched when the cops found 1.2 grams of crack cocaine "hidden between his buttocks." He pleaded guilty to possession of cocaine base, and because of nine prior felony convictions "alleged as strikes," was given a three strikes sentence of twenty-five-to-life.

Fryman appealed, claiming eligibility under Proposition 36. Subsequently, the Sixth District Court of Appeal declared that Fryman *was* eligible for treatment under Proposition 36 because "the drastic difference in treatment [between third-strike and Proposition 36 defendants] is the difference between incarceration for life, [and] release on probation. [And that] violates the constitutional guarantee of equal protection under the law." Tommy Lee had gotten lucky, or so it seemed.

André René Floyd had never been lucky. In April of 2000, Floyd's girlfriend died of natural causes. When the Bakersfield police arrived, Floyd was hovering over her body, crying. Then he coughed—a cough that would cost him the next twenty-five years of his life in state prison. The cough produced a plastic bag containing one quarter of a single gram of cocaine that landed on his girlfriend's lifeless body. The police arrested him, and Floyd—who'd been convicted of five felonies between 1981 and 1985—was convicted of simple drug possession and given a third strike twenty-five-years-to-life sentence. Like Tommy Lee Fryman, Floyd appealed.

Unlike the Sixth District Court of Appeal, however, the Fifth District was unmoved by the fact that the vast difference between a twenty-five-to-life sentence and drug treatment and no incarceration at all, was, in effect, simply a matter of timing. So it upheld his conviction.

Floyd appealed again, this time to the California Supreme Court. And in April of 2003, he received its verdict. The Court ruled six to one that, as Justice Marvin Baxter put it, "The act [Prop 36] was not intended to apply retroactively to this subset of cases . . . [it] means what it says, i.e. that except as otherwise provided, the act shall be applied prospectively."

But as his notably conservative colleague, Janice Rogers Brown, heatedly pointed out in her lone dissent, such a "narrow" interpretation of the law will cost taxpayers $24,000 a year to incarcerate people like Floyd, as opposed to $4,000 a year for treatment, and it "frustrates rather than promotes the purpose and intent of the initiative."

In her amicus brief supporting André René Floyd's appeal, Marylou Hillberg, Tommy Lee Fryman's attorney, laid out a strong but unsuccessful argument that Justice Brown was correct.

Sixty-one percent of the voters of this state declared [when they approved Proposition 36] their desire to halt the wasteful expenditure of hundreds of millions of dollars each year on the incarceration—and reincarceration—of nonviolent drug users who would be better served by community-based treatment.

Sixty-one percent of the voters said they did not want their tax dollars of $625,000 spent to keep appellant locked up for twenty-five years.

How do appellants' sentences of twenty-five years to life fulfill the desired goal of 61% of the voters of this state: "to enhance public safety by reducing drug-related crime and preserving jails and prison cells for serious and violent offenders, and to improve public health by reducing drug abuse and drug dependence through proven and effective drug treatment strategies"?

How else can [the attorney general] justify his position that would have appellants serve twenty-five years in prison, while identical defendants with the very same crime, and the very same prior convictions, sentenced after July 1, 2001 would now be placed on probation and placed in a drug program pursuant to the directive of the majority of the voters of this state?

Here we have a determination by the electorate that the draconian sentence of twenty-five years to life is no longer an appropriate sentence for someone with a small amount of drugs who has neither felony convictions, nor crimes causing the infliction of physical injury, within the preceding five years. There is nothing in this initiative that points to any intent or purpose to keep either Mr. Floyd or Mr. Fryman in prison for the rest of his life simply because he was sentenced before the initiative could become operative. Everything in the purpose and intent of this initiative points to the abolition of this kind of sentence under these circumstances.

A month earlier, a unanimous California Supreme Court had also ruled that a judge could not eliminate a prior strike of a suspect prosecuted for a low level drug crime and place him in a Prop 36 treatment program if the suspect had been convicted of a crime within the past five years, or had not been out of prison for five years. That a very conservative Court was able to rule as it did in both cases was no accident.

The authors of Proposition 36 had done extensive polling beforehand requiring at least a 60 percent positive rating in their polls before going ahead and spending the time and resources to have it placed on the ballot. "You have to draft something that people are willing to support," one of the initiative's creators, Bill Zimmerman, later said. "Giving people more than two chances at treatment, for example, was a breaking point for the voters we polled. If we had written the law with more than two chances, or made it more liberal in other respects, we would have lost significant support. There's no point in spending millions of dollars on an initiative that's going to lose." The justices of the California Supreme Court were making sure that André René Floyd, Tommy Lee Fryman, and many other "drug criminals" sitting crushed in their cells would pay for the trade off.

- - - -

Proposition 36 is just one of a series of drug reform ballot initiatives that had been proliferating around the country since the mid-1990s.

Nationally, about one million Americans are arrested annually on drug charges, *80 percent* of them just for marijuana, while the federal government has been spending $40 billion a year directly on our drug war, 80 percent of *that* targeted to marijuana. Two million Americans are now behind bars, giving the United States the highest per capita incarceration rate in the world. Forty percent of those two million are doing their time for drug offenses.

One of the key players behind the drug reform movement has been a tall, lanky, Santa Monica–based political consultant and long-time progressive political activist named Bill Zimmerman, who views America's drug crusade as "just another war, this one directed at America's poor and unemployed."

While Manley was working on the inside to change drug policy, Zimmerman and his colleagues in the drug reform movement began working from the outside. The prospect of making immediate change in federal law, they reasoned, was remote at best. So they decided to pursue reform on a state level, and to focus in particular on the twenty-five states that had a ballot initiative process.

In 1996, Zimmerman's group, the Campaign for New Drug Policies (CNDP), sponsored America's first successful marijuana initiative, California's Proposition 215, which allowed physicians to prescribe the drug to the seriously ill. From 1996 to the November 2002 election, CNDP and its New York–based sister organization, the Lindesmith Drug Policy Center, won twelve of the thirteen ballot initiatives they sponsored. Most of them were funded by the billionaire financier and social reformer George

Soros, his fellow billionaire Peter Lewis, and John Sperling, the founder of Phoenix University, who each contributed almost $1.2 million. In all, seventeen of their nineteen drug reform ballot measures passed.

The savvy that went into the *writing* of Proposition 36 was reflected in assuring that the *funding* for the implementation of the law would be there once it passed. One of its provisions stipulated that $120 million a year for the next five years had to be set aside solely for Proposition 36 programs. Consequently, when the state's budget deficit ballooned to $35 billion by 2003, Governor Davis was unable to slash Proposition 36's funding, as was done for most other state drug programs.

There had been plenty of opposition to Proposition 36: Davis and his fellow Democratic officerholders Attorney General Bill Lockyer and Senator Dianne Feinstein all condemned it, as did nine out of ten of the state's largest newspapers, including the *Los Angeles Times*, and fifty-seven of California's fifty-eight county sheriffs and district attorneys. (San Francisco was the lone exception.) The state's largest political donor, Don Novey's prison guards' union—wanting, as ever, to keep that maximum amount of new meat flowing into the state's meat-packing factories—gave $200,000 to the failed campaign against the law.

In short, Proposition 36 was politically toxic. It challenged the reefer madness that had dominated national drug policy for the preceding two decades—and had done so in a trend-setting state of over thirty million people. Consequently, it began generating tremendous opposition to similar proposed state initiatives nationwide. "There's this big misconception [in the rest of America], that we've legalized drugs here in California," says Kathryn P. Jett, the director of the California Department of Alcohol and Drug

Programs. "And they want to divorce themselves from us. There's this fear that if you do anything different from the way we've been doing business, that system will somehow break down."

People are also fearful, thinks Dr. David Deitch—a drug treatment pioneer and professor of psychology at the University of California, San Diego—of something else: "a serious, long-denied reexamination of America's drug policies. A discussion," he says, "that's never really been had. If we were fighting a true war," says Deitch, "we'd gather up all available information, strategically fund what works, and set out to win. Instead, we continue to feed the DEA and our local police money, while starving mental health and drug-prevention and treatment programs."

- - - -

Lenny Wilson, who was born in Salinas, California, cannot read or write. He's dyslexic, he says, and "also mental." He has "schizophrenia, paranoia, and [is] bipolar." He was first diagnosed as bipolar while in a mental institution in Georgia in the late 1970s. It was there that Lenny watched the guards beat a man to death with leather straps because he wouldn't stop flicking his cigarette butts; and there where he was first prescribed lithium—which he still takes, along with Arcane, the tranquilizer Vicerol, and Novane. "Now *that*," he says of the Novane, "is a reeeeeaaal tranquilizer, the one that keeps me from being so [manic]."

Lenny smoked his first joint at thirteen, then started taking bennies, dropping acid, and doing burglaries—about forty-five of them while still a teenager. He didn't do all the burglaries just for the money, however. It was also because of the edge on which he loved to walk, that danger zone. For Lenny, that edge was his bliss.

While in prison, says Lenny, he met up with Tex Watson, the Helter Skelter killer from back in the '60s, who'd become a prison chaplain. One day Tex looked him in the eye and gave him a piece of advice: "Lenny," he said, "don't you never come back here. Never!"

For a decade Lenny tried to take Tex's admonition to heart. He got a regular, long-term job as a caretaker "on a fifteen-and-a-half-acre ranch up in the mountains," and has calluses on his hands as thick as bricks to prove it.

The *problem*, he says, is that every once in a while he gets that urge, goes off his meds, gets good and high, and parties out on that edge. His last party would have been his final one, had it not been for Proposition 36, Judge Manley, and a DA who was likewise in tune with the spirit of the law.

In late September of 2002, Lenny finally got his new teeth and left the residential center. But then he had a stroke, one that affected his speech and partly paralyzed his hand and leg on one side of his body. He can still walk, but now has to drag his afflicted leg behind him. His speech is slurred, although he can still make himself understood. "He hasn't relapsed," says Bernie Saucedo, "but staying clean has been a real struggle for Lenny. He likes the isolation of working up in the mountains at that ranch, but it's also what makes him want to relapse so bad. You know how he loves that excitement."

- - - -

The long-running corridor along the string of courtrooms on the third floor of Los Angeles County's downtown Superior Court is filled as usual with black faces and LAPD blues—the cops there to testify, the faces to be processed through the system. With only ten minutes before the courts go into session on this Thursday morning in early December 2002, the place feels like the legal equivalent of a triage area in an emergency room.

Defendants wander about clueless, looking for their assigned courtroom; others stare uncomprehendingly when told they're three days late or a week too early for their court date. Overworked public defenders and blasé lawyers in red ties and worn, shiny blue suits hold whispered, three-minute-long impromptu interviews with their clients, while the cops waiting to testify have a few laughs over on the benches that line the walls.

Nancy Chand, an LA County public defender for the past sixteen years, hurries into courtroom 42—one of the two courts in downtown LA that handle Proposition 36 and drug court cases. Over any given *six-month period*, about eight hundred drug cases are processed through number 42, while its adjacent sister courtroom, number 40, deals with about nine hundred, the highest caseload in the state.

The scene is never-changing—a couple of women and a couple of Latinos, and fifteen or twenty tired black men, many of whom will soon be replaced in courts like this with yet another generation of their sons, nephews, younger brothers, and cousins.

Tall and thin with light brown hair worn long, Chand resembles one of those improbably pretty deputy DAs struggling to convict a monster serial rapist protected by some ridiculous constitutional safeguard on those network cop-prosecutor shows—the ones that pretend to be cynical so that you can feel so knowingly hip. But Chand's decidedly no prosecutor.

"I always wanted to be a public defender way back when I was in college," she says. "We help people. A lot of our clients need help—there are plenty willing to prosecute, but not many willing to help."

Chand walks away, and a few minutes later, Superior Court Judge Marcelita Haynes enters her Proposition 36 drug court courtroom. In her eyes is a touch of the wrath of God, in her demeanor the message that she has not arrived to play.

A meticulously coifed African American of an uncertain age, Haynes is adorned today in gold—gold earrings and eyeglasses, and a thin, barely detectable gold face mike winding past her cheek to the side of her mouth.

Wasting no time, Haynes gets right to it.

"Raul Sanchez . . . failure to appear, bench warrant issued.

"Jaime Sanchez, also a no-show, probation revoked, bench warrant issued."

A crew-cut, heavy-set Latino is up next. "You missed all of your twelve-step meetings, all your clinical groups . . . refused to take drug tests. . . ."

"He's promised to quit his job and devote all his time to his problem, your honor," a public defender tells her.

"If you don't want to be treated, that's fine with me, but you'll have to make up your mind what you want to do. . . . But you will take your drug tests. . . . If you fail . . . I *will* send you to jail."

All this is said with the stern, no-nonsense tone of your elementary school principal after your third grade teacher has sent you to the office for playing pocket-pool.

"Probation revoked and reinstated," she tells another man. "You willfully took yourself out of your program. . . . Your attitude is extremely poor this morning . . . I'm not here to be your friend. You quit. Do some jail time."

Then comes a string of failures-to-appear. In all, six out of sixteen defendants will fail to show up this morning—numbers that reflect both downtown LA's transient population and lack of funding. The money allocated for Proposition 36 treatment is proving inadequate, particularly when dealing with defendants living on skid row—the homeless, crackheads, winos, junkies, people with AIDS, and the dual-diagnosed long off their medications. Getting and maintaining them in treatment has been a frustrating and oddly unanticipated problem.

LA had been expecting a large number of recreational users to enroll in the Proposition 36 program, according to Lael Rubin, the special counsel in charge of Proposition 36 for the DA's office. But, as in San Jose, that hasn't been the case. Instead, most of the defendants have turned out to be the heavily addicted, the very people who require the longest, most expensive treatment—months in a residential facility as opposed to an out-patient twelve-step program—the very people most likely to be eligible for a three strikes sentence.

Next before Judge Haynes is John Washington (not his real name). This is his make-or-break day. The big-bellied, broad-shouldered, forty-six-year-old ex-marine is looking good today—especially compared to the guy who preceded him, who'd missed twenty of his twenty-four twelve-step appointments and severely riled the judge.

Standing there with public defender Nancy Chand at his side, Washington has what Judge Haynes describes as "a very good report," and "at the discretion of your program," she tells Washington, "you are transferred from level three to level one. Keep up the good work." In other words, he isn't going to jail. Clean and sober now for the past seven months, Washington is a happy and grateful man.

In 1987, after eight years in the Marine Corps, Washington was downsized out of the service. "I was going to make the Marines my career, but they told me I was 'expendable.' I can't say it made me do the things that I did, but it took its toll."

Ten years later, Washington was a homeless skid row crackhead "livin' in a big ol' dumpster—not exactly what you call clean. But, yeah, I went that low." Washington always had a hustle—stealing wooden pallets and then selling them back to local truck yards, buying and dealing—anything to make a buck, until he was caught by the LAPD.

Without Proposition 36, as he tells it, he would have done at least one year in county jail for being in possession of those "birds"—bundles filled with little rocks of crack cocaine that he tossed up in the air when the LAPD black-and-white spun around the corner and nailed him dead-to-rights.

Washington doesn't know how lucky he is. A year doing county time, in fact, would have been improbable. Probation was not even on the table. Prior to Proposition 36, with a record that included burglary, grand theft, vandalism, assault, and shoplifting, he would have been awarded a three strikes sentence.

"The Salvation Army program I'm in—over there at the Harbor Light shelter—is strict but good," he says. "A lot of people don't like it at first, they're in denial and don't like that discipline, don't like authority figures.

"In the program you detox first, then you go to classes within a therapeutic community—as many classes as the court deems fit. I'm a vet, and Harbor Light helped me get my benefits from the

Veterans Administration—which is helping me with my job preparation. They gave me a voucher to buy a suit, tie, and shirt for job interviews and showed me how to use a computer. But they do all that at Harbor Light even if you're not a vet.

"They're training me to be a truck driver now," he tells me, "right there in Skid Row, with winos and crackheads lyin' out in front of the door. It reminds me that I can't go back to that no more."

- - - -

Drug courts all around the country have already proved their effectiveness, and Proposition 36, when properly administered, is nothing other than a vastly expanded, statewide drug court system.

Studies over the past twenty years have shown that between 35 percent and 50 percent of people entering drug treatment programs complete and graduate from those programs. That success rate is comparable to those of programs for people with illnesses like hypertension and diabetes.

This doesn't mean that a positive view of Proposition 36 is guaranteed in the near future, however. Not if people who are willfully ignorant of the now overwhelmingly conclusive scientific evidence concerning the chemical, psychological, and physical nature of substance abuse are permitted to define its success.

This would include people such as Judge Michael A. Tynan. Tynan, who supervises all Los Angeles County drug court programs, told the *Los Angeles Times* in November of 2002 that "Proposition 36 was sold to voters as a way to keep true first- and second-time offenders out of prison. I think we're wasting an awful lot of money on people who can't benefit from such a light-weight program."

George Bush's drug czar John P. Walters agreed. And so did Republican governors and conservative DAs and law enforcement officials. Daniel Forbes, in a comprehensive Institute for Policy Studies report, characterized their opposition as a "crusade to scuttle [drug] reform initiatives around the nation." Walters and his allies stepped up an anti–drug reform media campaign begun by Bill Clinton's drug control policy adviser, Barry McCaffrey.

And in the November 2002 elections, they met with remarkable success. Drug reform measures similar to Proposition 36 were on their way to the ballot in Michigan, Florida, and Ohio. But a wall of opposition from those states' political and legal establishments arose, and only the CNDP's Ohio initiative made it to the ballot. And it went down to crushing defeat after a fierce counterattack organized by conservative Republican governor Robert Taft.

In Nevada, Lewis, Sperling, and Soros spent $1.7 million to qualify the most radical reform measure—a law legalizing up to three ounces of pot for personal use, which would have also required the state of Nevada to set up a system of legal distribution. It lost big. So did measures in North Dakota that would have eased the law on growing and using marijuana, and in Arizona, where an initiative to decriminalize possession of small amounts of pot was also soundly defeated. Dr. David Deitch's "serious, long-denied reexamination of America's drug policies," had, it seems, gone up in smoke.

26

THE MODIFICATION

"WE CAN'T AFFORD A FAILED PROSECUTOR with a soft-on-crime approach as Los Angeles County DA," declared a black-on-white campaign flyer. "Steve Cooley opposes our Three Strikes law . . . Cooley: Wrong for DA."

The amazing thing about the flyer, distributed in the heat of the 2000 campaign for district attorney of Los Angeles, was that the last minute mailing by Gil Garcetti against his Republican opponent, Steve Cooley, had no impact. In the end, Cooley, a low-key, highly regarded trial prosecutor and veteran of over twenty-five years in the DA's office, beat Garcetti by 27 percentage points.

Of course, it hadn't taken much to beat Garcetti. Just a credible campaign by a credible alternative. For Gil Garcetti was not just disliked by the Los Angeles electorate, he was despised. Not for his position on three strikes, but for his office's appalling incompetence during the O.J. Simpson debacle and for his leading membership in a political and criminal justice establishment that had miserably failed to hold a scandal-plagued LAPD account-able for decades. In 1999, the department's latest embarrassment, the Rampart brutality and corruption scandal, exploded, and Garcetti looked hapless and culpable in response. So bad, in fact, that seven months prior to his defeat, the *Los Angeles Times* ran an article accompanying a devastating poll the paper had conducted. "Garcetti," it read, "is in grim shape politically." Only 18 percent of those polled intended to vote for him for reelection. It was, the article pointed out, "a remarkable deficit for an incumbent."

But if Cooley's lopsided victory had more to do with Garcetti than him, it was nevertheless remarkable, and of more than local interest. During his campaign, Cooley had been aggressive and unequivocal in his criticism of Garcetti's indiscriminate prosecu-tions of three strikes cases. He spelled out that criticism in a cam-paign position paper: "The three strikes law provides a powerful tool to seek life sentences for repeat predators," wrote Cooley. "It is a necessary weapon, [but] one that must be used with precision and not in a scatter gun fashion. . . . I [always] felt that unless used judiciously, the law could result in injustice. . . . My fears were well founded. Because of the incumbent's misguided policies, I watched petty drug offenders and petty thieves sentenced to life terms. There has to be a strong sense of proportionality. I applied that approach as head deputy in the San Fernando branch office. Cases were efficiently settled because at an early stage prosecutors were empowered to fashion an appropriate evenhanded sentence in the interest of justice."

Then he laid out his future policy as DA: "If the potential third strike is a 'violent or serious' felony, the case will be *presumed* to be one that should be pursued as a third strike, meriting a twenty-five-to-life sentence. If it is not a 'violent or serious' felony, the case will be *presumed* to be one that should not be pursued as a third strike."

That Steve Cooley took a principled, reasoned stance, however, is not the point. What *is* the point is that it hadn't *hurt* him to take that stance. And *that* was an indication, like Dan Lungren's failure to coast into the governorship on a crime-fighting platform, that crime was no longer *the* dominant issue it had been back in 1994, and that the winds of fear and hysteria were cooling.

Steve Cooley proved true to his word. Third strike convictions in LA County dropped 39 percent at the end of his first year in office. But even before Cooley's change in policy, the number of three strikes prosecutions in LA County had begun to mirror a statewide trend. In the peak year of 1996, Los Angeles successfully prosecuted five hundred fifty-nine three strikes cases. In 1999, the number had fallen to three hundred ninety-five. In 2001, under Cooley, the figure was one hundred ninety-two. The rest of the state, meanwhile, was showing similar declines: seven hundred ninety-three cases in 1996; six hundred forty-nine in 1999; three hundred forty-four in 2001.

Crime hysteria had died down. The historic decline in the crime rate accounted for some of that decrease and, consequently, for the drop in three strikes prosecutions as well. Costly mandatory minimum sentences were being modified across the nation by state legislatures strapped for cash.

There was also a pragmatic problem contributing to the drop in three strikes prosecutions: taking a three strikes case to trial. Defendants prosecuted on a third strike almost always went to trial if not offered a plea bargain. With a twenty-five-to-life sledgehammer hanging over their heads, defendants would inevitably take the least bad choice—plea bargains that still guaranteed long stretches in prison. So why should prosecutors go through the expense of a trial?

A final, undeniable cause of the decline in prosecutions had to do with the law itself. There were already so many people with criminal records behind bars serving second- or third-strike sentences that the pool of potential candidates was getting harder to find.

- - - -

Shortly after Steve Cooley's 2000 election victory, Bill Jones, coauthor of the state's three strikes law and then California secretary of state, issued a press release: "Our crime rate is declining faster than anywhere else in the nation," it read, "in large part because of the deterrence provided by the strict implementation of Three Strikes. Criminals know there is no tolerance for repeat offenders in California." "District Attorney-Elect Cooley's anticipated blanket policy to let career serious and violent criminals off the hook because their third felony is a non-violent one is a dangerous abuse of discretion," the release continued, "and a flagrant disregard for the law that an overwhelming 72 percent of California voters supported in 1994. It's just a matter of time before one of these violent career criminals who could have been removed from our neighborhoods for a non-violent felony will be released to rape, rob, molest or murder innocent Californians."

Steve Cooley disagreed. "Of all the things I've done as a district attorney," he told the *Los Angeles Times* in 2003, ". . . there's not one that's been better received by the legal community and the public [than reform of LA County's three strikes policy]." Better received, at least for the present.

But what of the future? In 2002, the crime rate in the United States plunged to its lowest level in thirty years—the lowest since the Bureau of Justice Statistics began keeping records. From 1992 through 2002, crime decreased by a stunning and unprecedented *fifty* percent nationwide—and in every major property and violent crime category except murder, which rose only slightly. California has mirrored this trend. Between 1980 and 2002, the state's overall crime rate decreased by 51.8 percent.

Simultaneously, from 1980 to 2000, California's prison population rose by nearly 600 percent—nearly twice the national rate. By the turn of the twenty-first century, many of those locked up during the accelerated wars on crime and drugs during the '90s were being paroled back into their poor, minority communities unrehabilitated, with $200 in their pockets, and near zero prospects of finding a legitimate job.

By 2003, one out of every fourteen adult males in Oakland, California, was on either active parole or probation. More than ninety-eight people *per day* were being paroled back into LA County—more than in any other county in the nation. Meanwhile, six hundred and fifty-six murders occurred among the 3.8 million residents of the city of Los Angeles in 2002—placing it in strong competition with Washington, D.C., and Chicago for the dubious distinction of being the murder capital of America.

A 1997 California Department of Corrections survey found that 85 percent of the state's parolees were chronic drug or alcohol abusers, 50 percent were illiterate, 70–90 percent unemployed, 18 percent mentally ill and 10 percent homeless. They were being returned to the very streets that spawned them, to prey on the weakest and poorest among them, or to be preyed on themselves. The people with real power in California and the United States—the middle-class, white electorate and the corporate leaders whose money dictates the votes of America's politicians—seem perfectly content to confront this situation with one-stop-shopping, maximum-minimum laws such as Mike Reynolds's three strikes law.

The hard questions of how to otherwise deal with them on a meaningful, long-term, preventive basis are rarely being posed. Programs attempting to salvage the marginalized young people in America's ghettos, barrios and rural hovels—the Mexican and El Salvadoran kids lured into the *vato locos'* deadly gangs before they're twelve; the south LA ten-year-old bow tie–wearing little fifth-graders soon to turn into Niggas With Attitude; the crank-addicted grandchildren of the San Joaquin Valley's Ditch Bank Okies and Mexican stoop laborers—are being dismissed as just more of the same failed liberal bromides. What to do about their daily acculturation to crime and an accompanying highly sexualized, violence-glorifying hip-hop culture of niggas, 'hoes, bitches, ropes of neck gold, and bustin' caps in people's asses seems to have been settled, even as one doomed generation replaces the next.

Attempts such as Proposition 36 to treat instead of imprison the drug addicted are being fiercely fought throughout the nation. Dreams of solving America's homelessness tragedy are shattered by massive state and federal budget deficits and the slashing of social services for the poor.

In 2001, California's crime rate increased by 3.7 percent. Homicides went up 9.2 percent, robberies 7.2 percent. In 2002,

California's overall crime rate increased again by 2.4 percent. Granted, these are relatively small increases after a decade of dramatic decline. But the increase is there, despite the national trend, concentrated in the impoverished areas of cities like Los Angeles, Oakland, and Fresno.

The Steve Cooleys of California are rational people, but Cooley won't be the DA of Los Angeles County forever. What will happen when a politically ambitious replacement takes office and confronts a situation where crime is on the rise and gang killings are spilling out of their home turf and into middle-class neighborhoods? Or when another bout of media-induced mass hysteria such as the one that surrounded Polly Klaas's dreadful death occurs? Or a Willie Horton scenario again takes center stage, and a three strikes–eligible suspect is arrested for petty theft and is given a lesser sentence, gets out of prison, and commits a sensational murder?

It's easy to imagine Steve Cooley's successor reacting by replacing his three strikes policy and announcing—as did Gil Garcetti—that henceforth a new hard line will be in effect, and every crime committed by a three strikes–eligible suspect will be prosecuted as a third strike. Easier still to believe, with the Bill Joneses just waiting to pounce, that, as he put it, such a scenario is "just a matter of time."

And then the entire underbelly of LA—the people whom even liberals no longer have any sympathy for, the flotsam and jetsam of the Golden State—will be grist for California's three strikes mill: the greasy-clothed homeless, the shopping cart mentally ill, the kinetic speed freaks and pipe-sucking crackheads, the washed-out winos, the puncture-ridden junkies, Fellini's freaks, Charles Bukowski's bar flies—all the wizened old trash and the young wannabe's—will join the Gregory Taylors, Shane Reamses and three hundred and forty-four other inmates serving twenty-five years to life for petty theft with a prior, and the six hundred and forty-seven people doing the same time for simple drug possession.

In the meantime, three strikes remains a loaded gun that, at any moment, could be used again as it was in the peak years of '96 and '97.

27

SHANE AND A.J.

AS SUE REAMS HANGS UP THE PHONE, that slightly nauseated feeling in the pit of her stomach—that feeling that she always gets when it is time to make an appointment to see her son—momentarily subsides. The corrections officer she's just spoken to was "nice, very nice." By nice, Sue Reams means not unpleasant, not cold, distant, annoyed, and slightly hostile—not one of those guards who make you feel like you're somehow unclean because you have a relative or friend in prison.

Phoning ahead for a weekend appointment is Sue Reams's first step in the exhausting preparations she'll be making all week for her visit to see Shane and to celebrate his thirty-second birthday on January 31 of 2001. She's always very methodical when carrying out these tasks, doing everything in her power to ensure that nothing goes wrong. There's so much, after all, that's beyond her control. For example, the fact that Proposition 36, which passed in 2000 but wouldn't become effective until July 1, 2001, would only apply "prospectively," not "retroactively." And it would deal only with simple possession, not small-time dealing. It would not, therefore, apply to Shane. So his life, and that of his mother, would remain unchanged.

Her visits to Shane have to be not only carefully planned, but carefully budgeted as well. Her husband Wayne was recently unemployed, and she's only working part-time out of her home, doing headhunting web searches for an insurance company.

And inevitably, the long, arduous trip to Green Mountain Prison (not its real name) will cost at least $200, even if they watch every penny. The motel alone is $60 a night. Then there's the gas and food, and the stacks of quarters they have to bring to pay for the exorbitantly overpriced food they get from the prison snack machines. The planning is especially complex this trip because they are bringing Shane's son, A.J. (The name of Shane Reams's son has been changed to protect his privacy.)

When they go to pick up ten-year-old A.J. at his mother's house on Thursday evening, he is there to greet them. Shane is close to his son, as close as he can be considering he's been sitting in a prison cell since the boy was five.

A.J. is a handsome kid, "always immaculately dressed, with more the African American–type look of his mother than of Shane," says Sue Reams. He is also a kid with problems. He isn't doing well in school. Other kids pick on him and beat him up. But he hates to fight and is so emotional and sensitive that he seems unwilling to aggressively engage the world—just like his father.

While A.J. goes upstairs to take a bath, Sue Reams helps his mother pack. "No jeans this time," Sue tells her, "and no khaki. He's too old to wear that now, they don't want anyone even coming close to resembling a prisoner in uniform."

When he was younger, A.J. wanted to go and see his father

every chance he got. But recently he'd become more ambivalent, vacillating between wanting to go and wanting to stay, and trying to deal with his doubts. Those doubts, Sue was convinced, were directly attributable to the shame he was feeling about his father.

Once, A.J. had refused to do something his teacher had asked. "I don't have to do it," he said, "I'm going to live with my dad in prison." And, remembers Sue Reams, his mother "was just wounded."

When they get under way, it's raining hard, and Sue and Wayne are starting to get seriously concerned about the weather. They missed most of the downpour in San Diego, but soon after crossing over the LA County line, rain starts falling in torrents.

They're heading north and then inland into Mike Reynolds country—into the birthplace of three strikes, into the San Joaquin Valley—toward where Shane Reams languishes in a cell within the walls of a state prison. As usual, the Grapevine—that exhausting stretch of road cutting through the San Gabriel Mountains—is grim, wet, and foggy.

At the summit the sun sneaks through the clouds, revealing snow-capped mountains all around them. It's a spectacular moment, particularly for A.J., who's never before seen snow. But the moment, like the sun, quickly fades. Within an hour A.J. is complaining about the length of the trip. When they arrive at 1:00 P.M., having been on the road since 6 A.M., all three of them are exhausted.

By then, Sue is also becoming unglued at just the *thought* of entering the prison. She's never gotten used to it. But she *needs* to see her son. Wayne, for his part, hates everything about the trip. The ride, the travesty of justice he believes Shane's imprisonment to be, the harsh reality of Shane's prison life—he can find no justification, no logic, in any of it. All he can do is fall into a deep depression.

- - - -

Pulling into the entrance of Green Mountain State Prison is not the ordeal it is at other penal institutions Sue Reams has visited. There is no car search at the front gate to remind her who she is and where she is. She simply has to drive into the parking lot and walk about forty yards into the visiting room. Green Mountain is a new state prison, but its exterior is still grim, gray cement, topped by razor wire. Inside, it has that prison taste of cold metal.

They fill out visitors' slips, which are matched against their drivers' licenses, and a form allowing them to take A.J. with them into the visiting room. Then they take off their shoes, jewelry, glasses, belts, and jackets, and pull out their pockets before walking through a metal detector. On the other side, their right arms are stamped with a substance that can be seen only by black light. They put their shoes back on, and get redressed.

Inside, the visiting room resembles a huge cafeteria. Lined up along one wall is a bank of snack machines; along the other sits a long oval guard's desk with enough red and green flashing lights and equipment to launch a NASA mission to Mars.

About two hundred people are sitting at forty or so square tables with fiberglass or Formica tops, four chairs per table. All the inmates are seated on chairs facing the front door, as required by prison regulations.

When Shane arrives, they move to an area outside with a small patch of grass dominated by an expanse of cement. Like everything else, it's designed to be cold and impersonal, to break a man so he never wants to come back, to make his life as miserable as possible.

Sue and Wayne take a seat at one of the cement tables and watch Shane and A.J. toss around a Frisbee, and then a basketball. During the Frisbee-tossing, A.J. challenges Shane to a game: the first one who misses has to do push-ups. When Shane deliberately drops the Frisbee, A.J. orders him down to do forty.

Then it's time to eat. Their choices are soggy sandwiches, stale chips, or old candy from the prison's overpriced vending machines.

In fact, *everything* one can purchase in California's prisons—where money, needless to say, is scarce—is overpriced. As a lifer, for example, Shane is allowed just one phone call per month. And that call, with an automated voice breaking into the conversation every two minutes announcing that this call is being generated from a California state prison, costs a flat fee of $7.50 for a maximum of fifteen minutes. At the food machines, candy costs $.85, sandwiches $3.00. Despite the cost, the only item worth eating is the barbecue chicken wings at $3.50 per package. However, all Sue can choke down are the potato chips and Fritos. She can't stomach the rest, although Shane tells her it's far better than the food he gets inside. When Shane wants to purchase something for A.J. to eat, he asks Sue to fetch it, since inmates are never permitted to touch money.

Then, during a long, pleasant conversation over a late lunch, A.J. shatters the lie of the moment and says to Shane: "My mom says you're never coming home." As Sue Reams's eyes well up with tears, he adds the clincher: "Other people go to jail and they get out. If those guys get out, and you're a nice man, how come you can't get out?"

They leave the prison at 6:30 that evening. Like vending machine food and phone calls, hotels and motels around rural prisons are shamelessly overpriced. But, if you have no options, you *will* pay. Rooms shared with roaches go for $90 a night. Sue Reams already knows where her family is going to stay. Certainly not at the nice big hotel with the fine restaurant where the rooms start at $150 a night. Instead they decide on the cheapest option, Motel 6, right on the freeway. One room with two beds, $60 a night, right next door to a Denny's restaurant. A.J., who has no homework that weekend, watches *Zorro* on cable TV before the three head over to Denny's for dinner. By 9:30, they're all fast asleep.

Meanwhile, Shane is still on a high from seeing A.J. and his parents, despite the fact that he is once again locked up in his six-by-nine-foot cell. After spending half his life in prison, Shane has grown used to living in a claustrophobic cell; grown used to the cell designed for one man but, because of prison overcrowding, always shared by two; grown used to having to sleep on a metal slab with a mattress as thin as a sheet, while six inches away a roommate takes a dump.

Shane's been housed for three years with his current cellmate—a young guy from South Central whom he's taught to read, how to avoid prison politics, how to stay out of the mix in the yard, and how to deal with people demanding that he take sides.

"You've got to let them know," Shane told him, "that if you want to fight over a lousy table in a yard, go ahead and fight for it, but I've got a family I want to go home to, and I'm not getting involved." "Sometimes," he added, "they'll respect that, sometimes you'll get your ass whipped for not going along with their program, but you gotta take it if you want to get out of here as soon as you can."

Shane himself had set up his own little program to avoid the daily insanity that permeates prison life as a result of thousands of deprived, rebellious, unusually violent and sometimes psychopathic men being driven mad by the conditions of their lives. He leaves his cell only once a day, to jog the perimeter of the yard and then do his sit-ups and push-ups, before immediately returning to his self-imposed isolation, reading Tom Clancy novels, talking endlessly with his celly, hearing from few people other than his mother—the occasional letter from a stranger serving only as "a spark to a fading flame"—and "managing to keep his head up, hopeful for better days."

Shane Reams has also grown used to being told when to eat, sleep, and move by the often embittered, cynical corrections officers in a California penal system that stresses hard time. Hard time for guards too, who lack the opportunity or job description to help people rehabilitate themselves, or to add a touch of nobility, a small sense of doing something at least partly worthwhile with their lives. Instead, they do necessary, but ultimately ignoble, work that provides a secure job with extraordinarily high pay and benefits, but little else other than observing human misery.

Shortly after the passage of the state's three strikes law, for example, a couple of corrections officers at the California State Institute for Men at Chino described the protective emotional shields they donned daily before walking into temples of gloom and facing inmates who wished them dead. "I try to maintain some kindness in my heart for my fellow man," said Thomas Snipp, a Vietnam veteran in his forties who used to work for a linen-rental company, "but I've seen an awful lot of the worst of my fellow man, and the games that people play, the things that they do to play upon your kindness and humanity. And so, I try to maintain some equilibrium and not become totally hard and uncaring, but you're not going to allow yourself to be taken advantage of, you're not going to be a chump, you're not going to be a monk, and you're not going to be conned if you can help it."

Mark Hutton, another white officer who, like Snipp, attended college for a couple of years before dropping out, also had little empathy for his charges. "You are a criminal," said Hutton, who spent thirteen years in the termite and pest control business before going into corrections. "Sure somebody stole those items out of your locker, and I can sympathize with your feelings of frustration and rage . . . but in reality, you are in here for a burglary, so I don't have a lot of sympathy for you."

"Rehabilitation," added Sergeant Snipp, to nods of agreement and laughter from his fellow officers, "has been overused, because rehabilitation means returning someone to their former state. We *do* that. They go out just like they came in."

- - - -

By 9:30 Sunday morning, Sue and Wayne are back in the prison watching the day unfold while Shane plays with A.J., who is blessedly lost in the moment. Sue Reams herself has drifted off into a reverie, watching as a little girl of about four or five stands off to the side holding a Frisbee as Shane and A.J. play, longing to join in, but hesitant to do so. She's been wandering around by herself for several minutes—her parents engrossed in each other—when she catches A.J.'s eye. "Hey little girl, what you got there?" he asks her, indicating the Frisbee. "You got a pizza?" And Shane immediately joins in: "Oh, yeah, you want to make us a pizza?" The girl nods and begins placing rocks into the Frisbee, delighted with the game.

By two o'clock it is time to leave. A feeling of dread floods over Sue Reams as they head for the door, a feeling mirrored in her son's face. "Thanks for bringing my boy," he tells her, as if confirming the obvious: that bringing A.J. is the most she can ever do for him.

28

A "TALIBAN-TYPE" LAW

HURRIEDLY DRESSED in a pair of sweats and a T-shirt, Sue Reams is tense but focused as she weaves through traffic on the I-5 freeway on her way to LA. in April 2000, determined not to miss the bus awaiting her and her passengers in Los Angeles.

Like Reams, her passengers are both middle-aged women and members of FACTS. They'd left San Diego late because Sue Reams had insisted on waiting for several others who'd asked to ride with her to their ultimate destination—the state capitol in Sacramento, where they planned to stage a protest demonstration.

They're making the long, arduous trip in response to an announcement on the FACTS website. "The Assembly Public Safety Committee will have a hearing on April 4 [2000]," it read. "So, please, mark your schedules, set up a vacation day from work, and try to attend, and bring your family and friends."

The hearing is for a proposed bill to amend the three strikes law to require that a third strike be a "violent" or "serious" felony before a twenty-five-years-to-life sentence can be imposed.

After the hearing, Sue Reams plans on lobbying state legislators to support the pending bill, and she fills in her passengers as she drives. "We need to find out where their heads are," she tells them. "We need to know what kind of things a particular legislator is interested in, and how we can relate what *we're* interested in to what *they're* interested in. [Assemblywoman] Susan Davis is big on education. If we can talk to her about education, we can try to explain how the education budget is always short-changed because so much of the state's budget is going to keep so many people in prison."

"We need to get in there," continues Reams, "and not pound on the table and get angry at them because of their previous votes. Instead, we need to be dressed nicely and speak nicely, and show a professional appearance."

Susan Davis is a very conservative Republican, and her office had been noncommittal when Reams had called to make an appointment earlier in the week. And sure enough, when they called back, Reams was scheduled to meet with an aide, a clear sign, on an important issue like three strikes, that the meeting would be strictly pro forma. But Sue Reams does not mention this to her passengers. She is, after all, trying to pump them up, not deflate them.

She'd worked hard on behalf of the proposed bill, as she had on others, all of which had failed miserably. She'd written letters urging assembly members and state senators to support it—letters other FACTS members had then used as models. And on the weekends, she'd stood in front of the San Diego jail passing out flyers and telling jail visitors about FACTS.

The first two or three years, she'd had high hopes. But in time, she'd been exposed to the political reality of having to get a two-thirds vote of the legislature *and* the signature of a governor who was a passionate supporter of three strikes before even one word of the law could change. She had become deeply cynical about the inner-circle political players involved in the three-strikes debate—such as it was.

But Sue Reams says none of this to her passengers and tries hard to keep it out of her mind. She *has* to remain hopeful if she ever wants to see Shane outside of that electrified fence surrounding Green Mountain State Prison. She has willed herself "*not* to care if she winds up the only person at a demonstration." Even if only one person is watching, she has to be ready to stand there in silence holding up her "storyboard"—a large white piece of thin pressed foam mounted with a color picture of Shane, with his name in big block letters, and a pronouncement: "Twenty-five years to life for being a lookout on a $20 drug sale."

Sue Reams had been right to rush to LA. When she arrives in the parking lot of Hollman United Methodist Church at about 10:00 that night, there are only five or ten minutes left before two waiting buses carrying about fifty people each will depart for Sacramento.

At about 5:00 A.M., the buses arrive at the capital and stop at a Denny's for breakfast. Sue Reams immediately heads for the bathroom and changes into a pair of black slacks and a FACTS T-shirt, which she later supplements with a suit jacket and blouse when she goes to lobby for the bill.

- - - -

"I want to state up front," says Joe Klaas, a man born to the mike and the dramatic gesture, "that the murder, rape, and kidnapping of my granddaughter, Polly Klaas, was exploited by this three strikes bill—a bill which didn't stand a chance in hell of passing before Polly's killing."

As he lays out his bitter message to the members of the California assembly's Public Safety Committee, which is considering the amendments Sue Reams will lobby for, Joe Klaas's outrage seems to gush up from deep within his eighty-year-old bones. The insanity, the *injustice* of this "Taliban-type" law is an affront not only to twelve-year-old Polly's memory, but to the entire Klaas family. Polly—*his* granddaughter—had been used, they'd all been used, to get this "god-awful, unjust bill" passed. "Unjust, god-awful," that's exactly what he *felt*, exactly why he'd climbed into his silver '85 Buick Regal that morning and driven the two hundred miles from Carmel to speak at this hearing and to try and have the law changed.

But Klaas is not addressing the world as he was back in the front-page days of '94, when he had accused supporters of three strikes of "dancing a jig on Polly's grave." Precious few reporters had taken the time to attend today's hearing. Why bother? The chance of anything of lasting significance emerging from this or any other legislative hearing that dares consider modifying the state's three strikes law is next to zero. In the wider scheme of things, this hearing is little more than a bone tossed to a pleading dog.

Nevertheless, the members of the Public Safety Committee are mesmerized as they watch Joe Klaas from behind their dais. And so are Sue Reams and the other one hundred or so spectators seated in the stark hearing room beneath the splendid cupola of the neoclassical state capitol building. So tightly packed is the small room that people are standing at its edges and overflowing into the hallway outside.

Klaas continues to rivet his audience with the verbal agility of the talk show host he once was. "I belong to Citizens Against Violent Crime," he tells the committee. "There is no member of my family who's *not* opposed to violent crime or any other kind of crime. . . . We think that people who commit nonviolent crimes should get appropriate sentences. But we *don't* think that violence, [in turn] should be perpetrated upon them."

Upon *them*. That is typical Joe Klaas. For despite the unspeakable that has been done to his granddaughter, Joe Klaas remains an idealist. Joe Klaas doesn't just believe in the myth of World War II America, he *is* that America. The America that saved the world from the Nazis and Japanese warlords in order to ensure that his country would remain the land of the free and home of the brave, with liberty and justice for all.

What Joe Klaas does *not* believe in, however, he spells out to the committee as he continues. "As a former prisoner . . . of the Nazis . . . I can say that taking twenty-five years of somebody's life for committing a nonviolent crime is violence almost on the level with murder."

So blunt, so to the point, so unexpected is the line, that Reams and her fellow FACTS members spring to their feet and give Joe Klaas a "Standing O."

Applause and other such displays of emotion during hearings are a serious breech of assembly etiquette, however, and this one brings a quick, stern admonition from the committee chair.

"I'm sorry," Klaas snaps back, "but it *is* violence. [Sentencing someone] to twenty-five-to-life because he made a false statement on an application for a real estate loan, [or giving someone] twenty-five-to-life for taking aspirin out of a bottle and putting the bottle back on the shelf in a drugstore—now that *is* violence."

Joe Klaas feels *good*, feels victorious, as he strides out of the hearing room and onto the capitol steps. He had thought "this was such a dead issue," but looking around, he sees it is very much alive, at least for the FACTS members coming up to him, shaking hands, hugging him, letting him know how wonderful he was.

Among them are Sue Reams and Geri Silva, the chair of FACTS. Silva is a graying, vibrant woman in her early fifties, an impassioned radical who has been fighting for immigrants' and prisoners' rights and against police abuse since the early '70s, when the colorful LA beach town of Venice, where she'd grown up, was a cheerfully rundown hippie enclave and hotbed of counterculture politics. In '73, she'd taken some courses in Cal State LA's Chicano Studies Program that had raised her political consciousness, as they said back then. Now her energy is focused on getting somebody to do something to change the miscarriage of justice that is the three strikes law.

Silva is thrilled not just that Joe Klaas has come to the hearing, but that he has spoken with such power and eloquence. Joe Klaas is, according to Silva, "a star, a big-ticket item." As she explained later, "he came," after all, "from the other side. He could have been out there talking about how 'if we'd had this three strikes law earlier, his granddaughter would still be alive.' Instead," summed up Silva, "there he was in Sacramento, aligning himself with *us*. And *that* was major." But, in fact, nobody with any power to change things cared what Klaas had to say. Political decisions are based on votes, and how many votes did Joe Klaas have?

Nevertheless, Geri Silva's no fool. She's aware that today's hearing might not change anything. Not immediately. But each year, FACTS continues to grow, and each year, more and more people learn about FACTS and understand that it is a movement working to change the three strikes law. The word is getting out, she's certain. Hearings are being held and bills are being introduced to amend the law. Without FACTS, three strikes would be a dead issue. On the level of legislative change, nothing is going to happen any time soon. But it *will* happen. She has to believe that.

But when Joe Klaas steps out of the front door of the capitol building, the numbers, trends, and political winds are hardly drifting toward reform. In fact, were Silva more dispassionate, the tableau unfolding before her and Joe Klaas would only confirm the signposts of gloom. For there, displayed in all its sorrowful, touching impotence, a FACTS rally is being held—held with all the intense, righteous anger that only the truly outraged can muster, held with a determination not to recognize its utter irrelevancy. The fact that the organization is still pitifully small, ridiculously underfunded, and politically ineffective is enough to break the heart of anyone who has ever loved a loser.

The FACTS demonstrators are busy chanting in front of the capitol steps, busy carrying signs and lofting placards with blowups of third-striker husbands, sons, and brothers. "Reggie Allen, twenty-five-years-to-life for possessing a firearm," reads one. Nearby is a white banner with the names of third-strikers written all over it in black magic marker. Sue Reams is there, clutching her story board, marching with assuredness and certainty in front of the capitol steps with her fellow FACTS members. She'd been moved to tears when Joe Klaas spoke, crying in gratitude, crying because of the loneliness and frustration she so often felt.

Many of her family members, Sue Reams would later point out, as well as "friends and neighbors . . . don't even know about this work I do. They don't even know who I really am. And yet this is something I cling to. I feel I absolutely have to help fix this law. And to hear Joe Klaas, and to know that he cares . . ."

"Prisons for profits, you know you gotta stop it," chant the demonstrators. "Let the time fit the crime!" "Life is not a baseball game, three strikes is a goddamn shame!"

Earlier, wearing her story board, Reams had passed some women in a capitol hallway as she headed for the restroom. When they stopped and asked to talk to her, Reams was at first taken aback. It was "Crime Victims Week" at the capitol, and these women were from a crime victims group largely funded by CCPOA that rallied in front of the capitol building every year during the first week in April for new and tougher laws. Sue was "used to getting negative vibes from the 'crime victims' people," so she braced herself.

One of them, a slight, brown-haired woman about five-foot-four, looked at Sue's story board along with the others, and said that she and the others had originally supported three strikes, but now felt that Sue was doing the right thing in trying to change it, even though they had family members who'd been affected by violent crime. Shane's third strike, she said, certainly didn't fit into a violent category, and it wasn't what she had voted for. Then she said the strangest thing, at least strange to Sue Reams. "Thank you," she said. "Thank you for what you're doing."

- - - -

A year earlier, Reams and other FACTS members had gone to Sacramento to lobby for state senator Tom Hayden's three strikes amendment, which was similar to the one being introduced today. At a strategy session with some FACTS members, Hayden, the former antiwar leader and civil rights activist, had told them that changing the law would require a two-thirds majority vote in both of the legislative houses. To get that, added Hayden, they'd need Republican votes.

Once the FACTS members learned that Hayden hadn't even bothered to schedule lobbying meetings with Republican senators, however, they reasoned that Hayden's bill would be at best a ground-laying exercise and, at worst, a total waste of time.

And, in a sense, they were right. Hayden needed twenty-seven out of forty votes for his bill to clear the Senate. He got thirteen. But Hayden hadn't been shooting for an immediate, decisive victory. "Legislators rarely if ever take up bills which will only get thirteen votes," Hayden later explained, "because it's a sign of weakness and a setback for the cause. I introduced the bill as a tool for probing whether the other side might at some point be ready to compromise.

"For example, Steve Peace, who was one of the loudest supporters of three strikes in the state senate, was genuinely troubled by the long-term costs. Some prosecutors were open to reform for the same reason: resources. I reasoned that the other side might worry about a future court rejection of three strikes, or a future legislative effort to modify it. So for a year we kept a dialogue going, but the balance of forces remained unfavorable.

"The substance of the bill I introduced was to get a task force of parties with vested interests to explore a range of modifications of three strikes and see if there was any common ground. It could only be reformed if the proponents were on board. But by the time I [was term-limited out of office] the interest wasn't there."

Hayden had been one of the few politicians willing to stand up and say this law is *wrong*, something has to be done. It was just that nothing *could* be done. From 1996 to 1999, there had been four attempts, including his, to modify the three strikes law so it would apply only to "violent" and "serious" felonies, and not one of them had had a prayer.

The political forces they were up against were simply too powerful, their supporters too weak. "What we have in California," the liberal Democratic assemblywoman Jackie Goldberg once pointed out, "is a very, very polarized electorate. We have people who are either very supportive of three strikes or people who want to get rid of it. The people who want to get rid of it are not well organized and do not necessarily make major contributions to elected officials.

"The people who want to keep it are extremely well organized and make major contributions to elected officials. So what has happened is you have an enormous amount of [political] intimidation. People who are in assembly races know that they're term-limited [to two terms], know that they may want to run in a senate race a few years from now, and know that certain groups like police and prison guard unions, district attorneys, and crime victims' organizations will pay for [or against] campaigns."

Goldberg, a former '60s Berkeley free-speech radical turned public school teacher, Los Angeles school board member, and LA city councilwoman, had been elected to the assembly in 2000. Her interest in three strikes had started at the law's inception, but it really began in earnest during her run for the assembly.

A woman attending one of Goldberg's "campaign coffees" told her that her son had just been sentenced to his third strike for bouncing less than $200 worth of bad checks. "While I don't excuse him," the woman told Goldberg, "my son is basically just an alcoholic whose two previous strikes resulted from his trying to get some money for booze." "He stayed clean and sober for a while," continued the woman, "and then he fell off the wagon."

"The family got him into a treatment program," says Goldberg, "but they wouldn't give him any cash. So he decided to write some bad checks to liquor stores to get booze. Now, he's gone for the rest of his life.

"He has two children and a wife. He kept a job all through this. And now the wife doesn't have a job and is raising two small children. I kept saying to this mother: 'No, no. You must be wrong. I don't think you can go to jail for the rest of your life for writing less than $200 in bad checks.' And then I looked into it, and found that it was absolutely true."

One of the big reasons it's so absolutely true, and so hard to change, is the power of California's crime victims' organizations, whose expenses are paid for by Don Novey's prison guards' union.

"There are big rallies every year where all the crime victims come and push for hundreds of bills, all of which," says Goldberg, "have the same thing in common—enhancing sentencing. We are able to kill most of them, but a few of them get through every year because you just can't kill them all. It's just not possible. 'Sentence enhancement,' even outside of three strikes, continues every year.

"The people who are pushing these victims' crime groups and all the rest of this do not live in high-crime neighborhoods. For them, these laws represent job security and power for CCPOA and for police departments."

- - - -

As the rally unfolds, FACTS members take turns stepping up to a microphone set on a podium and telling their stories. A woman named Kelly Gillette talks about her brother receiving twenty-five-to-life for shoplifting at a Wal-Mart, and about how it is going to cost taxpayers $600,000 to keep him in prison for all those years. Wilana Richman speaks about her son, who's doing twenty-five-to-life "for slapping his girlfriend" during a domestic dispute. Gloria Watson tells of her son who is serving the same sentence for directing an undercover cop to a street drug dealer sitting at a bus stop.

The stories continue until interrupted by the arrival of Los Angeles assemblyman Rod Wright. Wright is the cosponsor of the current amendment, along with the rest of the assembly's Black Caucus. In the November 2000 election, he will be re-elected to his assembly seat with a 94 percent majority. But heavily black LA districts such as Wright's had been particularly hard hit by the three strikes law. A study of how the law had worked in Los Angeles County during its first year of implementation, for example, found that African Americans were thirteen times more likely to be sent to prison for twenty-five years to life than were whites. As a result, LA's black legislators were feeling the pressure.

The district attorney at the time was Gil Garcetti. Garcetti had originally spoken out against the Jones-Reynolds bill. It had seemed like a principled stand back in 1994. But 72 percent of California's voters had said, "Forget your principles," causing Garcetti to announce that he intended to prosecute every crime possible as a third strike. Soon, he was sending nearly *40 percent* of all of California's three-strikers into the gaping maw of the state's $3 billion a year penal system.

"You know," Assemblyman Wright tells the crowd as he steps up to the podium, "if you steal $10 worth of toilet tissue at the Rite Aid, that's not something we should put you in jail for life for. . . . But every now and then you like to have good news, and I'm proud to report today that . . . we got the fifth [majority] vote . . . [our bill] is moving out of the Public Safety Committee. . . . We're now over the first hurdle and onto the second."

Speaking next is Carl Washington, the chair of the Public Safety Committee. Washington, too, is a black assemblyman from an African American district in Los Angeles and a cosponsor of Wright's bill. "Let me tell you something," he says to the crowd. "If you have faith, if you believe that we serve an all-seeing God . . . [you know he'll answer]. My friends . . . this law is not fair. We're going to . . . make it so that society is protected, and, at the same time, that a man is given a second chance! . . . We all deserve that second chance. WE WILL GET ONE! God bless you."

It is a fine, exhilarating moment, underscored by the cheers of the crowd, fine enough to make it both unfair and uncharitable to call Wright's and Washington's words Holy Roller preachifyin' wrapped in political theater. Better to describe it as a rallying of the troops and the bolstering of morale by two well-meaning men in search of justice.

If it is just preachifyin', however, it is certainly understandable. Both men have districts with families suffering because of the three strikes law, but also peopled by a lot of folks—black, fearful, middle-class, voting folks—who are not very concerned about the issue. More than anyone else, they *crave* public safety, their neighborhoods being among the most dangerous to live in. That is Wright's and Washington's dilemma.

So, as Sue Reams and Geri Silva see it, instead of taking an *effective* stand and organizing an ongoing grassroots campaign around a law that symbolizes America's view of poor black and brown men as throwaways, they have chosen a route they know will be blocked every step of the way to its dead-end destination. Everyone knows their bill has zero chance of passing, yet they are acting like it was a done deal.

Three strikes, as Reams and Silva see it, is just politics to them. They, after all, don't have a son locked up for the best years of his life, and then some. But to be fair, what did Sue Reams and Geri Silva think these two rising young black politicians were capable of? If they can't muster the votes, they can't muster the votes. Had Hayden been able to? Had Goldberg?

- - - -

But power talks, and in the end, there will be no bill. True enough, Wright's legislation *did* clear the committee that Washington chaired. But it was all downhill from there.

When it became clear, as everyone already knew, that Wright's chance of getting two-thirds of the legislature and the signature of the governor on his reform legislation was about as likely as Ariel Sharon joining the PLO, Wright proposed codifying the California Supreme Court's emasculated *Romero* decision and requiring sentencing judges to give "great weight" in favor of eliminating a prior strike—*if* the third strike was "nonserious" or "nonviolent." But Wright wound up getting nothing. Even that failed to pass in the assembly, garnering only twenty-four of the forty-one votes needed for passage.

And who could blame those assembly members? What politician, after all, wanted to vote to soften a famous tough-on-crime law that been placed on a state-wide ballot and approved by 72 percent of the electorate and that was being given credit for a 41 percent drop in the state's crime rate?

But it was not just in California that the criminal justice machine continued at full throttle. In 1982, the federal government and the fifty states were spending a combined $36 billion on cops, courts, and prisons; by 1999, two years prior to 9/11, the nation was spending $147 billion. The business of crime prevention was booming. By the close of the '90s, one million police officers nationwide were on the job, seven hundred seventeen thousand guards worked in America's jails and prisons, and over four hundred fifty thousand were in its courts.

By the end of 2002, a record 2.1 million men and women were incarcerated in the United States—one in every one hundred forty-three people residing in the nation. As a *New York Times* editorial pointed out following the release of a Justice Department study reporting those numbers: "The population of federal and state prisons and local jails . . . has risen nearly 30 percent [since 1995]. . . . The nation's incarceration rate is among the world's highest, 5 to 10 times as high as in many other industrialized nations."

That same study revealed that over *10 percent* of black men between the ages of twenty-five and twenty-nine were in prison in the United States. *Ten percent.* As to be expected, California continued to lead the nation, imprisoning over one hundred sixty-two thousand people in 2002. And the state's three strikes law was the ultimate example of imprisonment as the answer to all problems.

So enshrined had three strikes become in California that, by 2000, when Wright's bill disappeared without a whimper, almost no one was arguing against the *concept* of three strikes, or making the case that the commission of a violent crime shouldn't result in a harsh three strikes sentence. In fact, two years later, when Erwin Chemerinsky stepped before the justices of the U.S. Supreme Court, the debate had come down to the composition of Mike Reynolds's human trash and just *who* should be swept off the streets and placed in prison for at least the next quarter-century.

EPILOGUE

ERWIN CHEMERINSKY IS ABOUT TO put his eight-year-old son on the 7:30 school bus that is just pulling up, when his cell phone rings. It's a reporter from the Los Angeles legal paper *The Daily Journal.* "You lost five to four," says the reporter. "Any comment?"

Chemerinsky's mind reels. All he can think about on this now grim day of March 5, 2003, is that if just one Supreme Court justice had voted the other way, Leandro Andrade would have been walking free within a matter of weeks.

Instead, Andrade, Gary Ewing (who'd also lost his case before the Court), and the over three thousand men and women whose third strikes had been nonserious and nonviolent—42.7 percent of California's three strikes inmates—would now be spending what amounted to the rest of their lives in prison.

Chemerinsky had planned on flying up to San Francisco that morning to speak at Hastings Law School about three strikes litigation. But halfway to the airport, he decides that he simply isn't up to it.

Hadn't the Court listened to *anything* he'd said? Hadn't he told them that Andrade's punishment "wasn't just 'cruel and unusual,' but 'cruel and unique'?" Hadn't he reminded them that the California attorney general's office could "not point to even one other person in the history of the United States who [had] received a sentence of fifty-years-to-life for shoplifting a small amount of merchandise"? Didn't they understand that "even in California, this sentence [was] much larger than, say, second degree murder, manslaughter, rape"? Didn't that indicate how "grossly disproportionate" the punishment was? Obviously not.

So he goes instead to his office at USC, where he winds up fielding phone calls for much of the day. Many are from friends phoning to commiserate and reporters asking for comments on the Court's ruling. Others are messages left on his answering machine, "really *nasty* messages from ordinary people," excoriating him for loving criminals, for being an ivory tower liberal, for being a fool, for putting their lives in danger. They needn't have bothered. The deed is done.

Several days later, Chemerinsky ponders an alternative argument. "There could remain some [slight] room for prisoners to argue 'cruel and unusual punishment' in *California* courts," he says. But, then, California courts have always been utterly unreceptive to that argument when it concerns three strikes. As Chemerinsky himself had earlier pointed out, "The California Court of Appeal had affirmed 100 percent of the sentences under the three strikes law for minor crimes; and the California Supreme Court had denied review in 100 percent of the cases as well."

- - - -

Mike Reynolds was fast asleep when he received *his* 7:30 A.M. media call. "Within seconds," as he'd later tell it, he was "going live on radio stations."

On the five talk shows he'd appear on that day, he made sure to stick to the particular cases in question—"golf clubs and the guy that stole videotapes. We pretty much spun their stories around," he'd later say. "The fact was that these people were up for third strikes. Why would they risk a twenty-five-to-life sentence over some minor crime? The answer to that is that they're criminals."

Soon CNBC called. Could he do a show at noon? Reynolds turned them down cold. He'd already made arrangements to go to "a small [local] high school to talk to a class of students, 99 percent [of whom] were Hispanic, with one black girl and one white boy."

But he suggested that CNBC give his son Christopher a call. And so Christopher, an attorney, went up against "liberal" political pundit Bill Press and "some lawyer out of Colorado. Pat Buchanan was the other conservative on the show."

Later that morning, Mike Reynolds left to speak at Caruthers High. On the way, he decided to savor the moment. "Just for fun," he stopped by a newsstand and picked up most of the major newspapers—the *New York* and *Los Angeles Times*, the *San Francisco Chronicle*, the *Modesto Bee*. "Our case," he said, "was on the front page of all of them." When he arrived at the school, Reynolds brought up the case of a guy out of Sacramento who got twenty-five-to-life for writing a bad check. "But," added Reynolds, "he had five prior homicides!" (Actually, the man, Robert Rozier, had killed seven people.)

"As a society," Mike Reynolds said, "we have to do something to deal with that. To *not* do something is to perpetuate it. Juvenile crimes become adult crimes; low-level adult crimes become great adult crimes. When do you say enough is enough?"

Of course, there's dealing with it, and then there's dealing with it. A year earlier, in Mike Reynolds's hometown of Fresno, the police launched what the *Los Angeles Times* called "the biggest gang crackdown in Fresno history." The crackdown, according to the *Times*, "followed forty murders in 2001, a 67 percent increase over the previous year."

The question isn't, as Mike Reynolds poses it, "When do you say enough is enough?" The question is, "When do you do something effective?"

- - - -

If Mike Reynolds's reaction to the Supreme Court's decision proves once again who he is, so does Joe Klaas's. "If life in prison isn't cruel and unusual punishment," asks Klaas, "what would be? The only other punishment is death. In the Middle East, you might get your hand chopped off for theft. Several family members I know have asked [their relatives in prison under three strikes]: 'If you had a choice of spending the rest of your life in prison or having a hand cut off, which would you choose?' The answer is almost always, 'Have a hand cut off.' So, the Supreme Court's decision is more cruel than having your hand chopped off."

Marc Klaas, according to his father, is "too busy to be involved in three strikes anymore. He doesn't even know much about what I'm doing now, working for a change in this god-awful law. He's busy going around the nation getting Amber Alert bills passed.

He's also started Beyond Missing, which offers coast-to-coast police notification within ten minutes of an abduction. He's almost a regular on Larry King . . ."

Joe Klaas says he now believes "that the public is really ready to accept the reform of three strikes. Jackie Goldberg has sponsored a bill that's going through the assembly right now [April, 2003]. It's already made it through one committee. She's trying to get the legislature to put three strikes reform on the ballot. I'm working with her."

In 2001, Goldberg had tried to get a measure passed that would have changed the three strikes law so that simple drug possession couldn't be used as a strike—no matter what. "That," she says, "was the only provision in the bill. I got it out of the [Public Safety and Appropriations] committees, but I was unable to get the votes on the floor."

By 2002, Goldberg had realized that it would be easier to get the legislature to *place a proposition* on the ballot in 2004 that would amend the three strikes law than to get them to amend it themselves. Her new proposal is similar to the one that Rod Wright had offered in 2000: All crimes filed as strikes had to be either "serious" or "violent."

A provision in Goldberg's bill also made any change retroactive, giving third-strikers already in prison for small-time crimes the chance to go to court for a resentencing hearing.

By using the ballot initiative strategy, Goldberg figured, she'd only need forty-one votes, as opposed to fifty-four—the difference between getting a two-thirds majority to amend the law and a simple majority to place it on the ballot. But her bill, says Goldberg, "didn't even get out of Appropriations. I had eleven votes, but I couldn't get two more," she adds, "so it died in committee."

Of course, there are other people and organizations from outside the legislature supporting reform—the ACLU, the Archdiocese of Los Angeles, Amnesty International, the Libertarian Party, and the *Los Angeles Times* editorial board. But who listens to *them* when it comes to proportional punishment, other than the already convinced?

Two years earlier, in 2000, they'd all voiced their support for a campaign independent of the legislature to place an initiative on the ballot to modify three strikes. But it had failed to gather even the 419,267 statewide signatures needed to make it eligible for the ballot. "We [just] didn't make it," Jan Tucker, the cofounder of the California Three Strikes Project, would later tell the *Oakland Tribune*. "I don't think we were [ever] close."

- - - -

When Geri Silva calls with the news, Sue Reams bursts into tears. She feels as though someone wearing a steel-toed boot has just kicked her in the stomach. As the pain subsides, Sue Reams starts thinking about something Justice Sandra Day O'Connor had said during the oral arguments last fall, and how stupid she'd been for ever holding onto hope. "We've [always] given great latitude to states," O'Connor had said.

Writing for the five-to-four majority when the decisions had been handed down, O'Connor made clear that the Court was again giving the states great latitude, and then some. "We do not sit as a superlegislature to second-guess [state] policies."

"Great latitude to states? If that's the case," thinks Reams, "then why do we even *have* a U.S. Supreme Court?"

That's *her* attitude. But Antonin Scalia—now it's impossible to say enough about *his* attitude. Scalia, of course, is not just another Supreme Court justice. He, along with the Court's Chief Justice, William H. Rehnquist, is the ideological leader of a Court majority who seem to consider criminal rights, and the rights of the accused, oxymorons.

Scalia was certainly operating at his creative best in concurring with O'Connor and sealing Leandro Andrade's cruel fate. Of course, to label it "cruel" or "unusual" would be precisely to miss Antonin Scalia's point. There are certain "modes" of punishment which violate the Eighth Amendment, and others that do not. And obviously, to Scalia, Andrade's sentence of fifty-years-to-life for shoplifting some kiddie videos does not.

In a previous, similar case, *Harmelin v. Michigan*, Scalia had gone to great, convoluted lengths to argue that no sentence was too long to be considered "cruel and unusual"—lengths so great, in fact, that he went all the way back to 1689 and the English Declaration of Rights (the antecedent of the U.S. Bill of Rights) to make his case. "The drafters of the Declaration of Rights did not explicitly prohibit 'disproportionate' or 'excessive' punishments," wrote Scalia. "Instead, they prohibited punishments that were 'cruell and unusuall.' . . . A disproportionate punishment can perhaps always be considered 'cruel,' " said Scalia, "but it will not always be . . . 'unusual.' "

Scalia went on to say that the Eighth Amendment's prohibition of "cruel and unusual punishments" is aimed at excluding only "certain *modes* of punishment," such as "drawing and quartering, burning of women felons, beheading, disemboweling, etc.," and is not a guarantee against disproportionate sentences.

On such reasoning, and on such a man, had the fates of Leandro Andrade and Gary Ewing hung.

Writing in dissent, Justice David H. Souter sounded like he had just flown into Scalia's world from Krypton. "If Andrade's sentence is not grossly disproportionate," he wrote, "the principle has no meaning."

- - - -

After calming herself, Sue Reams sits down and writes letters to Gary Ewing and Leandro Andrade. If the Court had voted in Andrade's or Ewing's favor, it would not have immediately helped Shane. Being a lookout on the sale of a $20 rock of cocaine is not a petty theft. Small-time drug cases like his, where Proposition 36 does not apply retroactively, have to be separately adjudicated. But what about Andrade and Ewing *now?* She can't wrap her mind around how despairing they must feel.

But her feelings of pity soon give way to a feeling more akin to that of Geri Silva's. Silva's reaction to the verdict had been to send out a press release on the very day she'd received the news. Under the FACTS logo, the headline had read, "Three Strikes Opponents Defiant After Supreme Court Ruling; Vow Push to Ballot in 2004."

"The U.S. Supreme Court this morning refused to overturn two 'three strikes' sentences," read the release, "indicating that only state-level efforts will be able to reform the three strikes law. . . . *Today's ruling reenergizes our campaign to bring three strikes reform to the ballot in 2004* [emphasis in original]. A new ballot measure is our best hope for reform."

But that hope may be no hope at all if Mike Reynolds has anything to do with it. And he will. In an October 1999 article in the Northern California online publication the *Lassen County News*, he mapped out the battle Silva and FACTS would face to get an initiative placed on the ballot.

Noting that it had cost about $1 million to place three strikes on the ballot in 1994, Reynolds predicts it will take twenty times that much funding to change the law. "If you've got enough money, you can sell steer manure to ranchers," says Reynolds. "But they'd have to totally distort the intent of three strikes [in order] to change public opinion. There are only three groups opposed to three strikes: the criminals, their families, and their attorneys. The question the people of California will have to answer is are we going to write laws the criminals and their attorneys like?"

Try as she might, moreover, it's extremely doubtful that Jackie Goldberg will get the two-thirds she needs for a ballot measure, "unless," says Tom Hayden, "the proponents are willing to retreat from the third strike provision of the law. Nevertheless," adds Hayden, "her bill will allow public hearings, grass roots organizing, lobbying, et cetera, until such time as we change the political winds. Surely the [U.S.] Supreme Court decision was a crushing blow, but the fight will continue. I feel really bad for the families, because it has become a way of life for them amidst a world of shrugs and rejections."

But Sue Reams intends to fight on. She's quit her job and is working full-time to get that referendum placed on the ballot. As

Reams and Silva calculate it, they have to raise $800,000 *minimum* to pay for the kind of professional help they need to make that happen. But that's where all Sue's emotion and energy are going—into that battle. "That's my flesh and blood in there," says Sue Reams. "My flesh and blood. I'm going to be doing this until my last dying breath."

NOTES

The notes below provide the sources for material in the text. Where a lengthy discussion in the text is taken from a few principal sources, a general statement of source is provided. However, when there is a direct quotation in the text, there is a specific note describing the source.

PROLOGUE

p. 1 *"Get back in line"*:   The scene at the Supreme Court is taken from the observations of Shannon Seibert, the author's graduate assistant, who was present and reporting on the arguments for the author.

p. 2 *They're bound together by Erwin Chemerinsky*:   Professor Chemerinsky's background and thoughts are taken from Erwin Chemerinsky, interviews by author, December 2001 and November 2002.

p. 3 *At about 6:30, a new group joins:*   The description of activities of the FACTS members is taken from Seibert's observations and the author's interview with Sue Reams, April 2003.

p. 3   *"the toughest in the nation":* Marc Peysert and Donna Foot, "Strike Three, You're Not Out," *Newsweek,* August 29, 1994.

p. 3   *"the only state in [the Union] in which a misdemeanor":* *Riggs v. California,* no. 98-5021 (1999).

p. 4   *Willie Turner:* Turner's alleged crime and sentence, and those of the others in this paragraph, are described at www.facts1.com (accessed February 2002).

p. 4   *72 percent of voters:* *Los Angeles Times,* August 1, 1996.

p. 5   *"political climate of fear":* Reams interview, April 2003.

p. 5   *"great set of facts":* Chemerinsky interview, November 2002.

p. 6   *$153.54 worth of videocassettes:* *Lockyer v. Andrade,* 123 S. Ct. 1166 (2003). Further details concerning Andrade are taken from the *Los Angeles Times,* April 7, 2002, November 5, 2002, and March 5, 2003.

p. 6   *"You know who the videos are for?"* *Los Angeles Times,* April 7, 2002.

p. 7   *In the appeal . . . Chemerinsky argued:* Transcript of oral argument before the Supreme Court in *Lockyer v. Andrade,* 123 S. Ct. 1166 (2003).

p. 7   *"cruel and unusual punishment":* *Lockyer v. Andrade,* 123 S. Ct. 1166 (2003) (dissenting opinion).

p. 7   *the forty-year-old Ewing:* The facts about the Ewing case are taken from *Ewing v. California,* 123 S. Ct. 1179 (2003), and *Los Angeles Times,* April 7, 2002.

p. 8   *"I don't have much time left":* *Ewing v. California.*

1. KIMBER REYNOLDS

p. 13   *As she locked the door:* Unless otherwise indicated, the descriptions of Kimber's background and of the circumstances leading up to her murder are taken from interviews of Mike Reynolds, summer 1998 and March 2003.

p. 13   *slim, self-possessed young woman:* *Fresno Bee,* June 2, 1992.

p. 13   *Kimber had always liked the Daily Planet:* Ibid.

p. 15 *two strangers sitting astride a stolen . . . motorcycle:* The description of the events surrounding Kimber's murder are taken from Mike Reynolds, Bill Jones, and Dan Evans, *Three Strikes and You're Out! A Promise to Kimber* (Fresno, Calif.: Quill Driver Books, 1996), 12–15.

p. 16 *he whipped out a .357 Magnum:* Joe Domanick, "Man with a Mission," *LA Weekly*, November 27–December 3, 1998.

p. 16 *At about 2:30 in the morning the phone rang:* The details concerning the aftermath of Kimber's murder are taken from Mike Reynolds, interviews by author, summer 1998 and March 2003, and Reynolds, Jones, and Evans, *Three Strikes and You're Out!* 13–15.

2. THE NATURAL

p. 18 *he was pissed, "really pissed":* The descriptions of Appleton's views and actions are taken, except where noted, from interview with Ray Appleton, March 2003.

p. 18 *"the only guy . . . to leave Fresno to spin":* Appleton interview, March 2003.

p. 19 *"a big, greasy man":* Catherine Campbell, "A Lesson in Politics," *CACJ/Forum* 25, nos. 2–3 (1998).

p. 19 *He regarded himself as "a conservative":* Appleton interview, March 2003.

p. 19 *"There were way too many people in talk radio":* Ibid.

p. 19 *"There isn't a damn thing that's easy":* Reynolds, Jones, and Evans, *Three Strikes and You're Out!* 17.

p. 20 *"But though one tragic death occurred":* Ibid.

p. 20 *"a flower that was really starting to bloom":* Ibid.

p. 20 *"He just basically announced to the world":* Appleton interview, March 2003.

p. 20 *"I've always been an extrovert":* Reynolds interview, March 2003.

p. 21 *It was a local snitch:* *Fresno Bee*, April 7, 1993, June 4, 1992.

3. JUSTICE SELDOM SEEN IN AMERICA

p. 22   *Joe Davis too was a native of the San Joaquin Valley:*   The description of Joe Davis is taken from Mike Reynolds, Bill Jones, and Dan Evans, *Three Strikes and You're Out! A Promise to Kimber* (Fresno, Calif.: Quill Driver Books, 1996), 11, 98.

p. 22   *"looked as if he might have been":*   Mike Reynolds interview, March 2003.

p. 22   *His accomplice in the killing:*   *Fresno Bee,* July 18, 1992.

p. 22   *earliest arrests had been for glue sniffing:*   *Fresno Bee,* December 3, 1992.

p. 22   *addicted not only to heroin:*   Reynolds, Jones, and Evans, *Three Strikes and You're Out!* 11.

p. 23   *a pattern he repeated at least seven times:*   Mike Reynolds interview, summer 1998.

p. 23   *Walker had been granted a temporary release:*   Reynolds, Jones, and Evans, *Three Strikes and You're Out!* 11–12; *Fresno Bee,* February 13, 1994.

p. 23   *part of a band of crystal-meth-speed freaks:*   Mike Reynolds interviews, summer 1998 and March 2003; Reynolds, Jones, and Evans, *Three Strikes and You're Out!* 11.

p. 23   *methamphetamine manufacturing capital . . . the drug of choice:*   *Los Angeles Times,* July 12, 1998.

p. 23   *"I've talked to family friends":*   Mike Reynolds interview, March 2003.

p. 24   *The officers' return fire:*   Tupper Hull, "A Father's Crusade to Lock up Criminals," *San Francisco Examiner,* December 8, 1993.

p. 24   *wounds undisguised by mortuary makeup:*   *Fresno Bee,* July 7, 1992.

p. 24   *"what happens when you abuse drugs":*   Ibid.

p. 24   *Walker was captured without a struggle:*   Reynolds, Jones, and Evans, *Three Strikes and You're Out!* 26.

p. 24   *There was talk at first of charging him with murder:*   *Fresno Bee,* December 2, 1992.

p. 24   *The night the murder occurred:*   Reynolds, Jones, and Evans, *Three Strikes and You're Out!* 27.

p. 24   *In a presentencing letter:*   *Fresno Bee*, December 2, 1992.

p. 25   *Mike and Sharon Reynolds were overjoyed:*   Reynolds interview, summer 1998.

p. 25   *"justice seldom seen in America":*   Ibid.

4. MIKE REYNOLDS'S WORLD

p. 26   *"Levine used to say":*   Catherine Campbell, e-mail correspondence with author, August 16, 2003.

p. 27   *Army Corps of Engineers:*   The description of the Central Valley in this chapter is taken from Marc Reisner, *Cadillac Desert: The American West and Its Disappearing Water* (New York: Penguin Books, 1986).

p. 28   *He'd grown up to be:*   The descriptions of Mike Reynolds in this chapter are taken from a combination of the author's observations and from the author's interviews with Mike Reynolds, summer 1998, March 2003, and August 2003.

p. 30   *"The state where lynching was most popular":*   David J. Garrow, "In the Bloody Hands of Hatred," *Los Angeles Times Book Review*, April 13, 2003.

p. 31   *Mike Reynolds wasn't . . . "the most likely to succeed":*   Reynolds interview, summer 1998.

p. 32   *She thought he was smart:*   Sharon Reynolds, interview by author, summer 1998.

5. MIKE REYNOLDS'S LAW

p. 37   *Reynolds invited about ten people to meet:*   The description of this meeting and of the personalities in attendance was taken from interviews with Mike Reynolds, summer 1998 and August 2003, and with Ray Appleton, March 2003.

p. 37   *Among them were a couple of local judges:*   Mike Reynolds interview, summer 1998, and "The Legacy: Murder, Media, Politics, and Prisons," *POV,* PBS, October 31, 2000.

p. 38   *From 1982 to 1992, the largest increase in crime:*   Crime statistics discussed here, unless otherwise noted, are taken from the *Los Angeles Times,* October 11, 1992, December 12, 1993, December 18, 1994, and May 22, 1995.

p. 39   *In 1990, homicides in Fresno:*   *Fresno Bee,* October 11, 1992.

p. 39   *Reynolds's murder helped boost the annual total:*   *Fresno Bee,* December 31, 1993.

p. 39   *"More than seven out of ten black children":*   *Los Angeles Times,* August 26, 2002.

p. 40   *"talked about the gambit":*   Reynolds interview, summer 1998.

p. 40   *"Right away, [they] began to zero in":*   Mike Reynolds, Bill Jones, and Dan Evans, *Three Strikes and You're Out! A Promise to Kimber* (Fresno, Calif.: Quill Driver Books, 1996), 31.

p. 40   *"I was at the meetings because of my mouth":*   Appleton interview, March 2003.

p. 41   *"[our] law was designed":*   Reynolds interview, summer 1998.

p. 41   *Instead, they settled on:*   John Clark et al., "Three Strikes and You're Out: A Review of State Legislation," National Institute of Justice, Research in Brief, September 1997.

p. 42   *He'd grown up on his family farm:*   The description of Bill Jones is taken from Bill Jones, interview by author, June 2002; Danielle Starkey, "The Race for Secretary of State," *California Journal* (1994).

p. 42   *Jones had always believed . . . "in certain fundamental rights":*   Jones interview, June 2002.

6. A MENACE TO SOCIETY

p. 44   *Sue Reams couldn't sleep:*   The material in this chapter is taken from the author's interviews of Sue Reams, December 2000, January 2001, February 2001, March 2002, July 2002, and April

2003, and from Shane Reams's statement, cited in his Orange County Probation Report, presented to Superior Court, Dept. 42, July 12, 1996, and from correspondence with Shane Reams, July 2003.

p. 45 *"Hawaiian complexion, base-tan skin":* Aubrey Nelson interview, fall 2002.

p. 46 *"He really did seem to start realizing":* Reams interview, March 2002.

p. 47 *"I can't wait":* Ibid.

7. CHILD OF THE '50S

p. 48 *"There's been this terrible crime committed":* Material about Dan Lungren, unless otherwise noted, is taken from Dan Lungren, interviews by author, August 1998 and June 2002.

p. 48 *a law enforcement colossus:* Joe Domanick, "California Scheming," *LA Weekly*, October 16–22, 1998.

p. 50 *"Iowa picnics, the flag, and fireworks".* Jan Hall interviews, April and July, 1997.

p. 50 *"When I went to [college at] Berkeley, it was a vastly different world":* Ibid.

p. 50 *John Lungren would serve Nixon:* Ernest Gualderon interview, July 1997.

p. 50 *John Lungren. . . "became prominent":* Jim Serles interview, July 1997.

p. 50 *"Nixon loved John Lungren":* Gualderon interview.

p. 51 *Lorraine Lungren was also a "very big force":* Ibid.

p. 51 *"his strongest feelings":* Serles interview.

p. 51 *"from the Holy Cross brothers":* Gualderon interview.

p. 53 *"Lungren . . . was the chief implementer":* Howard Berman interview, summer 1998.

p. 53 *The phrase . . . "had gone to the essence":* Lungren interview, August 1998.

p. 54   *George Will to gush over Lungren's . . . "robustness":*   Domanick, "California Scheming."

p. 54   *Lungren's looks were complemented:*   Ibid.

p. 55   *"His view was internment had been necessary":*   Berman interview.

p. 56   *The black rage that had been building:*   David Farber, *Chicago '68* (Chicago: University of Chicago Press, 1988), 57, 118.

p. 56   *"By 1970," Parker proclaimed:*   Joe Domanick, *To Protect and to Serve* (New York: Pocket Books, 1994), 185.

p. 56   *urban crime had grown by 88 percent:*   *Time* magazine, July 19, 1968.

p. 57   *"this looks like a proposal":*   Lungren interview, June 2002.

p. 57   *Lungren's lawyers then traveled down to Fresno:*   Ibid.

8. ROOTS OF THE BACKLASH

p. 58   *Deukmejian was both a mentor and a booster of Lungren:*   Unless otherwise noted, the information about Deukmejian in this chapter was taken from Joe Domanick, "California Scheming," *LA Weekly,* October 16–22, 1998; Jim Serles, interview by author, July 1997; *Los Angeles Times,* September 3, 1998; Clark McKinley, United Press International (BC Cycle), June 3, 1996.

p. 59   *Historians will differ:*   Countless volumes have been published on the criminal justice system and American politics and society during the last half of the twentieth century. The ones most useful to me for this book were Ken Auleta, *The Underclass* (New York: Random House, 1982); H. W. Brands, *The Strange Death of American Liberalism* (New Haven: Yale University Press, 2001); David Farber, *Chicago '68* (Chicago: University of Chicago Press, 1988); Peter Irons, A *People's History of the Supreme Court* (New York: Penguin Books, 1999); Richard Reeves, *President Nixon: Alone in the White House* (New York: Simon & Schuster, 2001); Jonathan Rieder, *Canarsie: The Jews and Italians of Brooklyn against Liberalism* (Cambridge, Mass.: Harvard University Press, 1985); and

Harris Wofford, *Of Kennedys and Kings: Making Sense of the Sixties* (New York: Farrar, Straus, Giroux, 1980).

p. 62 *Singleton picked up a hitchhiking fifteen-year-old:* The description of Singleton's activities is taken from the *Los Angeles Times*, January 1, 2002, and the *San Jose Mercury News*, January 1, 2002.

p. 62 *Singleton was caught and sentenced:* Alex Ricciardulli, e-mail to author, August 18, 2003.

p. 62 *Deukmejian again used crime:* Joe Domanick, "California Scheming."

p. 63 *A man named Charles Rothenberg:* *New York Times*, June 9, 2002.

p. 63 *"The real trouble lay":* Alex Ricciardulli, "The Broken Safety Valve: Judicial Discretion's Failure to Ameliorate Punishment under California's Three Strikes Law," *Duquesne Law Review* 41, no. 1 (fall 2002): 7.

p. 63 *Supreme Court Justice Rose Elizabeth Bird:* Preble Stolz, *Judging Judges: The Investigation of Rose Bird and the California Supreme Court* (New York: The Free Press, 1981).

p. 64 *he'd permitted the Los Angeles Police Department to run amok:* See the author's discussion of this point in Joe Domanick, *To Protect and to Serve: The LAPD's Century of War in the City of Dreams* (Pocket Books, 1994).

p. 64 *From 1979 through 1994, eleven hundred changes were made:* The statistics in this and the next paragraph were taken from the *Los Angeles Times*, November 16, 1994.

p. 65 *"While we were trying to 'understand' these criminals":* *Los Angeles Times*, June 15, 1990.

p. 65 *California would spend $10 billion . . . on new prison construction:* *Los Angeles Times*, October 16, 1994.

p. 65 *"The message has been clear":* *Los Angeles Times*, June 15, 1990.

p. 66 *Discipline . . . also consisted of:* *Los Angeles Times Magazine*, February 6, 1994.

p. 66 *During the mid- to late 1990s, eight guards at Corcoran:* *Los Angeles Times*, November 26, 1998.

p. 66 *"Since 1989, . . . thirty-nine inmates . . . have been shot":* Ibid.

9. THE NEW YELLOW PRESS

p. 67   *Mike Reynolds took his second trip to Sacramento:*   The material in this chapter is taken from interviews of Mike Reynolds, summer 1998 and March 2003, and from an October 31, 2000, Public Broadcasting System *POV (Point of View)* program entitled "The Legacy: Murder, Media, Politics, and Prisons."

p. 68   *"weird little ducks":*   Mike Reynolds, Bill Jones, and Dan Evans, *Three Strikes and You're Out! A Promise to Kimber* (Fresno, Calif.: Quill Driver Books, 1996), 44.

p. 68   *"I know you have kids":*   Reynolds interview, summer 1998.

p. 68   *"getting out of prison":*   Ibid.

p. 68   *"the one unindicted perpetrator":*   "The Legacy."

10. TOUGH LOVE

p. 69   *Sue Reams was nineteen:*   The information in this chapter on Sue and Shane Reams is based on information garnered from a series of interviews with Sue Reams and from Shane Reams's letter to the author, October 2003. The information on California prison statistics is discussed at length in Joe Domanick, "Straight Time: The Battle for Drug Treatment in California Prisons," *LA Weekly*, May 28–June 3, 1999.

p. 70   *Shane would describe Johnnie as "emotionless":*   Shane Reams, letter to the author, October 2003.

p. 71   *"using every avenue":*   Ibid.

p. 72   *He no longer knew "how to live":*   Ibid.

p. 74   *he'd do "anything to get drugs":*   Ibid.

p. 75   *"Empty the prisons in California":*   *San Jose Mercury News*, June 7, 1992.

p. 75   *"Two hundred dollars isn't much":*   Author's interview of Ricardo Hinojosa, December 1997.

11. "WEIRD DUCKS AND BLIND FOOLS"

p. 76 *Public Safety, like the assembly as a whole:* The description of the assembly and its Public Safety Committee is taken from interviews of Mike Reynolds, summer 1998 and March 2003.

p. 76 *"They were not just liberals":* Reynolds interviews, summer 1998 and March 2003.

p. 77 *Barbara Lee certainly was of a different persuasion:* The descriptions of Barbara Lee are taken from www.house.gov/lee; Susan McHenry, "Mounting a Serious Campaign to Replace Richard Nixon," *Essence,* December 2001; and "Profile: Barbara Lee," *California Journal Weekly,* March 21, 1994.

p. 77 *Her assembly colleagues, she would later bitterly complain:* "The Legacy: Murder, Media, Politics, and Prisons," *POV,* PBS, October 31, 2000.

p. 78 *And as far as Lee, Bates, and John Burton . . . were concerned:* Ibid.

p. 78 *Washington state voters had passed:* John Clark et al., "Three Strikes and You're Out: A Review of State Legislation," National Institute of Justice, Research in Brief, September 1997.

p. 78 *But there were also several provisions:* The descriptions of the provisions of the Jones bill are taken from Assembly Bill 971 (Jones/Costa, Chapter 12, Statutes of 1994–*Cal. Penal Code* sec. 667) and *Cal. Penal Code* sec. 170.12.

p. 78 *"Residential burglary runs the gamut":* Gary R. Nichols, interview by author, July 2001.

p. 79 *"The reason that residential burglary is a problematical prior":* Alex Ricciardulli, e-mail to author, August 18, 2003.

p. 80 *"There are over five hundred crimes in California":* "The Legacy."

p. 81 *"The beauty of three strikes":* Ibid.

p. 81 *"We ultimately decided to focus on":* Reynolds interview, summer 1998.

p. 82 *No suspending of sentences:* Samara Marion, "Justice by Geography?" *Stanford Law and Policy Review* 31 (winter 1999), and *Cal. Penal Code* sec. 667(b),(c)(2–8) (West 1998).

p. 82   *"the second strike was the true genius"*:   Reynolds interview, summer 1998.

p. 84   *As Gary Nichols noted:*   Nichols interview, July 2001.

p. 84   *As long as it's "easier to pick up a gun"*:   Reynolds interview, summer 1998.

p. 85   *children under the age of six:*   "The State of Our Children," report prepared by Children Now, reported in *Los Angeles Times*, June 21, 1991.

p. 85   *California tied with Louisiana: Los Angeles Times*, March 5, 1999.

p. 85   *"Whenever I spoke to people in Fresno"*:   Mike Reynolds, Bill Jones, and Dan Evans, *Three Strikes and You're Out! A Promise to Kimber* (Fresno, Calif.: Quill Driver Books, 1996), 44.

p. 86   *"terms like 'predator' and 'moral poverty' "*:   Catherine Campbell, "A Lesson in Politics," *CACJ/Forum* 25, nos. 2–3 (1998).

p. 86   *"a goddamn lie"*:   Reynolds interview, summer 1998.

p. 86   *In reaction to Reynolds's intractability:*   "The Legacy."

p. 86   *Reynolds blamed his defeat:*   Ibid.

p. 86   *"Unfortunately . . . news-wise"*:   Ibid.

p. 87   *"They got Bill Jones to carry [the bill]"*:   Ibid.

p. 87   *"the first time it came around"*:   Ibid.

p. 89   *"were able to take lapses in the law"*:   *Los Angeles Times*, March 7, 1994.

p. 89   *An initiative . . . can only be amended:*   California Constitution, Art. 18, Sec. 1 and Art. 2, Sec. 10(c).

p. 90   *She told him that she wanted no part of a public life:*   Mike Reynolds interview, summer 1998.

12. RIGHT OUT OF HER OWN BEDROOM

p. 93   *Richard Allen Davis's surreptitious entrance:*   The information for this chapter is based on interviews of Marc and Joe Klaas, and the reporting of Jeffrey Toobin in his definitive profile of Davis, "The Man Who Kept Going Free," in the February 7, 1994, issue of the *New Yorker*.

p. 93   *Shortly before . . . Davis had smoked a joint:*   *Los Angeles Times,* July 11, 1995.

p. 95   *"the last stop for many":*   Toobin, "The Man Who Kept Going Free."

p. 95   *As Davis himself tells it:*   The details of Davis's background are taken mainly from Richard Allen Davis, "Statement on His Childhood," written in response to letters he received questioning him about his childhood upbringing and posted on the web site of the Canadian Coalition Against the Death Penalty, www.ccadp.org/richarddavisstatementchildhood.htm (September 1, 2002); Davis, "Death Row—San Quentin, California," www.ccadp.org/richarddavis.htm (May 30, 2000); and Davis, letters to the author, July 23, 2003; and August 17, 2003.

p. 95   *His "family . . . was not":*   Davis letter, August 17, 2003.

p. 95   *"One Saturday morning":*   Davis, "Statement."

p. 95   *"gutter snipe dog bitch":*   Ibid.

p. 96   *"proved her [to be] unfit and immoral":*   Ibid.

p. 96   *"I don't think . . . that people can":*   Richard Allen Davis, letter to author, July 23, 2003.

p. 96   *"My father said it was time":*   Davis, "Statement."

p. 96   *"I have to work":*   Ibid.

p. 97   *He soaked cats with gasoline:*   Elizabeth Gleick, Tom Cunneff, and Johnny Dodd, "America's Child," *People* magazine, December 20, 1993.

p. 97   *At the age of twelve:*   Ibid.

p. 97   *After being booked, he'd invariably confess:*   Toobin, "The Man Who Kept Going Free."

p. 97   *"had the feeling she wanted something":*   Toobin, "The Man Who Kept Going Free."

p. 97   *"At that point, . . . he exposed himself":*   Ibid.

p. 98   *California's 1977 Uniform Determinate Sentencing Act:*   On this act, see "Three Strikes Laws: Are They Too Harsh?" *CQ Researcher,* May 10, 2002: 419–430, and Jerome H. Skolnick,

" 'Three Strikes, You're Out' and Other Bad Calls on Crime,"
American Prospect (spring 1994).

p. 98 *Prior to the law, judges had been able:* "Three Strikes Laws: Are
They Too Harsh?" *CQ Researcher*, May 10, 2002: 419–430.

p. 99 *During one incident:* Toobin, "The Man Who Kept Going Free."

13. ANOTHER PIERCING SCREAM

p. 100 *Marc Klaas was asleep in his bedroom:* The material in this chapter is taken from the author's interviews of Marc Klaas, May
1998, and Joe Klaas, July 2002.

p. 100 *"Polly's been kidnapped":* Marc Klaas interview, May 1998.

p. 102 *"Allied prisoners gunned down not fifty feet from him":* Joe Klaas
interview, July 2002.

p. 102 *"serving against everything [he] believed in":* Marc Klaas interview, May 1998.

p. 102 *"hippie trip around the world":* Ibid.

p. 103 *Klaas "stepped up . . . [and] caught Eve on the rebound":* Ibid.

p. 103 *Polly never got along with her stepfather:* The (Santa Rosa) Press
Democrat, December 10, 1993.

p. 104 *Meanwhile, a massive local effort:* Ibid.

p. 105 *"I have a daughter out there":* Ibid.

p. 105 *"a twelve-year-old prepubescent child":* Marc Klaas interview,
May 1998.

p. 105 *"If they believed that":* Ibid.

14. "GUNS DON'T KILL PEOPLE"

p. 107 *So he began to seek financial support:* Mike Reynolds interviews,
summer 1998 and March 2003.

p. 107 *A 1992* Los Angeles Times *poll:* *Los Angeles Times*, May 17, 1992.

p. 108 *If carrying a gun could save his life:* Ibid.

p. 108 *"proactive rather than reactive":* Mike Reynolds interviews,
summer 1998 and March 2003.

p. 108   *The NRA had accomplished:*   *Seattle Times,* November 9, 1993.

p. 109   *"the NRA was among the very first":*   Reynolds interview, summer 1998.

p. 109   *"my daughter was murdered":*   Mike Reynolds interview, summer 1998.

p. 110   *And never mind the parents, who . . . "come around the corner":* Joe Domanick, "The Reformer on a Honeymoon," *Los Angeles Times Magazine,* January 19, 2003.

p. 110   *Not after its initial contribution of $40,000:*   Catherine Campbell, "A Lesson in Politics," *CACJ/Forum* 25, nos. 2–3 (1998).

15. THE PRINCE OF "J" STREET

p. 111   *California Correctional Peace Officers Association:*   The material in this chapter is taken from the *San Francisco Examiner,* May 10, 1992; John Hurst, "The Big House That Don Novey Built," *Los Angeles Times Magazine,* February 6, 1994; and Joe Domanick, "Who's Guarding the Guards?" *LA Weekly,* September 2–8, 1994.

p. 111   *"the great historic trail of the Golden State":*   Don Novey, interview by author, July 1994.

p. 112   *A "fifth-generation Polish American":*   Ibid.

p. 112   *At the same time, he won unprecedented pay and benefits:*   *Los Angeles Times Magazine,* February 6, 1994; *San Francisco Examiner,* June 26, 1994.

p. 113   *Vasconcellos had ardently opposed:*   *Los Angeles Times Magazine,* February 6, 1994; John Vasconcellos, news release, February 17, 1994.

p. 113   *Novey decided to donate over $75,000:*   *Los Angeles Times Magazine,* February 6, 1994.

p. 114   *Novey gave almost $1 million:*   *San Francisco Examiner,* May 10, 1992; *Sacramento Bee,* August 14, 1992.

p. 114   *"Di-Fi gave me a plaque":*   Novey interview, July 1994.

p. 114   *CCPOA contributed over $1 million:*   *San Francisco Bay Guardian,* August 11, 1993.

p. 114   *$91,000 to Governor Wilson:*   *Sacramento Bee,* August 14, 1992.

p. 114   *Wilson then raised the salaries:*   Ibid.

p. 114   *"Supporting three strikes":*   Novey interview, July 1994.

p. 115   *contributing over $100,000 to the three strikes campaign:*   *Los Angeles Times,* November 16, 1994.

p. 115   *his would-be ballot initiative had garnered:*   Michael Vitiello, " 'Three Strikes' and the Romero Case: The Supreme Court Restores Democracy," 30 *Loyola Law Review* 1643, 1655 (1997).

16. POLLY KLAAS

p. 116   *"America's Child":*   The descriptions of events surrounding the abduction of Polly Klaas and the capture of Richard Allen Davis, except as otherwise noted, are taken from Elizabeth Gleick, Tom Cunneff, and Johnny Dodd, "America's Child," *People* magazine, December 20, 1993, and interviews of Marc Klaas, May 1998, and Joe Klaas, July 2002 and April 2003.

p. 116   *Bill Rhodes became the center:*   *The (Santa Rosa) Press Democrat,* December 10, 1993.

p. 116   *" a dynamic guy":*   Marc Klaas interview, May 1998.

p. 117   *"The Coast Guard had three hundred forty-one cadets searching":*   Joe Klaas interviews, July 2002 and April 2003.

p. 117   *over fifty FBI agents and local cops:*   *The (Santa Rosa) Press Democrat,* December 10, 1993.

p. 117   *"more than one hundred thousand flyers":*   Ibid.

p. 117   *"The search for Polly was about bringing":*   Mark Klaas interview, May 1998.

p. 118   *The luminous young actress . . . Winona Ryder:*   *The (Santa Rosa) Press Democrat,* December 10, 1993; *Los Angeles Times,* July 11, 1995.

p. 118   *"My greatest wish":*   *The (Santa Rosa) Press Democrat,* December 10, 1993.

p. 118 *Jeffrey Toobin did a lengthy profile:* "The Man Who Kept Going Free," *New Yorker,* February 7, 1994.

p. 118 *"we're going to use you to find Polly":* Joe Klaas interviews, July 2002 and April 2003.

p. 118 *"Everybody else was afraid of the media":* Ibid.

p. 119 *Bill Rhodes, who was playing:* Details on Bill Rhodes are from *The (Santa Rosa) Press Democrat,* December 10, 1993.

p. 120 *"There is a wild man on your property":* *The (Santa Rosa) Press Democrat,* December 10, 1993.

p. 120 *Just after midnight, two deputies . . . arrived:* The material on the deputies' interactions with Davis is taken from *The (Santa Rosa) Press Democrat,* December 10, 1993.

p. 120 *Lungren had earlier decided:* "Attorney General: Lungren gains re-election," *California Journal Weekly,* November 14, 1994.

p. 122 *"very disgusted with himself":* *The (Santa Rosa) Press Democrat,* December 10, 1993.

17. HAPPILY SHAKING FATE'S SORRY HAND

p. 123 *Mike Reynolds returned:* The events described in this chapter are taken, except as otherwise noted, from "The Legacy: Murder, Media, Politics, and Prisons," *POV,* PBS, October 31, 2000, and interviews of Mike Reynolds, summer 1998 and March 2003, Marc Klaas, May 1998, and Joe Klaas, July 2002 and April 2003.

p. 123 *"The hand of fate":* "The Legacy."

p. 124 *"I'm about to do a live, remote broadcast":* Joe Klaas interviews, July 2002 and April 2003.

p. 125 *"People were really into this Polly Klaas case":* "The Legacy."

p. 125 *President Clinton invited Reynolds:* *Los Angeles Times,* February 14, 1995.

p. 125 *"Three strikes and you're in—for life":* "The Legacy."

p. 126 *"Davis was a three strikes offender":* Ibid.

p. 126 *fifteen hundred people gathered:* The description of the Polly Klaas memorial service is taken from *The (Santa Rosa) Press*

Democrat, December 10, 1993; Joe Klaas interviews, July 2002 and April 2003; and Marc Klaas interview, May 1998.

p. 126 *"America Cries: Polly Is Dead":* The (Santa Rosa) Press Democrat, December 10, 1993.

p. 126 *Polly's death . . . "had bruised the psyche":* Los Angeles Times, December 12, 1993.

p. 127 *Both . . . "took the opportunity to pitch":* Marc Klaas interview, May 1998.

p. 127 *"We cannot call ourselves a civilized society":* Los Angeles Times, December 10, 1993.

p. 127 *"the stuff you yell at the TV screen in bed":* New York Times, August 3, 2002.

p. 128 *"It was such an easy call":* "The Legacy."

p. 128 *John and Ken were a "chain saw":* Mike Reynolds interviews, summer 1998 and March 2003.

p. 128 *"gang of three" in the state assembly:* "The Legacy."

p. 128 *"We generated so many calls":* Ibid.

p. 128 *"People actually called my office":* Ibid.

p. 129 *Huffington would prove ready to spend:* Los Angeles Times, December 24, 1995.

p. 129 *"Huffington didn't have much in the way of issues":* Mike Reynolds interview, summer 1998.

p. 130 *the NRA's combined donation of more than $90,000, and CCPOA's contribution of $101,000:* San Francisco Examiner, October 24, 1994.

p. 130 *Initially, the DAs didn't like Reynolds's bill:* Joe Domanick, "Random Retribution," *LA Weekly,* November 4–10, 1994.

p. 131 *"I do believe in the . . . principle":* Ibid.

p. 131 *"He didn't know a whole lot about the situation":* Mike Reynolds interview, summer 1998.

p. 132 *"Our daughters had been murdered":* Marc Klaas, reported by Joe Klaas, interviews July 2002 and April 2003.

p. 132 *"I am not going to let my daughter's death be in vain":* "The Legacy."

p. 132   *"What the hell is this business about serious":*   Joe Klaas interviews, July 2002 and April 2003.

p. 132   *"This isn't what everybody thinks it is":*   Ibid.

p. 132   *"through the goddamn roof":*   Interview with Joe Klaas, July 2002.

p. 133   *driving Mike Reynolds was "passion, not reason":*   Marc Klaas interview, May 1998.

p. 133   *"Polly was kidnapped by . . . a kidnapper":*   "The Legacy."

p. 133   *"integrity and ability to see through a lot of crap":*   Marc Klaas interview, May 1998.

p. 133   *He himself had "engaged in":*   Ibid.

p. 133   *"How much of the population can you put behind bars?":*   Ibid.

p. 133   *Sixteen new state prisons had been built:*   Ibid., and *Los Angeles Times*, October 17, 1994.

p. 134   *"I am hoping we raise enough money":*   *Los Angeles Times*, October 17, 1994.

p. 134   *"I've had my stereo stolen and I've had my daughter murdered":*   Marc Klaas interview, May 1998.

p. 135   *"Governor Wilson asked him to".*   Joe Klaas interviews, July 2002 and April 2003.

p. 135   *"They were used":*   Tom Hayden, e-mail to author, August 15, 2003.

p. 136   *"When we start adding amendments":*   *Los Angeles Times*, March 7, 1994.

p. 136   *Polls were showing 80 percent approval:*   Ibid.

p. 138   *"Police stoke fear":*   Beth Shuster, "Living in Fear," *Los Angeles Times*, August 23, 1998.

p. 139   *"In 1980":*   Hendrik Hertzberg, "Radio Daze," *New Yorker*, August 11, 2003.

p. 140   *cost the taxpayers of California a minimum of $600,000:*   "The Legacy."

p. 140   *"When education or health care or transportation issues":*   Ibid.

p. 140   *"Every goddamn politician in California":*   Marc Klaas interview, May 1998.

p. 140   *As strategized by Reynolds's group:*   Gordon Hawkins, Sam Kamin, and Franklin E. Zimring, *Punishment and Democracy: Three Strikes and You're Out in California* (Oxford: Oxford University Press, 2001), 11.

p. 140   *That same legislative session would see:*   *Los Angeles Times*, January 2, 1995.

p. 141   *More tough-on-crime legislation would pass:*   *Los Angeles Times*, March 13, 1995.

p. 141   *"Better get the hell out of the way":*   Hawkins, Kamin, and Zimring, *Punishment and Democracy*, 6, 12.

p. 141   *"They didn't get out of the way; . . . they jumped on the train":*   Marc Klaas interview, May 1998.

p. 141   *"The second time we went up there":*   "The Legacy."

18. CHECKING THE WEATHER VANE

p. 142   *So there stood Mike Reynolds:*   "The Legacy: Murder, Media, Politics, and Prisons," *POV,* PBS, October 31, 2000; *Los Angeles Times,* January 13, 1997.

p. 142   *"Three strikes and you're out":*   "The Legacy."

p. 142   *Fresno fund-raiser to collect $100,000:*   *Los Angeles Times,* January 13, 1997.

p. 143   *"a man who could not locate his motives":*   Sidney Blumenthal, "The Man Who Could Not Locate His Motives," *New Yorker,* October 30, 1995.

p. 143   *"There's a lot of Nixon in Pete":*   *Los Angeles Times,* January 13, 1997.

p. 143   *"It was his heart":*   *New York Times,* August 2, 1994.

p. 144   *Brown charged that Wilson was allowing:*   *Los Angeles Times,* September 17, 1994. On September 1, 1994, the California legislature passed the "One Strike Rape Bill," which called for a sentence of 25-years-to-life for sexual assaults involving torture and kidnapping. Under the law, lesser sex offenders receive fifteen-years-to-life.

p. 144   *"Brown's latest ads":*   *Los Angeles Times*, August 3, 1994.

p. 144   *Meanwhile, the crime rate:*   *Los Angeles Times*, August 31, 1994.

p. 145   *"I mean, . . . this is a crime issue":*   Mike Reynolds interview, summer 1998.

p. 145   *Then Mike Reynolds boarded a Queen Air plane:*   "The Legacy."

p. 145   *the eight hundred forty thousand petition signatures:*   Ibid.

p. 145   *Seventy-two percent of California voters:*   *Los Angeles Times*, August 1, 1996.

p. 145   *"It was sweet fruit for the GOP":*   Ibid.

19. LOOKING EAST, LOOKING WEST

p. 149   *Shane Reams was trying hard to stay straight:*   The descriptions of the events surrounding Shane Reams's arrest, conviction, and sentencing are taken from Sue Reams, interviews of December 2000, January 2001, February 2001, March 2002, July 2002, and April 2003; Orange County Probation Department, "Pre-sentencing Report," July 12, 1996 (Santa Ana Police Department DR #96–07063); and letters from Shane Reams to the author, July 2003 and October 2003.

p. 149   *"very high crime and very high narcotics area":*   "Pre-sentencing Report."

p. 150   *"Hey, what's happening?":*   Ibid.

p. 150   *"Give me twenty of rock":*   Ibid.

p. 150   *"constantly looking to his left and right":*   Ibid.

p. 150   *"hurry up [and] give him one":*   Ibid.

p. 150   *"his fingers were bigger than the container":*   Ibid.

p. 151   *"I may have been looking":*   Shane Reams letter, October 2003.

p. 151   *"Why can't their cases be separated?":*   Reams interview, December 2000.

p. 152   *a veteran of the LAPD—soon to become infamous:*   See stories on the Rampart scandal and the LAPD in the *Los Angeles Times*, 1999–2001, particularly those written by Matt Lait and Scott Glover.

20. SAY HELLO TO HITLER, DAHMER, AND BUNDY

p. 153   *"Fuck you"*:   Mark Klaas interview, May 1998.

p. 153   *"pierce my son through the heart"*:   Joe Klaas interviews, July 2002 and April 2003.

p. 153   *that "punk," that "monster"*:   Marc Klaas interview, May 1998.

p. 153   *lobbied publicly . . . for Davis to receive the death penalty:*   Modesto *Bee,* July 8, 1996.

p. 154   *In June, however, the jury had convicted:*   Elaine Lafferty, "Final Outrage: Facing Execution, Polly's Killer Lashes Back," *Time* magazine, October 7, 1996.

p. 154   *"Mr. Davis, . . . when you get to where you're going"*:   Ibid.

p. 154   *"I would like to state for the record"*:   *New York Times,* September 27, 1996.

p. 154   *"to emanate strange sounds"*:   Marc Klaas interview, May 1998.

p. 155   *"Mr. Davis, . . . this is always a traumatic"*:   *New York Times,* September 27, 1996.

21. PIZZA FACE

p. 156   *Life is tough for poor-boy Chicanos:*   Unless otherwise indicated, the description of Jesus Romero's background and events leading to his arrest and conviction are taken from Michael Butler, interview by author, July 2001.

p. 156   *Romero was meek, unhardened, and deferential:*   Maura Dolan and Tony Perry, "Justices Deal Blow to '3 Strikes': Lower Courts Allowed Discretion in Sentencing," *Los Angeles Times,* June 21, 1996, A1.

p. 156   *"I'm wiping my face"*:   Butler interview, July 2001.

p. 156   *the officer . . . found two small rocks:*   "Court Calls 'Three Strikes' Out," *Newsday,* June 21, 1996, A19.

p. 157   *Of five drug-related previous convictions:*   Alex Ricciardulli, "The Broken Safety Valve: Judicial Discretion's Failure to Ameliorate

Punishment under California's Three Strikes Law," *Duquesne Law Review* 41, no. 1 (fall 2002).

p. 157   *"wasn't offering jack shit":*   Butler interview, July 2001.

p. 160   *a case such as Romero's "was worth about sixteen months":*   *People v. Superior Court* (Romero), 13 Cal. 4th 497 (1996); Brief on the Merits of Respondent Jesus Romero, *People v. Superior Court* (Romero).

p. 160   *"present a brief to Mudd":*   Butler interview, July 2001.

p. 160   *had "a real desire to do justice":*   Ibid.

p. 160   *a law that "basically castrates":*   *Los Angeles Times,* June 21, 1996.

p. 161   *And Mudd decided to eliminate:*   *People v. Romero,* Superior Court of San Diego County, no. SCD 103345, Judge William D. Mudd (unpublished opinion), 1994.

p. 161   *"Michael Butler was an idiot":*   Butler interview, July 2001.

p. 162   *"is a judicial responsibility":*   *People v. Superior Court* (Romero).

p. 162   *"The Supreme Court could have left its decision":*   Gary R. Nichols, interview by author, July 2001.

p. 163   *"I'm very concerned":*   *Los Angeles Times,* June 21, 1996.

p. 163   *"we cannot tolerate a situation":*   Ibid.

p. 164   *"over-judicial discretion":*   Ibid.

p. 164   *the assembly . . . passed a bill:*   *Orange County Register,* July 17, 1996.

p. 164   *The defendant's offense had to be* "outside the spirit":   *People v. Superior Court* (Romero).

p. 164   *"personal antipathy for the effect":*   *People v. Superior Court* (Romero).

p. 165   *"I've been a public defender for twenty years":*   Nichols interview, July 2001.

p. 165   *give judges "broad authority":*   *New York Times,* January 17, 1997.

p. 165   *Writing in the* Duquesne Law Review: Ricciardulli, "The Broken Safety Valve," 29.

p. 165   *"I think the best example of a case":*   "Overturning the California Three Strikes Law," *Newshour Online,* KCET, June 21, 1996.

22. ANOTHER REYNOLDS BILL

p. 167   *Mike Reynolds's mind was racing:*   The quotations and descriptions in this chapter are taken from the author's firsthand observations and appear in a slightly different form in Joe Domanick, "Man with a Mission," *LA Weekly*, November 27–December 3, 1998.

p. 172   *"Second thoughts?":*   Ray Appleton interview, March 2003.

23. JEAN VALJEAN REDUX

p. 174   *Gregory Taylor was a young man:*   Unless otherwise noted, the material on Gregory Taylor is based on the reporting of Associated Press reporter Martha Bellisle in her definitive profile of Taylor, "Man Gets 25 Years to Life for Alleged Food Heist," in the *Los Angeles Times*, July 18, 1999.

p. 177   *he came to view Taylor as a "peaceful man":*   Graciela Martinez, deputy public defender and trial counsel for Mr. Taylor, Los Angeles County Public Defender's Office, December 11, 2001, as quoted in Alex Ricciardulli, "The Broken Safety Valve: Judicial Discretion's Failure to Ameliorate Punishment under California's Three Strikes Law," *Duquesne Law Review* 41, no. 1 (fall 2002): 25.

p. 178   *"to know bullshit when [he] heard bullshit":*   Statements from Dale Cutler and details about his prosecution of Taylor are drawn from his interviews with the author, August 2001.

p. 182   *With little chance of winning reelection, Reiner ceded:*   The description of Ira Reiner, his policies and his campaign against Gil Garcetti, are taken from the author's interview with Reiner, winter 1998; "Trouble at DA," *Los Angeles Magazine*, April 1988; Laureen Lazarovici, "Men with Convictions," *LA Weekly*, March 21, 1990; and Joe Domanick, *To Protect and to Serve: The LAPD's Century of War in the City of Dreams* (New York: Pocket Books, 1994), 409–11.

p. 183   *His office lost the first Menendez brothers trial:*   editorial, *Los Angeles Times,* February 27, 2000.

p. 183   *"In New York, . . . the cops hold the door for the DAs":*   James Fyfe, interview by author, winter 1989.

p. 184   *"Two decades ago, prosecutors and defense":*   opinion piece, *Los Angeles Times,* March 19, 2002.

p. 186   *Taylor's case was subsequently heard: People v. Taylor,* 71 Cal.App.4th, 693, as cited in Ricciardulli, "The Broken Safety Valve," *Duquesne Law Review* 41, no. 1 (fall 2002): 24.

p. 186   *Taylor . . . "may have honestly believed":*   Ricciardulli, "The Broken Safety Valve," 24.

p. 186   *Judge Earl Johnson wrote in dissent:*   Ricciardulli, "The Broken Safety Valve," 24.

p. 186   *AP reporter Martha Bellisle's profile of Taylor:*   *Los Angeles Times,* July 18, 1999.

p. 187   *When questioned by CNN . . . Garcetti replied:*   "Morning Show," CNN, April 30, 1999.

p. 187   *In the following year, 1998, 79 percent of LA County's third strike prosecutions.*   Howard Breuer, "Change Sought in 3-Strikes Law," Media News Group, April 29, 1999.

p. 187   *"as Klaas crossed the street":*   Marc Klaas interview, May 1998.

p. 188   *"My advice to parents":*   *Los Angeles Times,* February 14, 1995.

p. 188   *Attorney General Dan Lungren was getting applause:*   The description of Lungren's campaign is discussed at greater length in Joe Domanick, "California Scheming," *LA Weekly,* October 16–22, 1998.

p. 189   *"Nobody believes that three strikes":*   Peter Greenwood, interview with author, June 1998; Peter Greenwood and Angela Hawken, "An Assessment of the Effects of California's Three Strikes Law," Greenwood & Associates, http://greenwood associates.org, March 2002.

p. 190   *"So, all the public was exposed to":*   Greenwood interview, June 1998.

p. 190   *But it was also true that between 1993 and 1999:*   Federal Bureau of Investigation, "Crime in the United States," reports for 1993 and 1999, cited in Bill Jones, press release, February 7, 2002.

p. 190   *the end of the crack wars:*   *New York Times,* October 27, 1997.

p. 191   *"If California's crime decline":*   Janet Gilmore, "State's Three Strikes Law Strikes Out," *Berkeleyan,* November 10–16, 1999.

p. 191   *"before three strikes:*   Ibid.

p. 191   *Zimring also found that "before three strikes went into effect":*   Ibid.

p. 191   *"over the last twenty years, the homicide rate":*   *New York Times,* July 22, 2001.

24. THE MORE COMMITTED EXECUTIONER

p. 195   *It's a sunny morning in August of 1998:*   The material in this chapter on Dan Lungren's campaign for the governorship is taken from the author's firsthand observations and is discussed at greater length in Joe Domanick, "California Scheming," *LA Weekly,* October 16–22, 1998.

p. 196   *"I read this audience":*   Lungren news conference, August 1998.

p. 196   *"How many of you are from a large family?":*   Author's observations, August 1998.

p. 197   *"Some people say that if you're a Republican":*   Ibid.

p. 198   *$2 million the union would contribute to Davis's campaign:*   Dennis Duncan, president of FACTS, at a rally after speaking to the Public Safety Committee in Sacramento in favor of amending the three-strikes law, April 2000, www.facts1.com/events/00-04-04.htm.

p. 199   *So when the debate was joined:*   *Los Angeles Times,* August 19, 1998.

p. 199   *Gray Davis then repaid Don Novey:*   Gary Delsohn and Sam Stanton, "Rolling Back Three Strikes," www.salon.com, May 9, 2000.

p. 199   *"As long as you have me":*   Ibid.

25. LENNY, DRUG COURT, AND THREE STRIKES

p. 200   *"Graduating? I don't believe it!":*   The description of California drug courts in general and Judge Manley's in particular is taken from Joe Domanick, "High on Justice," *LA Weekly*, May 9–15, 2003. All unattributed quotations are taken from this source.

p. 201   *Most of them . . . are "one-rock people"*:   Bernardo Saucedo, interview by author, August 2002.

p. 202   *For almost a decade, Manley . . . has been a leader:*   author interviews of Stephen Manley, August 2002, and David Deitch, March 2002.

p. 202   *"over 100,000 offenders [nationwide] have participated"*:   "What Are Drug Treatment Courts?", DEA web site, www.dea.gov/ongoing/treatment.html.

p. 203   *"I'd seen a lot of programs"*:   Joe Domanick, "Straight Time: The Battle for Drug Treatment in California Prisons," *LA Weekly*, May 28–June 3, 1998.

p. 203   *Charles Dederich, Sr., a self-destructive alcoholic:*   David Deitch, interview by author, March 2002.

p. 203   *The proof had been the notorious inability:*   Domanick, "Straight Time."

p. 204   *"I knew that I had two hundred guys"*:   Ibid.

p. 205   *about thirty-six thousand Californians a year were being incarcerated:*   The statistics on the California prison population and incarceration for drug possession are taken from Domanick, "Straight Time."

p. 205   *almost five hundred eighty people had been sentenced:*   "May 31: Drug Treatment Initiative (Prop. 36) That Affects 3-Strike Law Gathers Enough Signatures for November Ballot," FACTS Web site, www.facts1.com.

p. 206   *"We do coerce and hold people accountable"*:   Manley interview, August 2002.

p. 206   *Hunched in the back is Bernardo Saucedo:*   The descriptions of Saucedo and of Lenny Wilson (pseudonym), his story and his circumstances, are taken from interviews of them by the author in August 2002.

p. 207   *"The guy was throwing gang signs"*:   Saucedo interview, August 2002.

p. 207   *"See you next time":*   Ed Bervena, interview by author, August 2002.

p. 208   *"Yo, Ed":*   Ibid.

p. 208   *But Lenny had gotten lippy:*   Lenny Wilson, interview by author, August 2002, and Saucedo interview, August 2002.

p. 209   *"Prior to Prop 36, we . . . would have had to":*   Saucedo interview, August 2002.

p. 209   *1.2 grams of crack cocaine "hidden between":*   "Equal Protection Clause Requires Retroactive Sentencing Measure, Appeals Court Rules," Metropolitan News-Enterprise, May 1, 2002.

p. 209   *"the drastic difference in treatment":*   People v. Floyd, 31 Cal. 4th 179, 2003.

p. 210   *André René Floyd had never been lucky:*   Material in this chapter about André René Floyd is taken from Kenneth Ofgang, "Proposition 36 Not Retroactive," *Metropolitan News Enterprise,* July 22, 2003, www.metnews.com/articles/floy072203.htm, accessed on August 29, 2003; *People v. Floyd,* 31 Cal. 4th 179, 2003, amicus brief filed by Marylou Hillberg, attorney for Tommy Lee Fryman; and David Kravets, "Court: Drug Leniency Not Retroactive," *San Jose Mercury News,* July 22, 2003.

p. 210   *"The act [Prop 36] was not intended":*   People v. Floyd, 31 Cal. 4th 179, 2003.

p. 210   *"frustrates rather than promotes":*   David Kravets, "Court: Drug Leniency Not Retroactive," *San Jose Mercury News,* July 22, 2003.

p. 211   *"Sixty-one percent of the voters":*   Amicus brief filed by Marylou Hillberg, attorney for Tommy Lee Fryman, in *People v. Floyd,* 31 Cal. 4th 179, 2003.

p. 212   *"You have to draft something":*   Bill Zimmerman, interview by author, July 2002.

p. 213   *Nationally, about one million Americans are arrested:*   The statistics about incarceration and the discussion of Bill Zimmerman's role in the drug reform movement are taken from Domanick, "High on Justice," and Zimmerman interview, July 2002.

p. 213   *"just another war":*   Zimmerman interview, July 2002.

p. 214   *who each contributed almost $1.2 million*:   "Top Ten Contributors to California Propositions," www.calvoter.org.

p. 214   *"There's this big misconception"*:   Kathryn Jett interview, March 2002.

p. 215   *"a serious, long denied reexamination"*:   David Deitch, interview by author, March 2002.

p. 215   *He has "schizophrenia, paranoia"*:   Lenny Wilson interview, August 2002.

p. 215   *"Now that," he says of the Novane:*   Ibid.

p. 216   *"Lenny, . . . don't you never come back here"*:   Ibid.

p. 216   *"He hasn't relapsed"*:   Saucedo interview, August 2002.

p. 217   *"I always wanted to be a public defender"*:   Nancy Chand, interview by author, December 2002.

p. 218   *Haynes enters her Proposition 36 drug court courtroom:*   the description of the scene in Judge Haynes's courtroom is taken from the author's personal observations, December 2002.

p. 219   *LA had been expecting a large number:*   Lael Rubin interview, November 2002.

p. 220   *"I was going to make the Marines"*:   The description of John Washington (pseudonym) and his background is taken from the author's interview with John Washington, December 2002.

p. 220   *"The Salvation Army program"*:   Ibid.

p. 221   *Studies over the past twenty years have shown:*   The discussion about the effectiveness of drug courts and efforts to pass Proposition 36 is taken from Domanick, "High on Justice."

p. 221   *"Proposition 36 was sold to voters"*:   *Los Angeles Times*, November 27, 2002.

p. 222   *"crusade to scuttle [drug] reform initiatives"*:   The full text of Daniel Forbes's report, "The Governor's Sub-Rosa Plot to Subvert an Election in Ohio," can be found at www.ips-dc.org/projects/drugpolicy/ohio.pdf.

26. THE MODIFICATION

p. 223   *"We can't afford a failed prosecutor"*:   campaign flyer, Los Angeles County District Attorney election, 2000.

p. 224   *"Garcetti . . . is in grim shape"*:   *Los Angeles Times*, April 10, 2000.

p. 224   *"The three strikes law provides a powerful tool"*:   Steve Cooley for District Attorney campaign, "Position Paper 5: Three Strikes Policy," 2000.

p. 224   *"If the potential third strike is a 'violent or serious' felony"*:   Cooley for District Attorney campaign, "Position Paper 5."

p. 225   *Third strike convictions in LA County*:   *Los Angeles Times*, May 27, 2003.

p. 225   *the number of three strikes prosecutions in LA County*:   California Department of Corrections, as quoted in *Los Angeles Times*, May 27, 2003.

p. 226   *"Our crime rate is declining faster"*:   Bill Jones, news release, November 29, 2000.

p. 226   *"Of all the things I've done as a district attorney"*:   *Los Angeles Times*, May 27, 2003.

p. 227   *In 2002, the crime rate in the United States*:   *Los Angeles Times*, August 25, 2003.

p. 227   *Between 1980 and 2002, the state's overall crime rate*:   "Crime in California, 2002 Advance Release," released by Office of the Attorney General of California, Bill Lockyer, July 1, 2003.

p. 227   *Simultaneously . . . California's prison population*:   Scott Duke Harris, "Listening to Oakland," *Los Angeles Times Magazine*, July 6, 2003.

p. 227   *with $200 in their pockets*:   "Hard Time: California's Criminal Justice Build Up and Its Consequences," Liberty Hill Foundation, April 2003.

p. 227   *By 2003, one out of every fourteen adult males*:   Scott Duke Harris, "Listening to Oakland," *Los Angeles Times Magazine*, July 6, 2003.

p. 227   *More than ninety-eight people* per day: "Hard Time."

p. 227   *A 1997 California Department of Corrections survey*:   Ibid.

p. 228   *In 2002, California's overall crime:*   "Crime in California, 2002 Advance Release."

p. 229   *such a scenario is "just a matter of time":*   Bill Jones, news release, November 29, 2003.

27. SHANE AND A.J.

p. 231   *As Sue Reams hangs up the phone:*   Unless otherwise noted, the material in this chapter is taken from Sue Reams, interviews with author, December 2000, January 2001, February 2001, March 2002, July 2002, April 2003.

p. 236   *"You've got to let them know":*   Sue Reams interviews.

p. 237   *"I try to maintain some kindness":*   Thomas Snipp interview, summer 1994.

p. 238   *"You are a criminal":*   Mark Hutton interview, summer 1994.

p. 238   *"Rehabilitation . . . has been overused":*   Snipp interview.

28. A "TALIBAN-TYPE" LAW

p. 240   *Three months later:*   The material in this chapter is taken, except where otherwise noted, from the author's interviews of Sue Reams, March 2002, July 2002, April 2003; Joe Klaas, July 2002 and April 2003; and Geri Silva, June 2002.

p. 240   *"The Assembly Public Safety Committee":*   Families Against California's Three Strikes (FACTS) Web site, www.facts1.com, accessed spring 2000.

p. 241   *"We need to find out":*   Reams interviews.

p. 242   *She has willed herself "not to care":*   Ibid.

p. 243   *"I want to state up front":*   Joe Klaas, speaking before the Public Safety Committee in Sacramento in favor of amending the three strikes law, April 4, 2000, www.facts1.com/040400/0129291.htm

p. 243   *this "Taliban-type" law:*   Joe Klaas, KOVR 13 News, January 15, 2002.

p. 243   *"god-awful, unjust bill"*:   Ibid.

p. 243   *"All these supporters of three strikes"*:   *Los Angeles Times*, October 26, 1994.

p. 244   *"I belong to Citizens Against Violent Crime"*:   Joe Klaas, Public Safety Committee.

p. 244   *"As a former prisoner . . . of the Nazis"*:   Ibid.

p. 245   He had thought *"this was such a dead issue"*:   Joe Klaas interviews, July 2002 and April 2003.

p. 245   *"a star, a big-ticket item"*:   Geri Silva interview, June 2002.

p. 247   *"friends and neighbors . . . don't even know"*:   Reams interviews.

p. 247   *"Thank you for what you're doing"*:   Ibid.

p. 248   *"Legislators rarely if ever take up bills"*:   Tom Hayden, e-mail to author, August 15, 2003.

p. 249   *"What we have in California"*:   The material about Assemblywoman Goldberg is taken from the author's interviews with Jackie Goldberg, May 2002.

p. 250   *"There are big rallies every year"*:   Goldberg interviews, May 2002.

p. 251   *Wright is the cosponsor*:   AB 2447, introduced February 24, 2000, www.assembly.ca.gov/acs/acsFrameset2text.htm.

p. 252   *"You know, if you steal $10 worth of toilet tissue"*:   Rod Wright, at a rally after speaking to the Public Safety Committee in Sacramento in favor of amending the three strikes law, April 4, 2000, www.facts1.com/040400/0129291.htm.

p. 252   *"If you have faith"*:   Carl Washington, ibid.

p. 253   *When it became clear . . . that Wright's chance*:   "May 15: California 3-Strikes bill—AB 2477—gutted because of Gov. Davis," FACTS Web site, www.facts1.com/events/chrono3.htm.

p. 254   *sentencing judges to give "great weight"*:   Alex Ricciardulli, "The Broken Safety Valve: Judicial Discretion's Failure to Ameliorate Punishment under California's Three Strikes Law," *Duquesne Law Review* 41, no. 1 (fall 2002): 36.

p. 254   *Even that failed to pass*:   "June 1: AB 2 477 Does Not Receive Enough Votes in Assembly for Passage," FACTS Web site, www.facts1.com.

p. 254 *By the end of 2002, a record 2.1 million men and women:*   *New York Times,* April 7, 2003.

p. 254 *"The population of federal and state prisons":*   *New York Times,* August 1, 2003.

p. 254 *That same study revealed:*   *New York Times,* July 28, 2003.

EPILOGUE

p. 257 *Erwin Chemerinsky is about to:*   The material in this chapter is drawn from the author's interview of Erwin Chemerinsky, November 2002.

p. 257 *"You lost five to four":*   Chemerinsky interview, November 2002.

p. 257 *42.7 percent of California's three strikes inmates:*   "Second and Third Strikers in the Inmate Population," California Department of Corrections, Policy and Evaluation Division, June 30, 2002. Report can be found at www.corr.ca.gov/OffenderInfo Services/Reports/Quarterly/Strike1/STRIKE1d0206.pdf.

p. 258 *could "not point to even one other person":*   Opening arguments, *Lockyer v. Andrade,* 123 S. Ct. 1166 (2003).

p. 258 *"really nasty messages":*   Chemerinsky interview, November 2002.

p. 258 *"There could remain some [slight] room":*   Ibid.

p. 258 *"The California Court of Appeal had affirmed 100 percent":*   Chemerinsky interview, December 2001.

p. 259 *"Within seconds . . . going live on radio stations":*   Mike Reynolds, interview by author, March 2003.

p. 259 *"golf clubs and the guy that stole videotapes":*   Ibid.

p. 259 *"a small [local] high school":*   Ibid.

p. 259 *"some lawyer out of Colorado":*   Ibid.

p. 259 *"Our case . . . was on the front page":*   Ibid.

p. 259 *"But . . . he had five prior homicides!":*   Ibid.

p. 259 *Robert Rozier, had killed:*   *Sacramento Bee,* June 29, 2000.

p. 259 *"As a society, . . . we have to do something":*   Reynolds interview, March 2003.

p. 260 *"the biggest gang crackdown":*   *Los Angeles Times,* February 25, 2002.

p. 260   *"When do you say enough is enough?":*   Reynolds interview, March 2003.

p. 260   *"If life in prison isn't cruel and unusual":*   Joe Klaas, interview by author, April 2003.

p. 260   *"too busy to be involved in three strikes":*   Ibid.

p. 261   *"that the public is really ready to accept":*   Ibid.

p. 261   *In 2001, Goldberg had tried:*   The information in this chapter about Goldberg's role is taken from Goldberg, interviews by author, May 2002.

p. 262   *But it had failed to gather:*   Josh Richman, "The Three Strikes Act of 2000," June 15, 2000.

p. 262   *Sue Reams bursts into tears:*   Reams, interview by author, April 2003.

p. 262   *"We've [always] given great latitude":*   Lockyer v. Andrade, 123 S. Ct. 1166 (2003), and *Los Angeles Times*, March 6, 2003.

p. 263   *"Great latitude to states?":*   Reams interview, April 2003.

p. 263   *"The drafters of the Declaration of Rights":*   Harmelin v. Michigan, 501 U.S. 957 (1991).

p. 263   *aimed at excluding only "certain modes":*   *Los Angeles Times*, March 6, 2003.

p. 264   *"If Andrade's sentence is not grossly disproportionate":*   Lockyer v. Andrade, 123 S. Ct. 1166 (2003); *Los Angeles Times*, March 6, 2003.

p. 264   *"The U.S. Supreme Court this morning":*   FACTS, press release, "Three Strikes Opponents Defiant After Supreme Court Ruling," March 5, 2003.

p. 265   *he mapped out the battle Silva and FACTS would face:*   Sam Williams, "Initiative to Amend Controversial Law May be on Next Year's Ballot," *Lassen County News*, October 1999, www.lassennews.com/news_archive/news/283.htm, accessed December 22, 2001.

p. 265   *"If you've got enough money":*   *Lassen County News*, November 1999.

p. 265   *"unless," says Tom Hayden, "the proponents are willing":*   Tom Hayden, e-mail to author, August 15, 2003.

p. 266   *Reams and Silva calculate:*   Reams interview, April 2003.

p. 266   *"That's my flesh and blood":*   Ibid.

SELECTED SOURCES

BOOKS, ARTICLES, AND FILMS

Auleta, Ken. *The Underclass.* New York: Random House, 1982.

Baum, Dan. *Smoke and Mirrors: The War on Drugs and the Politics of Failure.* New York: Little, Brown and Company, 1996.

Brands, H. W. *The Strange Death of American Liberalism.* New Haven: Yale University Press, 2001.

Burton-Rose, Daniel, Dan Pens, and Paul Wright. *The Celling of America: An Inside Look at the U.S. Prison Industry.* Monroe, Maine: Common Courage Press, 1998.

Cole, David. *No Equal Justice: Race and Class in the American Criminal Justice System.* New York: The New Press, 1999.

Domanick, Joe. *To Protect and to Serve: The LAPD's Century of War in the City of Dreams.* New York: Pocket Books, 1994.

Donziger, Steven A., ed. *The Real War on Crime: The Report of the National Criminal Justice Commission.* New York: Harper Perennial, 1996.

Farber, David. *Chicago '68.* Chicago: University of Chicago Press, 1988.

Gest, Ted. *Crime & Politics: Big Government's Erratic Campaign for Law and Order.* Oxford: Oxford University Press, 2001.

Gilens, Martin. *Why Americans Hate Welfare*. Chicago: University of Chicago Press, 1999.

Gottlieb, Stephen E. *Morality Imposed: The Rehnquist Court and Morality in America*. New York: New York University Press, 2000.

Hawkins, Gordon, Sam Kamin, and Franklin E. Zimring. *Punishment and Democracy: Three Strikes and You're Out in California*. Oxford: Oxford University Press, 2001.

Irons, Peter. *A People's History of the Supreme Court*. New York: Penguin Books, 1999.

"The Legacy: Murder, Media, Politics, and Prisons." *POV*, Public Broadcasting System, October 31, 2000.

Mauer, Marc. *Race to Incarcerate: The Sentencing Project*. New York: The New Press, 1999.

Parenti, Christian. *Lockdown America: Police and Prisons in the Age of Crisis*. London: Verso, 1999.

Reeves, Richard. *President Nixon: Alone in the White House*. New York: Simon and Schuster, 2001.

Reisner, Marc. *Cadillac Desert: The American West and Its Disappearing Water*. New York: Penguin Books, 1986.

Reynolds, Mike, Bill Jones, and Dan Evans. *Three Strikes and You're Out! A Promise to Kimber*. Fresno, Calif.: Quill Driver Books, 1996.

Ricciardulli, Alex. "The Broken Safety Valve: Judicial Discretion's Failure to Ameliorate Punishment under California's Three Strikes Law," *Duquesne Law Review* 41, no. 1 (fall 2002).

Rieder, Jonathan. *Canarsie: The Jews and Italians of Brooklyn against Liberalism*. Cambridge, Mass.: Harvard University Press, 1985.

Stolz, Preble. *Judging Judges: The Investigation of Rose Bird and the California Supreme Court*. New York: The Free Press, 1981.

Wofford, Harris. *Of Kennedys and Kings: Making Sense of the Sixties*. Farrar, Straus, Giroux, 1980.

INTERVIEWS

Appleton, Ray (talk show host, Fresno, Calif.). March 2003 (interview by
Shannon Seibert).

Berman, Howard (congressman, D–Los Angeles). Summer 1998

Bervena, Ed (probation community worker, San Jose, Calif.). August
2002.

Butler, Michael (deputy public defender, San Diego). July 2001.

Chand, Nancy (deputy public defender, Los Angeles County). December 2002.

Chemerinsky, Erwin (counsel for Leandro Andrade; Sydney M. Irmus
Professor of Public Interest Law, Legal Ethics, and Political Science
at the University of Southern California). December 2001, November 2002.

Cooley, Steve (district attorney, Los Angeles County). October 2000,
January 2001, February 2001.

Cutler, Dale (deputy public defender, Los Angeles). August 2001.

Deitch, David (professor of psychology, University of California, San
Diego). March 2002.

Fyfe, James (professor of criminal justice, Temple University). Winter
1989.

Garcetti, Gil (district attorney, Los Angeles County). October 2000.

Giarretto, Gary (probation officer, San Jose, Calif.). August 2002.

Goldberg, Jackie (assemblywoman, 45th Assembly District, California).
May 2002.

Greenberg, Charles E. (attorney, Long Beach, Calif.). July 1997.

Greenwood, Peter (president, Greenwood & Associates, Inc.). June
1998.

Gualderon, Msgr. Ernest (Lungren family friend). July 1997.

Hall, Jan (Republican Party consultant). April 1997, July 1997.

Haynes, Marcelita (Superior Court judge, Los Angeles County). December 2002.

Hinojosa, Ricardo (ex-prisoner and recovering addict). December 1997.

Hutton, Mark (corrections officer, State Institute for Men, Chino, Calif.). Summer 1998.

Jett, Kathryn P. (state coordinator, Proposition 36; director, California Department of Alcohol and Drug Programs). March 2002.

Jones, Bill (secretary of state, California). June 2002.

Judge, Michael (public defender, Los Angeles County). November 1997.

Keiso, Doug (attorney; co-chair, FACTS [Families Against California's Three Strikes]). March 1999.

Klaas, Joe (grandfather of Polly Klaas). July 2002, April 2003.

Klaas, Marc (father of Polly Klaas). May 1998.

Lessem, Mark (deputy public defender, Los Angeles County). December 2002.

Lungren, Dan (former attorney general, California). August 1998, June 2002.

Manley, Stephen (Superior Court judge, Santa Clara County; presiding judge, drug court). August 2002.

Nelson, Aubrey (ex-girlfriend of Shane Reams). Fall 2002.

Nichols, Gary R. (deputy public defender, San Diego, Calif.). July 2001.

Novey, Don (president, California Correctional Peace Officers Association). July 1994.

Reams, Sue (mother of three-strikes offender Shane Reams). December 2000, January 2001, February 2001, March 2002, July 2002, April 2003.

Reiner, Ira (district attorney, Los Angeles County). Winter 1998.

Reynolds, Mike (moving force behind three strikes law). Summer 1998, March 2003 (interview by Shannon Seibert), August 2003.

Reynolds, Sharon (wife of Mike Reynolds and mother of Kimber). Summer 1998.

Ricciardulli, Alex (deputy public defender, Los Angeles County; adjunct professor, Loyola Law School and University of Southern California Law School). March 1999, June 1999.

Rubin, Lael (special counsel, LA district attorney's office). November 2002.

Saucedo, Bernardo (deputy public defender, Santa Clara County). August 2002.

Schiraldi, Vincent (director, Justice Policy Institute). Lecture, June 2002.

Serles, Jim (former Republican candidate, Long Beach City Council). July 1997.

Silva, Geri (chair, FACTS [Families Against California's Three Strikes]). March 1999, June 2002.

Snipp, Thomas (corrections officer, State Institute for Men, Chino, Calif.). Summer 1994.

Taqui-Eddin, Khaled (policy analyst, Justice Policy Institute). March 1999.

Taylor, Whitney (director of Proposition 36's implementation for the Drug Policy Alliance). Fall 2002.

Vasconcellos, John (D–San Jose; chair, California State Assembly Committee on Ways and Means). July 1994.

Washington, John (pseudonym of drug court defendant). December 2002.

Wilson, Lenny (pseudonym of drug court defendant). August 2002.

Zimmerman, Bill (executive director, Campaign for New Drug Policies). July 2002.

INDEX

AA (Alcoholics Anonymous), 203
ACLU (American Civil Liberties
    Union), 66, 181, 262
Agricultural Labor Relations
    Board (ALRB), 170
Alcoholics Anonymous (AA), 203
Alulo, Johnnie (pseud.), 69, 70–71
Amber Alert program, 260
American Civil Liberties Union
    (ACLU), 66, 181, 262
American Graffiti (film), 94
"America's Most Wanted" (televi-
    sion show), 118
Amity Foundation, 204
Amnesty International, 262
AM talk radio. *See* talk radio
Andrade, Leandro, 5–6, 203, 257,
    263, 264. See also *Andrade v. the
    Attorney General of the State of
    California; Lockyer v. Andrade*
*Andrade v. the Attorney General of
    the State of California:* appealed
    to the Supreme Court, 7; back-
ground of case, 5–6; Constitu-
    tional defense in, 7. See also
    Lockyer v. Andrade
Anti-Terrorism Bill (1996), 189
Appleton, Ray: on crime in Fresno,
    18; on England's two strikes
    law, 173; on Richard Machado,
    38; on Kimber Reynolds's
    death, 19–20; self-image of, 19;
    three strikes role of, 40–41, 67,
    125–26
Arax, Mark, 39
Ardaiz, James, 38, 41
Army Corps of Engineers, 27
Autry, Alan, 168

Baez, Joan, 126
ballot initiatives. *See* initiative pro-
    cess
Banales, Richard, 4
Baron, Ruth, 97
Barrales, Ruben, 196
Barsamian, Ron, 170

Bates, Tom, 76–77, 78, 128
Baxter, Marvin, 210
Beccaria, Cesare, 83
Bellisle, Martha, 176, 177, 186
Benscotter, Scott, 4
Berkeleyan (weekly newspaper), 191
Berman, Howard, 53, 55
Bervena, Ed, 207–8
Beyond Missing program, 261
Bird, Rose Elizabeth, 63–64
blacks: gang violence of, 174–75,
    182–84; integration backlash
    against, 60–61; leadership role
    of, 180–81; percent of, in
    prison, 254; as political cam-
    paign issue, 137–38; public
    safety concerns of, 253; in riots,
    56; third strike convictions of,
    251; in Tulare County, 39
Bloods (gang), 175
Blumenthal, Sidney, 143
Bradley, Tom, 62, 63, 64
Brennan, William, 59
Brown, Janice Rogers, 210
Brown, Jerry, 88
Brown, Kathleen, 143, 144
Brown, Pat, 55
Brown, Willie, 141, 171
Buchanan, Pat, 259
Burton, John, 78, 128
Bush, George, 137, 222
Bush, George W., 181
Butler, Michael: proposal of, to
    Judge Mudd, 160–61; Jesus
    Romero case of, 157–58

Cadillac Desert (Reisner), 27
Cain, Bruce, 89
Calderon, Greg, 13–14, 15, 16
California: crime rate statistics in,
    144, 188, 189–91, 227, 228–29;
    criminal justice policies of,
    29–31; number of drug courts
    in, 202; polarized electorate of,
    249; prison population of, 64,
    205, 227, 254–55; third strike
    prosecutions in, 225–26
California Correctional Peace Of-
    ficers Association. *See* CCPOA
California Court of Appeal: Fifth
    District, 210; Fourth District,
    161; Second District, 186; Sixth
    District, 209–10. *See also* Ninth
    Circuit Court of Appeals (U.S.)
California Department of Correc-
    tions: budget of, 1984–1994,
    65; pilot therapeutic commu-
    nity (TC) program of, 204–5;
    survey on parolees by, 227
California District Attorneys Asso-
    ciation, 130
California Men's Colony (CMC),
    95
California State Institute for Men
    at Chino, 237–38
California Supreme Court: on ju-
    dicial discretion, 161–63,
    164–65; on Proposition 36's ap-
    plication, 210–12
California Teachers Association,
    130
California Youth Authority (CYA),
    72
Campaign for New Drug Policies
    (CNDP), 213, 222
Campbell, Catherine, 19, 26–27,
    86
Canadian sentences, 171–72
Catholic Archdiocese of Los Ange-
    les, 262

CCPOA (California Correctional
Peace Officers Association),
107; contributions to three
strikes campaign, 114–15, 130;
Gray Davis's ties to, 198, 199;
political influence of, 112–14,
250–51; salaries of members of,
112
Chand, Nancy, 217–18, 219
Chemerinsky, Erwin; and Andrade
three strikes cases, 5–7, 8–9,
255, 257–58; background of,
2–3; Eighth Amendment posi-
tion of, 7; on U.S. Supreme
Court ruling, 257–58
Chiampou, Ken, 127
child molestation: Canadian sen-
tences for, 171; as prior strike,
79–80
Chino state prison, 237–38
Chisholm, Shirley, 77
Clark, Marcia, 183
Clinton, Bill, 64, 125, 126, 138,
180, 222
CMC (California Men's Colony), 95
CNBC, 259
CNDP (Campaign for New Drug
Policies), 213, 222
CNN, 125, 126
Cochran, Johnnie, 183
Collaborative Justice Courts. See
drug courts
Collins, David, 104
Community-oriented Policing
Task Force (C.O.P.), 150
Comprehensive Crime Control
Act (1984), 52, 53–54
Conservative Opportunity Society,
52
Contract with America, 52, 129, 139

Cooley, Steve, 223–27
C.O.P. (Community-oriented
Policing Task Force), 150
Corcoran State Prison, 66, 187
Cordell, LaDoris H., 80
Costa, Jim, 43
Court of Appeal(s). See California
Court of Appeal; Ninth Circuit
Court of Appeals (U.S.)
Cox, Robert Lee, 150–52
crime: California's statistics on,
144, 188, 189–91, 225, 227,
228–29; exploitation of, for
profit, 138–39; federal expendi-
tures against, 254; in Fresno,
38–39, 260; integration's impact on, 60–61; 1994 cam-
paigns against, 143–44; 1994
legislation on, 140–41; as Re-
publican wedge issue, 62–63;
137–38; talk radio's focus on,
18, 67–68, 139
Crime Control Act (1984), 52,
53–54
crime victims organizations:
CCPOA's link to, 112–13,
250–51; sentencing enhancement rallies of, 247, 250–51
Crime Victims United, 112
Crime Victims Week, 247
Crips (gang), 175
"Crossfire" (television show), 125
"cruel and unusual punishment":
Chemerinsky on, 7, 258; constitutional prohibition of, 84;
Joe Klaas on, 260; Antonin
Scalia on, 263–64
Cruz, C. Christian, 6
Cubie, Bernice, 4
Cutler, Dale, 178–80, 185

CYA (California Youth Authority), 72

The Daily Journal (legal paper), 257
Daily Planet restaurant (Fresno), 13–14, 15–16, 167–68
Dass, Ram, 126
Davis, Gray, 195, 198, 199, 214
Davis, Joseph Michael, 21, 22, 23–24, 25, 68
Davis, Richard Allen: abduction/homicide by, 93–94, 119–22; childhood of, 95–97; pathological behavior of, 97–98, 99; as three strikes offender, 126; trial/sentencing of, 153–55
Davis, Robert R., 95–97
Davis, Susan, 241
Day Top (therapeutic community), 204
DBOs (Ditch Bank Okies), 23
death penalty: and homicide statistics, 191; in Lungren-Davis race, 198–99
Dederich, Charles, Sr., 203
Deitch, David, 215, 222
Dellums, Ron, 77
Democratic Party: crime issue vulnerability of, 62–63, 137; crime legislation by, 138, 140–41, 144
determinate sentencing, 98–99
Deukmejian, George, 55; criminal justice policies of, 64–65; 1982 campaign issue of, 62–63; political background of, 58–59, 61–62
di Blasi, Robert, 4
Ditch Bank Okies (DBOs), 23

Dole, Bob, 125
drug courts: clientele of, 201, 218–19; coercion element of, 206; of Stephen Manley, 200–202; number of cases in, 217; probation community workers of, 207–8; success of, 202, 221; therapeutic community concept of, 203–5
drug offenders: annual arrests of, 213; in drug court, 201, 217, 218–19; methamphetamine use by, 23; numbers of, in prison, 74–75, 133, 205–6, 213; as percent of parolees, 227; prison recidivism of, 23, 74–75; therapeutic communities for, 203–5; with third strike, in LA County, 187; "tough love" approach to, 71–72; treatment for, under Proposition 36, 205, 208–10, 220–21
drug possession: Jackie Goldberg's bill on, 261; incarceration for, 205; treatment for, under Proposition 36, 205, 208–10
drug reform initiatives: drug treatment provisions of, 205, 208–10, 220–21; funding sources of, 213–14, 219; political opposition to, 214–15, 221–22; success of, 213; voter polling on, 212
drug treatment programs: coercion element of, 206; for the mentally ill, 215–16; under Proposition 36, 205, 208–10, 220–21; success rate of, 221; therapeutic community concept of, 203–5; three strikes law's approach to, 83

Dukakis, Michael, 137
Dunn, James, 185–86
Duquesne Law Review, 165

education. *See* schools
Edwards, Sue, 99
E! Entertainment, 118
Eighth Amendment, 7, 84, 263–64
Eisenhower, Dwight D., 51
Ewing, Gary, 7–8, 257, 264

FACTS (Families Against Califor-
    nia's Three Strikes), 3, 251; bal-
    lot initiative goal of, 264–66;
    Tom Hayden's work with,
    248–49; size/impact of, 246–47;
    at three strikes amendment
    hearing, 240–41, 244–45
FBI, 100–101, 104, 105
Feinstein, Dianne, 144; Michael
    Huffington's race against, 129;
    at Polly Klaas's memorial, 127;
    1990 gubernatorial race of,
    113–14; on Proposition 36, 214
felonies: Steve Cooley's policy on,
    224–25, 226–27; petty crime
    "wobblers" as, 81, 165; residen-
    tial burglaries as, 78–80; statis-
    tics on, after three strikes law,
    191
Fernandez, Joey Arthur, 4
Fifth District Court of Appeal,
    210
Floyd, André René, 209, 210–12
Forbes, Daniel, 222
forced school busing, 61
Fourth District Court of Appeal,
    161
Fresno: criminal justice policies of,
    29–30, 85; Daily Planet restau-
    rant in, 13–14, 15–16, 167–68;
    description of, 26–28; farming
    business of, 27, 42–44; KMJ
    talk radio in, 18–19; Richard
    Machado's role in, 37–38; vio-
    lent crime statistics in, 38–39,
    260
Fresno Bee, 24
Fryman, Tommy Lee, 209–10
Fyfe, James, 183

Gallup Poll (1968), 56
gangs, 174–75, 182–84
Gann, Paul, 88, 89
Garcetti, Gil, 131, 181, 182;
    cases lost by, 183; Steve Coo-
    ley's race against, 223–24;
    gang violence policy of, 184;
    on Gregory Taylor case, 187;
    third strike prosecutions by,
    251–52
Garrow, David J., 30
Giarretto, Gary, 206
Gillette, Kelly, 251
Gingrich, Newt, 52, 129, 139
Goldberg, Jackie: on political
    obstacles, 249–51; three
    strikes reform bill of, 261–62,
    265
government housing projects, 61
Greenberg, Jack, 3
Green Mountain State Prison
    (pseud.), 232, 234–37
Greenwood, Peter, 189–90
Gualderon, Msgr. Ernest, 50–52
gun crimes: *Los Angeles Times* poll
    on, 107–8; "Ten, Twenty, Life"
    law on, 168–69
gun rights lobby, 107, 109–10
Guthrie, Woody, 27

Hall, Jan, 50
Harbor Light shelter (Los Angeles), 220–21
Harmelin v. Michigan, 263
Hastings, Thomas C., 154, 155
Hayden, Tom, 135–36, 248–49, 265
Haynes, Marcelita, 218, 219
Hertzberg, Hendrik, 139
Hillberg, Marylou, 211–12
Hinojosa, Ricardo, 75
Holliday, George, 182
Holy Cross brothers, 51–52
homelessness, 176, 227–28
home sentencing (Canada), 171
homicide statistics: in death penalty states, 191; in Fresno, 38–39, 260; in Los Angeles, 227
Horton, Willie, 137
House, Skip, 125
Huffington, Arianna, 129
Huffington, Michael, 129–30, 144
Hutton, Mark, 237–38
Human Rights Watch, 66
Humphrey, Hubert, 60
Hurtt, Rob, 164

Ibarra, Ruben, 149–50, 152
initiative process: amendment requirements of, 89–90, 145; antitax movement's use of, 88; costs of, for three strikes reform, 265, 266; drug reform's use of, 213–14; for Jackie Goldberg bill, 261–62; origin of, 87; signature requirements of, 106–7. *See also* drug reform initiatives
integration movement, 59–61

Jacobs, Greg, 153
Jacob's Center (San Jose), 207–8
Jaffee, Dana, 119–20, 121
James, Michael, 4
Japanese internment, 55
Jarvis, Howard, 88, 89
Jett, Kathryn P., 214–15
"John and Ken" (talk radio show), 127–28
Johnson, Earl, 186
Jones, Bill: on judicial discretion ruling, 164; on nonviolent third felonies, 226; political priorities of, 41–43; on three strikes' simplicity, 81; as three strikes sponsor, 43, 48–49, 53, 57, 87
Jones-Reynolds bill. *See* three strikes law
judges: appointments of, 1984–1994, 65; reaction of, to three strikes law, 159; sentencing discretion of, 83, 161–65
Justice Policy Institute, 87
juvenile facilities initiative, 169

Kennedy, Robert, 56
KFI (radio station), 127
KGO (radio station), 123
King, Martin Luther, Jr., 56
King, Rodney, 64, 181–82
Klaas, Joe: on Richard Allen Davis, 153; on Jackie Goldberg bill, 261; at Ron Owens's broadcast, 124–25; personal background of, 101–2; on Rainey bill, 135; on search for Polly, 117, 118–19; on three strikes law, 132–34, 243–45; on U.S. Supreme Court ruling, 260

Klaas, Marc: crime prevention efforts of, 188, 260–61; at Richard Allen Davis's trial, 153–55; FBI interrogation of, 104, 105; learning of Polly's abduction, 100–101; learning of Polly's murder, 121; at *Little Women* premier, 187; personal background of, 102–4; on Polly's memorial service, 127; on Rainey bill, 135; on search for Polly, 117–18; on three strikes bill, 131–34, 140, 141

Klaas, Polly: abduction/murder of, 93 94, 100–101, 119–22; memorial service for, 126–27; parents of, 103; search for, 116–18; three strikes law's exploitation of, 123–26, 128, 135–36, 243

Klaas, Violet, 103, 188

Klaas Kids Foundation, 188

KMJ (radio station), 18–19

Kobylt, John, 127–28

Landa, Rene, 4

LAPD (Los Angeles Police Department), 56, 64, 145, 183, 224

Lassen County News, 265

Lee, Barbara, 76–78, 128, 140

"The Legacy" (film), 80, 125, 128

Levine, Philip, 26–27

Levis, Buck, 38

Lewis, Peter, 214, 222

Libertarian Party, 262

Lightner, Candy, 88–89

Lightner, Cari, 88

Limbaugh, Rush, 18, 19, 67, 127, 139

Lindesmith Drug Policy Center, 213

Lindner, Charles, 184

Little Women (film), 187

Lockyer, Bill, 5, 7, 172, 214

Lockyer v. Andrade: as appeal of *Andrade v. the Attorney General of the State of California*, 7; reactions to ruling on, 258–60, 264–66; U.S. Supreme Court ruling on, 257, 262–64

Lombardi, Vince, 49

Long, Jeff, 87

Long Beach, 49–51

Los Angeles: black leadership of, 180–81; black third strike offenders in, 251; district attorney's office of, 181–82, 183–84; drug court cases in, 217; gang violence in, 174–75, 182–84; homelessness in, 176; homicides in, 227; parolees released in, 227–28; third strike prosecutions in, 187, 225 26, 251

Los Angeles Police Department (LAPD), 56, 64, 145, 183, 224

Los Angeles Times articles, 54, 141, 259, 262; on Leandro Andrade, 6; on blacks in poverty, 39; on citizen-driven movements, 89; on Steve Cooley, 226–27; on exploitation of crime, 138–39; on Fresno's homicide rate, 260; on Gil Garcetti, 224; on gun violence, 107–8; on Marc Klaas, 187, 188; on Polly Klaas, 118, 126; on LA district attorney's office, 184; on "No on Proposition 184," 134; on prison treatment, 66; on Proposition 36, 214, 221–22; on Pete Wilson, 143

Lucas, George, 94, 126
Lungren, Dan, 58, 144, 170, 225;
    criminal justice policies of,
    48–49, 52–53, 188–89; and
    death penalty, 198–99; discre-
    tionary spending by, 120–21;
    education platform of, 195–97;
    Peter Greenwood on, 190; gu-
    bernatorial aspirations of,
    54–55; Marc Klaas on, 133;
    personal background of, 49–52;
    on three strikes bill, 53–54, 57;
    on tobacco lawsuit, 198
Lungren, John, 50–51
Lungren, Lorraine, 51
lynchings, 30

Machado, Richard, 37–38, 41
MADD (Mothers Against Drunk
    Driving), 88–89
Manley, Stephen V., 207, 208; on
    coerced treatment, 206; drug
    court of, 200–202
The Many Faces of Judge Lynch
    (Waldrep), 30
marijuana: drug reform initiatives
    on, 213–14, 222; Dan Lungren
    on, 198; number of arrests for,
    213
Marshall, Thurgood, 3
Martinez, Graciela, 185
Massachusetts crime rate, 190
Mays, Frances, 97–98
McCaffrey, Barry, 222
McCoy, Rev. Allan, 177, 185
McElroy, Leo, 134
Menendez brothers, 183
mentally ill persons, 83, 215–16,
    227
methamphetamine, 23

misdemeanors: judicial discretion
    ruling on, 165; prosecuted as
    felonies, 81
Les Misérables (Hugo), 186–87
Modesto Bee, 259
Mothers Against Drunk Driving
    (MADD), 88–89
"MTV News," 118
Mudd, William, 160–61
murder statistics. See homicide sta-
    tistics
Myers, Deanne, 8

National Association of Drug
    Court Professionals, 202
National Rifle Association. See
    NRA
Newark riots (1964), 56
Newsweek, 3
New York crime rate, 190
New Yorker, 95, 118, 143
New York Times, 191, 254, 259
Nichol, Allan, 100, 130
Nichol, Anne, 103
Nichol, Eve, 103, 105, 154
Nichols, Gary, 84; on judicial dis-
    cretion ruling, 162–63, 164–65;
    on residential burglary offense,
    78–79
Ninth Circuit Court of Appeals
    (U.S.), 5, 7
Nixon, Richard M., 27–28, 77; and
    John Lungren, 50–51; presi-
    dential campaign strategy of,
    60–61; and Pete Wilson, 143
"No on Proposition 184" cam-
    paign, 129–30, 134
Novey, Don, 142; and Gray Davis's
    election, 198, 199; personal
    background of, 111–12; politi-

cal influence of, 112–14,
250–51; on three strikes bill,
114
NRA (National Rifle Association),
106; on gun control, 107; three
strikes funding by, 109, 110,
115, 130; Washington state
campaign of, 108–9

Oakland parolees, 227
Oakland Tribune, 262
O'Connor, Sandra Day, 262, 263
one strike law, 144
O'Reilly, Bill, 19
Owens, Ron, 123, 124, 125–26

Parker, William H., 56
parolees: under determinate sentencing act, 98–99; drug testing
of, 23; in LA County, 227–28;
in Oakland, 227; parole violations by, 74
Patriot Act, 7
Peace, Steve, 248
Pelican Bay State Prison, 65–66
People (magazine), 97, 116, 118
Petaluma, 94, 124–25
Phoenix House, 204
Pico Union ghetto (Los Angeles),
110
plea bargaining: Ira Reiner's policy
on, 182; three strikes law's impact on, 83–84, 130, 157–58
police: number of, nationally, 254;
traits of, in California, 30–31.
See also LAPD
Polly Klaas Foundation, 119
Pounders, William, 165–66
poverty: in Los Angeles, 174–76,
182–83; of parolees, 227–28;

rate of, 1980s–1990s, 85; in Tulare County, 39
Press, Bill, 259
preventive detention, 8–9, 84
prior strikes: judicial discretion on,
160–63, 164–66; and nonvio-
lent third strike, 253–54; as
percent of felony arrests, 191;
residential burglaries as, 78–80;
retroactive application of,
81–82; sentencing mandates
for, 82
prisons: black inmates in, 254;
CCPOA's support of, 113; construction costs of, 205; construction of, 1984–1994, 65;
corrections officers of, 237–38;
drug offenders in, 74, 133,
205–6, 213; early release from,
63, 141; housing costs of, 140;
motel accommodations near,
236; parolees released from,
227–28; population of, in California, 64, 205, 227, 254–55;
population of, nationally, 254;
recidivism rate in, 74–75; sec-
ond/third strike offenders in,
189; state budget for, 65,
188–89; TC programs in,
204–5; treatment of prisoners
in, 65–66; visiting areas of,
234–35; for worst offenders, 95
prison terms. *See* sentences
Proposition 13 (tax limitation),
87–88
Proposition 36 (Substance Abuse
and Crime Prevention Act),
200; drug treatment provisions
of, 205, 208–10, 220–21; funding of, 214, 219; political oppo-

Proposition 36 (*continued*)
sition to, 214–15, 221–22;
prospective application of, 210;
voter polling on, 212; voter
support of, 205. *See also* drug
courts
Proposition 184. *See* three strikes
law
Proposition 215 (medical use of
marijuana), 213
Public Safety Committee (California assembly): Joe Klaas's ad-
dress to, 243–45; liberal members of, 76–77; three strikes
modification by, 86; three
strikes vote by, 136

Quirino, Johnny, 3

R. J. Donovan Correctional Facility, 203, 204–5
racial integration, 59–61
Racketeer Influenced and Corrupt
Organization (RICO) statutes,
52
Rainey, Richard, 131, 134–35
Rampart scandal (Los Angeles),
224
RAND Institute, Criminal Justice
Program, 189–90
Ratelle, John, 203, 204–5
Reagan, Ronald, 49, 61, 94, 176
Reams, Shane, 5, 203, 205; childhood of, 69–70; criminal behavior of, 71–73; drug addiction of, 44–47; mother's prison
visits to, 231–32, 233–35,
238–39; ten-year old son of,
232–33; in undercover drug
bust, 149–52

Reams, Sue, 4, 5, 44, 46, 47; at
amendment hearings, 243–45,
246–47; dealing with son's offenses, 71–73, 151; first marriage of, 69–70; legislative lobbying by, 240–42; prison visits
by, 231–32, 233–35, 238–39;
and Supreme Court ruling on
Lockyer v. Andrade, 262–63, 264,
265–66
Reams, Wayne, 44, 70, 71, 151,
233–34, 235
Rehnquist, William H., 263
Reiner, Ira, 181–82
Reisner, Marc, 27
Republican Party: crime issue of,
62–63, 137–38; criminal justice
policies of, 52–53; in Long
Beach, 50–51
residential burglary offense,
78–80, 131, 133
Reynolds, Christopher, 33, 259
Reynolds, Kimber, 20, 33; killer of,
21; personal background of,
13–15; shooting death of,
15–17, 23–24
Reynolds, Michael (Mike
Reynolds's son), 33
Reynolds, Mike, 37, 101, 141, 145,
265; bill drafting meetings of,
39–41, 57; at bill signing ceremony, 142; on bill's initial defeat, 86–87; on Canadian sentences, 171–72; criminal justice
philosophy of, 84–86, 168–69;
and Daily Planet's owner,
167–68; and daughter's death,
16–17; on Joe Davis, 22–23, 25,
68; funding resources of,
106–9, 110, 114–15, 129–30;

on gun control, 109–10; on judicial discretion ruling, 163; and Polly Klaas's abduction, 123–25; Marc Klaas's response to, 131–33; on Barbara Lee, 76–77; on Bill Lockyer, 172; personal background of, 14–15, 29, 31–33; on second strike sentences, 82; as Dave Stirling supporter, 170–71; on "Street Sweeper" name, 82–83; talk radio appearances of, 18, 19–21, 67–68, 128; on Art Torres's amendment, 136; on U.S. Supreme Court ruling, 259–60; on Douglas Walker, 68

Reynolds, Sharon, 14, 16–17, 25, 32, 90, 106, 171

Rhodes, Bill, 116–17, 119

Ricciardulli, Alex, 63, 79, 165

Richman, Wilana, 251

RICO (Racketeer Influenced and Corrupt Organization) statutes, 52

Rojas, Julio, 108

Rolls, Dwight, 4

Romero, Jesus, 203, 205; discretionary sentencing of, 160–61, 162–63, 165; third strike offense by, 156–58

Ronstadt, Linda, 126

Rothenberg, Charles, 63

Rozier, Robert, 259

Rubin, Lael, 219

Ryder, Winona, 118, 187

San Francisco Chronicle, 259

San Joaquin Valley: description of, 26–28; farming business in, 27, 42–43; impoverished blacks of,

39; Richard Machado's role in, 37–38; methamphetamine use in, 23. *See also* Fresno

Santa Rosa Press Democrat, 117

Saroyan, William, 26, 27

Saucedo, Bernardo, 201, 206–7, 209, 216

Scalia, Antonin, 263–64

Schiraldi, Vincent, 87

Schlessinger, Laura, 127

schools: gun crime videos in, 169; Dan Lungren's platform on, 196–97; Proposition 13's impact on, 88; reading scores in, 85

Second District Court of Appeal, 186

second strikes: percent of inmates sentenced on, 189; sentencing mandates for, 82. *See also* prior strikes

Second Vatican Council (1962), 55

sentences: in Canada, 171–72, crime victims' rallies on, 247, 250–51; as "cruel and unusual punishment," 7, 84, 258, 260; "determinate" law on, 98–99; Deukmejian's policy on, 64; of federal prisoners, 53; good time provision of, 63, 141; gun crimes law on, 168–69; in high profile cases, 62–63; with judicial discretion, 160–66; without judicial discretion, 83, 159; Joe Klaas on, 244–45, 260; plea bargaining for, 83–84, 130, 157–58; with prior strikes eliminated, 161, 253–54; in Rainey bill, 131; Antonin Scalia on, 263–64; for second strikes, 82; for third strikes, 3–4, 78, 82, 157

Serles, Jim, 50, 51
Shuster, Beth, 138–39
Silva, Geri, 245–46, 262, 264–65, 266
Simmons, Eric, 4
Simpson, O. J., 183, 223
Singleton, Lawrence, 62
Sixth District Court of Appeal, 209–10
Skelton, George, 143
Snipp, Thomas, 237–38
Snoop Doggy Dogg, 183
Soros, George, 213, 222
Souter, David H., 264
Spears, Susan, 178
Sperling, John, 214, 222
St. Joseph's Catholic Church (Los Angeles), 177–78
Stevens, John Paul, 3
Stirling, Dave, 170–71
Stirling, Stephanie, 170, 171, 172
Stokes, Doug, 68
Substance Abuse and Crime Prevention Act. See Proposition 36
Synanon, 203–4

talk radio: Ray Appleton of, 18–19; incendiary rhetoric of, 127–28; political impact of, 67–68, 139; Mike Reynolds's appearances on, 19–21; right-wing, 139; three strikes role of, 123, 124–25, 128
Taylor, Dwight, 176, 177
Taylor, Gregory: Dale Cutler's prosecution of, 178–80; personal background of, 174–75, 176–77; third strike offense of, 177–78; trial/sentencing of, 185–87

TCs (therapeutic communities), 203–5
"Ten, Twenty, Life" law, 168–69
three strikes: blacks convicted for, 251; Steve Cooley's policy on, 224–26; Gil Garcetti's policy on, 187, 252; and jury verdicts, 152; misdemeanors as, 81; number of, for drug offenses, 205–6; percent of, as nonviolent, 187, 257; percent of inmates sentenced on, 189; without plea bargain, 157–58; proposed sentencing amendment on, 240–41; sentencing mandates for, 78, 82, 157; types of offenses as, 3–4, 78–81
three strikes amendments: ballot initiative costs of, 265, 266; by Jackie Goldberg, 261–62; Tom Hayden on, 248–49; Joe Klaas's support of, 243–45, 260; legislative hearings on, 240–42; political obstacles to, 249–51; Rod Wright's sponsorship of, 251–54. See also drug reform initiatives
Three Strikes and You're Out! (Reynolds), 85, 86
three strikes law: as ballot initiative, 89–90, 106–7; Willie Brown on, 141; Steve Cooley's policy on, 224–25; crimes covered by, 3–4, 78–81; defeat of, in 1993, 86–87; drafting of, by Reynolds, 39–41, 57; dubious impact of, 189–91; FACTS against, 3, 246–47, 264–65; federal proposals for, 125; financial contributors to, 106–9, 110,

114–15, 129–30; Tom Hayden's opposition to, 248–49; Bill Jones's sponsorship of, 43, 48–49; judges' reaction to, 159; judicial discretion rulings on, 162–66; Joe Klaas on, 132–34, 243–45; Marc Klaas on, 131–34, 140, 141; Polly Klaas's exploitation by, 123–26, 128, 135–36, 243; Dan Lungren on, 53–54, 57, 189; misdemeanor provision of, 81; plea bargaining impact of, 83–84, 130, 157–58; preventive detention notion of, 8–9, 84; Proposition 36's modification of, 205, 208–10, 220–21; vs. Rainey bill, 131, 134–35; retroactive application of, 81–82; sentencing mandates of, 78, 82; signing of, 142; and street gangs, 184; as "Street Sweeper," 82–83; talk radio's promotion of, 67–68, 123, 124–25, 128; Art Torres amendment to, 136; U.S. Supreme Court ruling on, 257–58, 260, 262–64; as violation of Eighth Amendment, 7, 84; voter support of, 4, 140, 145; in Washington state, 41, 78, 108–9, 131. *See also* prior strikes; three strikes; three strikes amendments
Toobin, Jeffrey, 95, 97, 99, 118
Torres, Art, 136
"tough love" philosophy, 71–72
Tucker, Jan, 262
Turner, Willie, 4
Turning Point shelter (San Mateo), 95

"20/20" (newsmagazine show), 125
Twin Towers Correctional Facility (Los Angeles County), 176
two strikes law (England), 173
Tynan, Michael A., 221–22

Uniform Determinate Sentencing Act (1977), 98–99
U.S. Supreme Court decision on three strikes law, 257–58, 260, 262–64

Vasconcellos, John, 113, 172
Virco Company (Torrance), 195–96
Virtue, Bob, 195–96
Virtue, Doug, 195–96

Walden House, 204
Waldrep, Christopher, 30
Walker, Douglas, 22–23, 24, 68
Wallace, George, 61
Walters, John P., 222
Warren, Earl, 55, 59
Wasco State Prison, 22
Washington, Carl, 252–53
Washington, D.C., crime rate, 190
Washington, John (pseud.), 219–21
Washington Citizens for Justice, 108
Washington state, three strikes law in, 41, 78, 108–9, 131
Watson, Gloria, 251
Watson, Tex, 216
Watts riots (1965), 56
Werdegar, Kathryn Mickle, 162
Will, George, 54
Wilson, James Q., 75
Wilson, Lenny (pseud.), 208–9

Wilson, Pete, 55, 65; bill's signing by, 142; CCPOA's support of, 114; crime issue strategy of, 143–44; on judicial discretion ruling, 163–64; at Polly Klaas's memorial, 127; and Richard Rainey, 135

"wobblers" (petty crimes), 81, 165
Woods, Fred, 186
Wright, Rod, 251, 252–54, 261

Zimmerman, Bill, 212, 213–14
Zimring, Frank, 190–91

COMPOSITOR: BINGHAMTON VALLEY COMPOSITION, LLC
INDEXER: PATRICIA DEMINNA
TEXT: 10/15 JANSON
DISPLAY: INTERSTATE LIGHT AND REGULAR
PRINTER AND BINDER: MAPLE-VAIL MANUFACTURING GROUP